D0708717

Cubs on the Loose

To Shiela—

Thank you and best regards.

Lyle P. Shaler

Cubs on the Loose

Old Airplanes—New Adventures

As told by NC-87881
to Lyle Wheeler

AMEA Cottage

ISBN: 0-9709890-0-8 hardcover
ISBN: 0-9709890-1-6 softcover
Library of Congress Control Number: 2001-132351
Cover design: OspreyDesign
Cover photo: Jim's Camera House
Typesetting, design and production: Tabby House
Printed in The United States of America

All events discussed or described herein took place prior to July 1997.
Quality of service rendered or the condition of physical properties of any
and all airports, aircraft landing sites, businesses, and fixed base operators,
referred to may have greatly changed for better or worse since that time.

Publisher's Cataloging-in-Publication
(*Provided by Quality Books, Inc.*)

Wheeler, Lyle (Lyle D.)
    Cubs on the loose : old airplanes--new adventures /
As told by NC-87881 to Lyle Wheeler. -- 1st ed.
    p.cm
    LCCN 2001132351
    ISBN 0-9709890-0-8 (casebound)
    ISBN 0-9709890-1-6 (trade paperback)

    1. Piper airplanes. 2. Private flying--United
States. 3. United States--Description and travel.
    4. Antique and classic aircraft--Popular works.
    5. Air shows--United States. I. Title

TL686.P5W44 2001   629.133'343
             QB101-700694

AMEA Cottage
4410 Camino Real
Sarasota, FL 34231
(941) 922-0182

To my wife, Pat, and our children, Chris, Kathy and Scott.
Their unconditional love and understanding
have facilitated my avid pursuit of a lifelong mistress—
the Wonderful World of Flight.

Contents

Preface

Piper Cub airplane. My goodness, the number of meanings those three words have to different people! To the uninformed non-aviation person, they generally mean anything that flies other than either a military aircraft or an airliner traveling at several hundred miles per hour at very high altitude. To many members of the airline and corporate aviation communities, they are slow-moving obstructions to the wheels of progress as their big jets move travelers, cargo, and indispensable members of corporate staff to and from meetings, etc. Even new members of the aviation family at the grassroots level have no idea or understanding of those three words, other than the fact they represent something from the Stone Age of aviation.

However, scattered and buried within the many groups of intrepid birdmen and birdwomen around the world can also be found a small, close-knit fraternity who find their pulse increasing, eyes twinkling, and excitement level at a new high at the mention of the three words—Piper Cub airplane. Even though there are many models of the Piper Cub—J-2, J-3, J-4, J-5, PA-11, PA-12, PA-18 (Super Cub) to list a few—some members of this clan think only of the J-3 Cub when hearing those three cherished words. Could that be because we J-3 Cubs taught so many people the fine art of flying before, during, and after World War II? Yes, we were one of the primary players in that era of world aviation. In this day and age of controlled airspace, whistles, buzzers, and gee-whiz gadgets of modern aviation, it is we Cubs and our cousins (the Taylorcrafts, Aeroncas, and other tube-and-rag aircraft of yesteryear) that still offer flight to our humanoids for the pure joy of it.

Our niche in present-day aviation circles is becoming harder and harder to carry forward. Most Johnny-come-lately aviators do not understand that even though most of us Cubs do not carry, nor wish to carry, all of the modern-day avionics equipment, which they feel is necessary for traversing this world's airspace, we are still able to cross great distances with no problems. Proof of this statement will be found in the pages that follow.

Fate, friendships, and mutual friends played important roles in bringing the players involved in these true adventures together for the first time on a small private airstrip near Frostproof, Florida, in March 1993. Three months later would find six Piper Cub "sisters" winging their merry way northward as they started on their first great adventure. These six intrepid voyagers are all of the J-3 lineage with birth dates ranging from 1938 through 1946. Thus, at the time, the youngest of the flock was only forty-seven-years-old while the oldest was a mere fifty-five years of age. None are equipped with nor allowed to use any form of modern electronic navigation system or communication equipment. These trips are conducted as was originally done when we were newborn Cubs, fresh from the factory.

Cradled within the snug cockpit of each Cub is its own beloved "humanoid." These creatures of the human race consisted of one each of the following—a certified public accountant; a high school teacher; a computer consultant; a building contractor; a real estate developer; and an old "graybeard" retired Boeing 747 captain from a major world-wide airline. On later trips, a retired RV resort park manager/developer would ride along as a passenger in one of the Cubs. The various flight experience tallies for these individuals ranged from a low of about 700 hours to a high of over 42,600 hours. Each knew and understood that there is always something new to be learned about flying an airplane and that a J-3 Cub could be a very tough teacher as is very subtly demonstrated on occasion.

Obviously, science and knowledge dictate that machines, such as Piper Cubs, do not possess senses, the ability to have feelings, or the power to show affection. However, any humanoid involved in aviation who is not afraid to allow their imagination and inner self the luxury of giving these lovable creations their freedom, will find them to be a very understanding, caring, and loving creation. This characteristic is quite apparent as each of these odysseys come to life. Sex, violence, deception, and foul language find no place in these accounts. Fact is—none is required, because my goal is to tell of the pure unadulterated joy that is experienced during these flights of fancy. Yes, entwined within these pages, can be found the thread of love between humanoids, flying machines, flight itself, and the challenge of the adventure. True, on occasion a torrid love scene between Cub and humanoid will be revealed, but this is a normal phenomena within such a bonded group. The adventures chronicled in the following pages are as we Cubs saw and experienced them.

As we all know, many of us airplanes do not survive into a real life of retirement. Most of us are melted down and recycled into other things—maybe some parts do actually return to service on other aircraft. A very small number of us may wind up in a museum where we are very seldom—if ever—allowed to fly again. However, some of us are lucky enough to find ourselves in the hands of loving humanoids who treat us as actual living members of their family. These beloved friends make a habit of keeping us in tip-top health, and fly us on a regular basis. Yes, we even find ourselves at various air shows and "beauty contests." But most of all, those of us who are blessed with being found and acquired by such a person, almost without exception, find ourselves being flown for the pure pleasure and enjoyment of flight. Sometimes these flights turn into the most enjoyable and relaxing flying we have ever done in our lifetime.

The lost art of low and slow long-distance flight in an old airplane using nothing but a sectional chart, plotter, compass, and watch, coupled with a touch of barnstorming atmosphere, presents good exposure to a long past—all but lost—era of aviation. My desire to share with others the challenge of the journey, love of planes, and love of flight itself is why I, an inanimate Piper J-3 Cub airplane, chose this media to communicate with you the reader. I hope you enjoy the following true adventures.

NC-87881

Introduction

Hi there—my name is NC-88474 (474 for short) and I am a Piper J-3 Cub. A few years ago, some of my brothers and sisters, along with our humanoids, got together at Clinch Lake, Florida, and talked about making a barnstormer-type trip—you know—grass landings, and sleeping under our wings. Well, it happened and was it great. We had so much fun that I can hardly keep my tail feathers still when I think about it and I really think the story should be told—especially in this day and age of all-business flying and very little real fun flying happening.

Actually, you need a score card to know the players, so I will list my sisters by name and throw in their ever-present humanoids—yep— we really are stuck with them! Let's see now, there was NC-22726 (Leighton Hunter from Venice); NC-87881 (Lyle Wheeler from Sarasota): NC-25885 (Jim Sprigg from Dade City; NC-70209 (Dennis and Nancy Garrett from Hudson); NC-7398H (Dirk and Donna Leeward from Ocala), and of course myself, NC-88474 (Paul Wenz from Frostproof)—all from Florida. Even though there were eight humanoids involved there were only six of those of us who really mattered— thus we voted to be known as the Cub Six-Pack. From that point, until the trip described by my very eloquent sister, 881, in the first chapter was completed, we insisted on being called by our real names—the last three digits in our tail numbers. Goodness, how our humanoids complained about not being recognized as the real subjects on this trip. We Cubs held the spotlight and that was proven at every stop that we made on this once-in-a-lifetime journey. No one gave a hoot about anyone in the group other than the Cubs!

During the course of these adventures, our humanoids had some excursions of their own in which we Cubs could not be involved. Rather than interrupt 881's excellent narrative, commentaries by hu-

manoid Lyle about these events are footnoted at the end of their respective chapters.

As you will read, 881 traveled sometimes without me. Although I
wasn't always with them in person, my sister's words make me soar.

NC-88474

And Away We Go!

The Great Adventure of the Cub "Six-Pack"

We Piper Cubs were made for barnstorming. Our humanoids were curious to see what those days were like—flying without modern-day navigational conveniences of a radio, Loran or GPS, landing on grass, and sleeping under our wings. And so the great adventure was conceived.

The humanoids from Florida: Leighton Hunter, Venice, (NC-22726); Lyle Wheeler, Sarasota, (NC-87881—that's me); Jim Sprigg, Dade City, (NC-25885); Dennis and Nancy Garrett, Hudson, (NC-70209); Dirk and Donna Leeward, Ocala, (NC-7398H) and Paul Wenz from Frostproof (NC-88474), had decided to fly as a Six-Pack with no particular destination in mind and without modern technology.

Only 885 had any of the banned instruments and we told her that if she even once turned them on, we would take out her fuses at the next stop. She gladly agreed to our demands. However, 209 and 98H were very ashamed of their humanoids—all four of them went to a bed and breakfast instead of camping out—and on the first night out. It only happened once, so we let it go—that time.

During the early stages of planning, we did not have a destination, so we were just going to drift around the country. However, about a month before departure, we all received an invitation to attend the Annual Cub and Short Wing Piper Fly-in at Gadsden, Alabama. Now we had a final destination—so it was a simple matter to figure out where the grass was located and who would allow us to spend the night on their nice grass with tents or sleeping bags under our wings.

As had been planned, by 10:00 A.M. on June 10, 1996, all six of us had met and were taxiing out for takeoff at Crystal River, Florida. Since this was to be a very relaxed journey, we decided to stop and see as many airports as we could and still cover a reasonable distance each day. Thus our first destination was Live Oak, Florida. It was further agreed that we would be flying a buddy system—209 and 98H would be together, 885 and 474 would be together, and 726 would be with me. All seemed well and it really

"Six-Pack" ready to depart, Crystal River, Florida

did feel good to be on the wing with five of my sisters—what fun we were going to have during the next few days!

Seven-two-six and I arrived at Live Oak on schedule, the beautiful grass beside the runway tickling the little fat donuts we call tires as we gently touched down. About five minutes later 98H came to the gas pumps—alone. She had no idea where the other three were as she had not seen them in the last thirty minutes. We waited, but nothing. We were not really concerned yet—but where were they?

About this time a snooty little Cessna 150 came up to us, making like he was really teaching a student to fly (Ha, little did he know!) and asked if we were "looking for three more of us funny-looking little yellow airplanes with our wheels on the wrong end." We ignored his snide remark and admitted that we were indeed wondering where our sisters had strayed. He informed us that they were at least ten miles west and still headed north.

Good grief. Where were they going? They didn't have enough gas to get very far! Nothing to do now, but wait and hope they came back. Sure enough, about fifteen minutes later, here they came. It seemed that 885's humanoid had taken the wrong river and 474 and 209 had blindly followed. None of them did that again.

Fueled and ready to go, we waited patiently while our humanoids bickered good naturedly over the navigational error of the past leg. As they approached us it was announced that I would lead the group even though 726 had made the contact for our next port of call—Spence Airport, Moultrie, Georgia. That's right, the Maule Aircraft factory. It seemed that since I had been the only one not "lost" getting this far, I should be the one to lead. My humanoid really was griping—something about not being the "trail boss."

Airborne again, we were one of the loosest formations of Cubs to ever fly. As soon as Spence came into sight, 726 moved to the front as she knew where the grass for landing was located. Once on the ground, it was like going through a complicated maze to get to the Maule ramp. Once there, it was really great fun to see that we Cubs outnumbered the parked Maules. I think every employee of the factory was standing around admiring our bright yellow plumage with our bold black lightning stripes.

After our humanoids took a brief tour of the factory, it was fun time again. We were told that rather than spend all that time on the ground getting back to the runway, we could depart from the ramp. Knowing us Cubs as you do—we jumped at the chance to show our stuff by taking off from the ramp.

This next leg was to be our last one for the day. After a quick call to Petecraft Aviation, on Peterson Field, at Plains, Georgia, telling them that we would be there by 4:00 P.M., we were on our way. Again, I was in the lead, but this time I heard no complaints from my humanoid as we had made the arrangements for this overnight stop.

Peterson Field was one of the few remaining all-grass commercial airports in the United States, and we were going to get to spend the night basking in its unequaled serenity. As the six of us taxied to the vicinity of the gas pumps, the lovely Martine Peterson met us. She apologized for the fact that Tom, her husband, was gone on a charter, but said that he would be back by nightfall. We were invited to make ourselves at home and feel free to tie down and pitch our tents anywhere we wanted—other than on the runway! She even drove a scouting party to the other end of the airport to check out the possibility of camping in the woods. Since we Cubs could not be part of that program, it was decided to stay on the civilized part of the airport. (Gosh, our humanoids really do love us.)

Martine loaned the humanoids two cars and told them of the different things to do while we were visiting her great little airport. She explained that there was a small bed and breakfast in town—where some of President Carter's family had lived in the past—if anyone was interested in spending the night there. Two-zero-nine and 98H drooped their wings in sorrow when they heard that their husband and wife humanoids chose to go to town for the night.

After we were all secured for the night, the two couples took one of the cars and were on their way. The remaining four of us had great fun watching tents being set up under our wings and a makeshift shower being erected out of a garden hose and an engine hoist. Seven-two-six had brought along one of those portable showers and it was filled with hot water from the rest room in the office—so the shower really was not half bad. Our campsite was soon in order and our four humanoids quickly departed in the second car, leaving us to relax and remember the fun we had had during the past few hours.

The entire entourage of humanoids met at Mom's Kitchen in Preston, Georgia, for one of the most enjoyable family-style meals any of them had eaten in quite a while. This little family-run restaurant had its own little historical mystique. It seemed that Mom, herself, had shot and killed her husband in that very same establishment. I guess there must have been a good reason as she was still making some of the best "vittles" this gang had ever eaten.

Soon the humanoids of 726, 881, 474, and 885 were back at the campsite relaxing with us in the long shadows of the low evening sun. Two local families drove in with their children and wanted to take a good look at us. It seems that word had gotten out that we were in the area and these people wanted to show their children some "real airplanes." We nearly burst our bungee cords with pride as they admired us in our natural surroundings.

Shortly after the sun had set, 209 and 98H's humanoids drove into the parking lot. Two-zero-nine's humanoid shouted something about "she is here and she is yellow, and that is all the reason I need" as he bounded toward her. Shortly they were airborne and proceeded to make five touch-and-go and one full-stop landing within the next ten minutes. Talk about your torrid love affair—that takes the cake! They were both in complete ecstasy.

Before everyone turned in for the night, it was decided that a dawn patrol flight was mandatory for the next day. So it was with great anticipation of an early frolic that the Six-Pack of Cubs and our humanoids settled in for the night.

Sleep did not come easy for any of us that night. Here we were, six sisters, tied on beautiful grass out in the country between peanut and wheat fields with a great big silver moon shining down from above. It was so still that you could imagine you could hear the grass grow. Then there were the real sounds of crickets chirping and an occasional deer dashing through the area. The excitement of what was in store and the beauty of the setting removed all thoughts of sleep. Life just does not get any better than this.

Long before the sun even thought of getting up, we were all ready for the dawn patrol takeoff. Only four of us would be making this flight as 209 and 98H's humanoids were still in town—no doubt asleep as they did not have the tranquil beauty to excite them. Just as soon as there was legal light, the four of us (726, 474, 885, and myself) were in the air headed for Americus, Georgia, airport. (That was the airport where Charles Lindberg soloed so many years ago.) By the time the sun was just breaking the horizon, we had explored the workings of a large fleet of Polish-built ag planes parked on the Americus airport and left a note on another of our sisters to join us on our journey if she got up early enough.

It was time for breakfast, so it was a quick takeoff from the taxiway and we chased each other back to our great little campsite at Peterson Field. Well, with no one around and such a nice grass runway, we had to make several passes around the pattern before parking didn't we? Tom and Martine Peterson lived on their nice little airport, so it went without saying that our little group had them up long before their normal rise-and-shine hour. They made no objection as they really enjoy Cub noise.

As we were parked and our humanoids headed for the Country Citchen, in Plains, for breakfast, 209 and 98H were happy to see their humanoids round the corner because they knew they would soon be on their way to retrace the paths that we had just completed.

It was 10:00 A.M. on the morning of June 11. Two-zero-nine had some important business to take care of before she could leave, so 98H elected to stay with her while the rest of us headed on out. We agreed to meet in Clanton, Alabama, before heading over to Ware Island, (located in the Coosa River), our destination for the day. At the insistence of the others, I was in the lead again. My humanoid put on quite a show about not wanting to be the trail

Departure time from Peterson Field, Plains, Georgia.
Credit, Petecraft Aviation Services, Inc.

boss or wagon master, but down deep, he really considered it an honor to be asked to lead this fine group of Cubs across the miles.

Tuskegee, Alabama—if you have never been there, make a point of doing so. That is the place where many of our brothers were used to train the famous Tuskegee Airmen. The four of us had again used the nice grass beside the runway for our landings and were now gathered around the gas pumps waiting for a nice drink of fuel. Little did we know what was in store for us during the next hour or so.

To add a touch of humor to this stop, a prissy little Cessna 150, who had seen us land on the grass, came up and wanted to know what was wrong with us. Didn't we know that there was a beautiful 5,000-foot concrete runway out there that we should be using? Knowing he would not understand, we informed him what it was like to land on grass. He just put his tail higher in the air and turned on all of his electronics and moved away. Poor guy, he will never know what it is like to truly fly—just you and the wind.

Back to the surprise that was waiting for us. The original chief flight instructor of the Tuskegee Airmen, C. A. "Chief" Anderson, had watched us land and he came to the airport to see us. This man was a walking history book and he could have kept us in awe for hours with his stories. His students were all trained in Cubs, just like us—same color and everything. Just seeing his eyes when he looked at us made our tail feathers wag as we could tell there was a lot of compassion for us within him. His gentle hands didn't just touch us, they caressed us as he embraced our cowlings and props. It made every spar quiver with excitement. What an honor just to be here with him. We wanted so much to let him fly one of us, but

Lyle Wheeler, "Chief" Anderson and "726."
Credit, Leighton Hunter.

25

we were concerned just where some shyster attorney would take us if anything should happen.

As a farewell salute to Chief, we were given permission to make a low pass on our departure. Unknown to us, 209 and 98H were in the area as we made our pass over the Chief and they fell in behind us so he got the full Six-Pack flyby salute! They landed for fuel and the rest of us headed for Clanton.

En route to Clanton, my sisters and I decided we would have a little fun with our humanoids. We decided that if we could get the wind gods to help us out a little, we would take them down a little. They were getting a little cocky and it was time to show them who was boss. All went as we planned. There was a model airplane meet in progress at the airport, so many people were there to watch our little show. The wind gods were very helpful as they arranged a couple of 180-degree wind shifts just as we landed, in trail formation. Seven-two-six was very gentle and did not create any problem for her humanoid. Eight-eight-one managed to turn about forty-five degrees to the right and almost got off the runway before she laughingly straightened out down the runway. Eight-eight-five managed to almost make it off the left side of the runway before she too started laughing about the situation and went straight down the runway. Four-seven-four was the winner on this one as she managed to make it all the way around—yep, a complete ground loop—directly in front of the crowd. We didn't do any damage, but we sure got the attention of our cocky humanoids. Oh boy! What fun! (There was no grass available here which made our little trick much easier.)

After a wait of about thirty or forty minutes, 209 and 98H were back with us and we were ready to head for Ware Island. However, one of those little black clouds decided to cry all over the route to the island so we had to continue to wait for it to regain control of its emotions.

Four-seven-four and her humanoid were well known around the area of Clanton and Ware Island as they had been here before. For this reason, they both took much kidding about their little "loop-dee-loop" in front of the crowd. Also, this good relationship with the local citizens made it possible for us to be invited to spend some time on the island. You see, Ware Island is a private island, most of which is owned by an old gray beard Waco (UPF-7, I think) and his partner, a very attractive young lady Stinson 108 on floats. (I have forgotten their names as I failed to write them down.) I did know their humanoid was Dr. Richard Meyer who was assisted by the lovely Betty Norris. Mr. Waco rules the island and one does not land on his property without a proper invitation. Thanks to 474, we all had that invitation and just as soon as that stupid cloud stopped sniffling we would be on our way.

Within about thirty minutes, the bright sunshine had convinced the cloud that life really wasn't so bad; it stopped crying and we were on our way. It was about twenty miles to the island and 474 should have been leading as she was the one who made all the arrangements for this overnight. But no, she would have nothing to do with that—claiming that she would get lost—and insisted that I once again be in the front. (This prompted much grumbling again—something about not being the trail boss.) Once the island was sighted, 474 moved to the front, leading us to a fantastic grass, lighted, runway that had been hacked out of a growth of sixty- to eighty-foot-high trees. Settling onto that green velvet was like descending into a deep canyon and putting our donut tires onto a soft, beautiful, scenic fairway. It was fantastic!

Our Shangri-la, Ware Island. Credit, Leighton Hunter.

The "Six-Pack" campsite at Ware Island. Credit, Leighton Hunter.

The campsite was quickly selected and we were all beginning to relax when we heard the first sounds of it. At first it was difficult to determine just what it was, but in short order, we all knew it was the purring sound of one of Mr. Franklin's engines—no doubt in the front of one of Mr. Stinson's creations. Sure enough, it was a Stinson 108-1 and here she came right down the runway at full bore! Her name was N-9101K, and she was a very dear friend of 474. Along with her humanoids (Keith and Karen Carden) she brought a load of Kentucky Fried Chicken with all the trimmin's. My, what a party we had that evening! After the party was over, 01K departed for home with the promise that she would be here the next evening to greet us when we returned from the fly-in.

The hour was quite late now. We Cubs were standing guard over each of the tents pitched under our wings. That's right, we each had a tent tonight. Again the moon was smiling on us, the beauty of the river, we six Cubs parked in the grass by the forest, and the quiet tranquil surroundings were enough to make any being glad to be alive. It was beautiful. We keep saying it couldn't get better than this—but it did.

Tomorrow is the big day—we get to see all of our long-lost brothers and sisters that would be at the Gadsden Cub Fly-in. The original plan had been to spend one night on the island and the next on the grass at the Gadsden airport. However, we liked the island so much that with the blessings of our host and hostess, we would be returning after the gathering. Fact is, we had decided to spend the next two nights here.

Earlier in the evening, plans were made for our final leg to the fly-in. Everyone agreed that since we are the Cub Six-Pack we should make some sort of grand arrival. It was decided that we should be in some sort of formation, even though few of us had had any formal training in that type of flying. Thus, an in-trail, follow-the-leader thing would probably have to do. The officials at the fly-in had been told that we would arrive about 10:30 A.M., so we had all better get some sleep as it will be an early departure. Again with fond memories of our great adventures of this day and great anticipation of what was to come on the morrow, our humanoids drifted off to sleep while we sisters continued to enjoy our intoxicating surroundings.

The clear early morning dawn of June 12 found much activity around the campsite. Breakfast, consisting of whatever happened to be brought along for that purpose, was consumed amid much merriment, because soon we would be on our way. The tents would stay as we would be back again tonight. Since there was no fuel available on the island, and some of us had overindulged the evening before by chasing each other up and down the river, we would have to make a gas stop at Sylacauga, Alabama.

By 7:00 A.M. all of our Continentals were ticking over warming up for the upcoming flight. Finally, my humanoid accepted the fact that I would be the leader! Nothing more was mentioned about the formation flying, but as we proceeded toward Sylacauga, I noticed that everyone was moving in a little closer and maintaining a much more stable condition of flight.

The "gas man" at Sylacauga had been to a party the night before, and we had to wake him up in order to get our energy supply replenished. While we were waiting for him to get to the airport, one of our distant cousins, a BC-12D Taylorcraft, stopped to visit. She was carrying a ten-year-old future pilot and his father who wanted to show his son all of these pretty little yellow airplanes. We nearly burst our rib stitches with pride from the compliments that BC-12 gave us. Lovely young lady, she was.

We were now less than twenty miles from Gadsden, and the closer we get, the tighter our formation is becoming. By the time we were ten miles out, I could see 474 and 98H tucked in *very* tight in an echelon from my left wing. To the other side, also tucked in just as tight in echelon from my right wing were 726 and 209. Where the heck was 885? Finally, I spotted her shadow on the ground and she was tucked in real nice and tight in the "slot."

Over the boundary of the airport we were as one, so it was down to 100 feet over the grass just off the ramp for the grand arrival of the Cub Six-Pack from Florida. Eat your hearts out Blue Angels and Thunderbirds—you may make a lot more noise and move a lot faster, but you will never be as slow and nostalgic as my sisters and I were right now! Following the break, the nice soft grass was soon caressing our gear and we were on our way to the parking area.

Much to our surprise, people were waving and clapping their hands as we passed them en route to park with the rest of our brothers and sisters. The official greeters expressed delight in our arrival. Hey, we didn't do anything—we were just having fun! After we had registered, the airport manager asked if we would be so kind as to do our little formation show again. With due respect for her request, we turned her down because we were not that experienced in formation flying and to try to form up that tight in a very short time after takeoff would not be safe. We did agree to do some sort of in-trail thing upon departure and she said that would be fine—anything we wanted to do would be all right.

We all had a ball during the day. Being the sport jock of the group, 98H decided she would enter the bomb drop and spot-landing contests. The fly-in also had a balloon-bursting competition, but she did not enter that event. Thank goodness we had others who actually dropped bombs, because 98H really didn't do too well in that event. By the time it was her turn to make the spot landing, someone had hurt the feelings of a little ol' cloud and it was crying so hard that 98H could barely see the runway and nothing of the spot. Oh well, she had a good time and we all enjoyed watching her try her best.

By the time an excellent barbecue meal had been consumed it was time to award the prizes that had been won during the event. None of the Six-Pack won any of the beauty contests or the sporting events. However, when the distance awards came up, we made quite a stir. We all were given nice certificates for the furthest distance, but when it came to the trophy, there was a little problem. Both 726 and I had come from Venice, which was the furthest distance. Now there was a problem as there was only one trophy and which one of us should get it? The final ruling was made that since 726 resided in a hangar that was eighty feet further south than my homesite, she would be given the prize. No one will ever believe that I lost a long-distance trophy by just eighty feet! We all had a good laugh about the situation and started saying good-bye to our newfound friends and long-lost brothers and sisters, before heading back to camp.

Our departure from Gadsden was not as spectacular as our arrival had been, but as we passed single file over the crowd, they were all waving good-bye to us. What a warm feeling we all had as we pointed our spinners south, which in reality was the start of a much-too-soon journey home.

A quick stop at Pell City, Alabama, gave us enough energy to make it back to our island paradise, after going around a couple of very angry giants with fire flashing around them. (Good grief, there is no reason to be that angry. We wouldn't think of infringing on their territory.) Even though we were enjoying our return flight just as much as ever, there was an underlying sadness tugging at our oil pumps. We all knew that this big day had been the apex of our adventure and we must now start thinking of going home.

Spirits soared again as we rolled into our campsite on the island because, as promised, there sat 01K with another load of great food for another evening of merriment. Even better, she was prepared to spend the night with us, too. All indications were that tonight's event was going to be even better than the night before, and we were not disappointed. Many additional humanoids came to the island by boat and our host and hostess joined in the festivities around us within our cozy little nesting place.

There were now seven of us, counting 01K, basking in the luxury of silver moonlight reflecting from our fabric-covered wings. Happy thoughts of the day's events, and the gentle rustling of the night zephyr through the pines soon had us all asleep, trying our best to put off thoughts of what must happen tomorrow.

June 13 dawned crisp and clear as had the other mornings. This being Sunday, our humanoids were all sleeping in—or were they trying their best to avoid the inevitable? Business commitments required 209 and 98H to start for home this morning. They needed to be home by nightfall, so they had a long day ahead of them. Yes, the Six-Pack was starting to break up.

Seven-two-six, 474, 885, and I had a few more days to play, and we decided to spend one more day in our island Shangri-la. We bid an early farewell to 209 and 98H as they were breaking camp, and along with our new friend, 01K, jumped over to Clanton for a big breakfast and to get some laundry done. (It was about time for that.) The Giant Scale Model Airplane Meet at which we had performed a couple of days earlier was still in progress, so we enjoyed that event, too, before returning to our favorite getaway. Zero-one-kilo came with us and we spent the rest of the day relaxing and enjoying life. By early evening, it was decided that 01K would return to the nearest Pizza Hut and bring back some pizza and a very special treat of fresh peaches and ice cream for the evening meal. Those of us who stayed behind watched as another one of those pesky dark clouds formed in the direction of our friends' journey and we knew she could never make it back. That did not discourage her humanoids as they risked their very lives in order to return when they came by ground-bound means. This truly was not the proper way to spend our last night on the island, but it would have to do.

Things were pretty gloomy on the morning of June 14. Not only were the tents being folded in solemn silence, but Mother Nature seemed to know our feelings and she followed suit. This was the only day she decided to give us lowered ceilings and reduced visibility. It was not all that bad—just not up to what we had been enjoying.

Shortly after consuming another breakfast of eat-what-you-brought, the four remaining members of the Six-Pack were lined up on our takeoff roll. We lifted out of the canyon of trees, made a wide turn around and came back down through the canyon in a farewell salute to our host and hostess who were standing beside the vacant campsite waving to us. We rocked our wings in return—thanking them again for such a wonderful interlude in our lives.

Today's destination was Thomasville, Georgia. There were a couple of reasons for this and the number one was the fact that the FBO had a full-size shower with hot and cold water available for guests. (All of those cold showers were great, but our humanoids knew some hot water would feel good!) The second reason was that they had nice grass to land on and, we believed, nice grass to tie down and camp on, too.

After energy-replenishing stops at Wetumpka and Eufala, Alabama, and Camilla, Georgia, we were gathered around the gas pump by mid-afternoon at Thomasville. Much to our surprise, the ground was too firm to allow us to install our tie-down stakes. Not wanting to be left untied, we had to be put on that hard ol' concrete ramp. It was ironic that the spaces in which we were tied formed a perfect diamond formation. This was to be to our advantage later in the evening.

A suitable grass area for pitching the tents was found nearby, so things weren't as bad as they could have been. As soon as all tents were erected, our humanoids departed in the loaner car for downtown and a nice hot evening meal. They returned within a couple of hours.

The flying today had been as much fun as ever, but due to the fact that we all knew we were on the downhill side of our great adventure, the usual jovial attitude was somewhat subdued. We all knew this portion of the trip would come, but it still was not exactly what we wanted. Come morning, 726 and I would have to depart for home—thus there would be only two of the Six-Pack still drifting around the countryside.

We were positioned well away from the main part of the ramp, and as darkness crept around us, ramp lighting—sodium vapor fixtures located some distance from us—began to function. Now, with only stars in the heavens, we found ourselves in an area of very soft subdued light, not unlike the glow surrounding a nice big campfire. What was this? Here came our humanoids, carrying chairs, and they seated themselves exactly in the center of the diamond that our tethered positions created. They spent the next two hours just sitting there talking about flying, airplanes, and us. Talk about affection for Cubs—gosh we *were* lucky!

Sunrise the next morning, June 15, found 726 in the lead and me tucked close in under her right wing as we made a low pass over 885 and 474, bidding them so long for now, as we head for home. (Finally someone else was leading!) They planned to spend a couple more days, just drifting, before going home. (We were to learn later, that 474 had a humanoid who developed a malfunction, so they returned home the next day in order to get him a mechanic who could make the needed repairs. He recovered nicely.)

Anyway, on this final day of our little outing, our conduct was a little more orderly. I guess we were kind of like a couple of horses going to their barn—we were headed home now, so might as well get there as quickly as possible. By midday, I was tucked into my home, and 726 was resting at ease in her abode, which is eighty feet further south—with her long distance trophy! *Just kidding, Sis.*

There is no way to express the feeling of camaraderie that had developed between our humanoids in just these few short days. (Four months ago, only two of them knew each other.) Yes, I know the world believes that we machines have no feelings, but you cannot tell me that after the last few days there wasn't something special among those of us Cubs who were privileged to live through all the events that happened—moonlight nights with tents under our wings—the dawn patrol flight—the loving look of Chief Anderson as he remembered bygone days—our chasing each other up and down the river and through the tree canyon—the formation flyby at the Gadsden gathering—and the many joyous moments when humanoids looked at us and remembered or told their sons and daughters about adventures they had known with our sisters and brothers. You had to be there to understand.

Well, it is nice to know that we did hear much conversation about where we will go next year. Hot dang, it could happen again!

Eight-Eight-One Sees Sun-'n-Fun

You know—we Cubs are really not much different from the young child who has been playing and gotten a little "soiled" and his parent has insisted he takes a bath. The child never feels there is a need for this distasteful task—so it was with much the same feeling that I was forced to endure the unwanted scrubbing my humanoid, Lyle, bestowed upon me. This was something that I had to put up with on occasion and I felt it was just another one of those clean-up jobs until he brought out the polishing wax.

Then it hit me. It was almost the first of April 1994, and that meant it was almost Sun-'n-Fun time. Oh, boy, I'm ready! I'm ready. Bring on the water, wax and anything else to make me look pretty for that great event. Oh boy, let's do it.

Within a couple of days, I was sparkling like a newborn star, and my adopted brother, the big Stearman next door, was given the same treatment. Then Lyle disappeared. He actually locked our doors and never came back. One week passed. Then two weeks passed—where was he? We felt we had been betrayed and were not going to be allowed to make the journey to Lakeland, Florida—what a letdown after all of that cleaning and waxing.

Two more days passed—nothing. Then, about midday on the third day, I heard the sound of a strange engine come to a halt in front of my door. Soon I heard the key in the lock and the door rolled open. There stood my Lyle with another humanoid who had flown him back from Lakeland in his Thorp T-18 just to get me. It seems that my humanoid had been working at the Sun-'n-Fun site getting it ready for the big show and that explained his absence.

Without delay, we were on our way to Linder Airport. I could hardly wait. Big brother Stearman would have to wait until Lyle's offspring, Chris, could get the time to fly him to the big fly-in.

Arrival at Lakeland was uneventful. In my baggage compartment was a coveted piece of paper giving me special authorization to use the Sun-'n-Fun grass runway. I had also sent my NORDO card to the control tower so there was no reason to be concerned that I had no avionics. My humanoid had driven a few wooden stakes to mark where the runway was to be before coming after me, and it had not been lined yet when we landed. Thus, I had the honor of being the first 1994 arrival on the grass runway.

Much to my disgust, we had gotten to Lakeland four days before the program started so there was not much airplane activity at the time. To make matters even worse, I was put into a strange dark hangar. I hated it. I heard some conversation about keeping me out of the hot sun, but I wanted to be out where I could see what was going on. If only I could make my wishes known—I would be out of this black box and enjoying the activity.

The sun had not even started to creep above the eastern horizon on Sunday, the first day of the big show, when the doors to my prison opened and Lyle and two other humanoids helped me free my bonds. Soon I had a second row seat in the Antique/Classic area where I really could be in the midst of everything. Maybe it was worth all of the wait after all.

By the time I was secure in my spot, the eastern sky was getting quite bright and I could now make out what was going on. Much had changed since my arrival a few days earlier. There were now brothers and sisters, uncles and aunts, as well as many cousins parked all over the place. What was this? Out in the center of the field directly in front of me was a large growth of balloons beginning to take shape. They were in many shapes and colors. There was one that looked like a hamburger. No kidding. *Oh look! Over there! See that one! It looks like a big sneaker.* Wow! I had never seen anything like this. What beauty as they drifted to the west in the first rays of the rising sun.

With the departure of the balloon brigade the whole sky seemed to open up and drop airplanes onto Linder Field. There were the antiques, classics, and contemporaries filling the area around me, each one dressed in their best Sunday-go-to-meetin' clothes. On the other side of the commercial area, the ground was literally being covered with beautiful homebuilts of all sizes and descriptions. Out behind, where we were camped, you could see Paradise

City with the hordes of ultra-lights flitting here and there, and across the taxiway, the warbirds were coming to roost. Such excitement and activity I had never seen. It was better than any other year that I had attended!

OK. It was time to settle down for a while. Here came the judges to look me over. My, I was glad that I had that beautiful new coat of wax. I must do my best because these guys really give us all the "acid test." I had won in the past, but from the looks of things, it was going to be pretty rough competition this year. Some of my sisters sure had wonderful face-lifts. *Quiet now, while they do their thing.* At last the judging was over and now I could go back to enjoying the show. We would not know if I had won until the last night of the program.

Mid-afternoon brought the best airshow in the world. The twists and turns, rolls and loops, vertical climbs and descents, inverted passes, and many tumbles made by my distant cousins would make anyone's gyros spin. How they managed to do those things I will never understand. I guess they drink lots of 100-octane and use quarts of super lube in order to keep their strength up. For three and one-half hours they carried on. My, what stamina!

The sun had descended below the western horizon now and it was starting to cool down a little. Now I could understand why I was put in that ol' dark hangar. It was very hot and the dust was terrible, but boy was it fun. As I drifted off to sleep, surrounded by many friends and relatives, I thanked my lucky stars that I had a humanoid who enjoyed these events as much as I did.

Two days later brought us to Tuesday. Without a doubt, this day was the most exciting of my stay on the Sun-'n-Fun grounds. Along with eighteen of my relatives, I had been chosen to fly in the History of Flight Parade. Hot dang! I was going to be part of the airshow. Actually, this parade was during the morning hours and gave everyone a chance to see from where they have come. I was so excited that I forgot to remember who participated in this grand parade! I do know the oldest one of us was a 1933 OX-5 Curtis Robin and the youngest was a grand lady from 1956—a Cessna 195. What a striking picture we made, with our multi-hued plumage, lined up waiting to take to the air.

The parade was fantastic. We were to depart from the paved runway 09, fly a rectangular pattern to the south, make one low pass along the show line and then come back in and land on the grass runway. All the time, an announcer broadcast a brief history of each of us as we made our pass along the show line. We were all so proud that without exception, we almost burst our wing cords.

All went as planned. However, as I turned onto the short final for the grass runway, cousin Cessna 140 got so excited that he jumped in front of me for the landing. I got quite a kick out of this because I then had to add power and make another flyby along the show line. So, I actually got to make two low passes.

The next time around, the way was clear and I could make my landing. That's when I got to do my one and only airshow act. There was quite a strong crosswind blowing, so I was able to put only my right wheel on the soft grass and let it roll until I was almost stopped before allowing the other two wheels to touch the ground. My what fun. After that, we proceeded to our respective positions on the grounds and settled in for the rest of the show. I had the honor of having several humanoids leave notes in my cockpit saying how much they enjoyed seeing me fly. (You see, I was the only J-3 Cub in the parade.)

Wednesday dawned bright and clear as usual. Every day was a repeat of the day before—except better. There has been an open spot to my right for the last two days and bright and early this morning I have found out why. Much to my delight, big brother Stearman came rolling to a stop next to me. My, I was proud of him in his bright navy uniform! He, too, was to be judged so I had to prod him a little about not relaxing just yet. Since he would only be there for one day, he really wouldn't have much time to enjoy himself due to the constant pressure from the judging. Luck would have it that he would be judged before the airshow, so he could relax and enjoy the program after all.

Immediately after the airshow, big brother Stearman had to depart as his humanoid, Chris, had to be back at work the next morning. Needless to say, he wanted to stay for the awards on Saturday night just in case he had won something, but there was not enough time. Down deep, I felt that he should stay, because I was certain he had won something.

The sun had set and the darkness of Wednesday night was starting to come upon us, when all of a sudden up pops a *huge* hot-dog-shaped balloon! What an unusual sight—a big glowing

*Adopted brother Big Stearman, his humanoid, Chris, me, 881, and my
humanoid, Lyle. Credit, Bill Kilborn.*

wiener anchored to the ground. Every time the burner was turned
on, the flame made the balloon glow. We were told that there were
to be several participants in this "balloon glow" event, but the
only one to show up was the hot dog.

Suddenly, all was quiet and all spinners turned toward the dark
evening sky, watching and waiting. Then as if by magic two small
comets appeared high above us. Actually, it was the fireworks fas-
tened to the wing tips of our motorless friend, the sailplane, doing
her night aerobatic act. What beauty and grace—it was indeed
fascinating.

When she had finished her routine, the silence was shattered
by the roar of the big AT-6 Texan as he put on his night display.
Those Texans always do things in a big way. Again, it was fascinating to watch the streaks of lights and fireworks in the night
sky—seemingly controlled by some magical force—dancing to
their own drummer. All too soon it was over and the sky was given
back to the stars and moon.

After the night show, my humanoid took me back to the dark
ol' hangar. I really did not want to go, but I must say, it did feel
good to get in out of the hot sun and dust for the next three days.

It was mid-afternoon on Sunday, after Sun-'n-Fun closed on
Saturday night, when I moved out of my temporary hangar. My,

what a transformation had taken place on the airport. Hardly any of my friends and relatives were still there. All that remained were outlines in the grass where they had rested and the earth was lined with tire tracks and footprints. I observed all of this as I gained altitude after takeoff from runway 09, and headed for home. It really was sad, but then there is always next year and you can bet your bottom dollar I would be there if at all possible.

By the way, I must admit that my stay at Sun-'n-Fun had made me quite dirty—what with all of the dust blowing around, and you know what? I was ready for a nice bath this time.

Oh, I almost forgot! I did not win anything this year, but that was all right—my humanoid still loves me anyway. Big brother Stearman did win—he came home with the Best Bi-Plane award. Gosh I'm proud of him.

Six-Pack (Minus Two) Flies Again

It goes without saying that we Cubs really have to put up with some weird activities by our humanoids. So it was with much wonderment that I found my humanoid, Lyle, changing my oil when it still had over nine hours of flying time left on it before the next scheduled change. Not only that, but he also removed my front control stick—boy, he really had flipped his cork this time!

My older sister, N-22726 (Leighton Hunter), who resides near me on the Venice airport, found herself being treated in much the same manner. Was it possible that both of our humanoids had flipped out at the same time?

Clues to this unusual behavior started to surface in the pre-dawn darkness of June 4, 1994. In the wee hours of that Saturday morning, 726 and I found ourselves being loaded with all sorts of supplies and camping gear—the reason our front sticks had been removed. By the time the sun was starting to crack the horizon, we were winging our way to the northeast and we both finally realized that we might be off on another great flying adventure. I guess our humanoids weren't as crazy as we thought.

Since 726 can run faster than I, she charged on ahead. I did not know when or where I would catch up with her, but I did know it would happen before long. Sure enough, within an hour or so, I saw her go into a lazy orbit in the vicinity of Clinch Lake, and by the time I fell in behind her, we could see another of our sisters, NC-88474 (Paul Wenz), moving out to takeoff from her beautiful grass home. Oh boy, oh boy! Could it be another great trip like last year? I sure hoped so

As 474 climbed out, we proceeded to turn north toward Kissimmee, Florida. I could hardly contain myself as I was beginning to realize that this really is the beginning of another great adventure. There were now three of us and I was wondering where the rest of the gang would join us. *Hot dang, we were doing it again! Yes! Yes! Yes!*

As we entered the pattern at Kissimmee, we could see NC-25885 (Jim Sprigg) on the ramp, patiently waiting for us. They had left Plant City, Florida, very early in the morning also. Needless to say, 885 was rarin' to go, too, with her new prop and everything!

But wait—what was this? There was N-1524Y (George and Murray Sellers) of Touch-'n-Go Florida fame parked beside 885. What the heck was she doing there? She knew a Cessna couldn't go with us. As it turned out, s he just wanted to give us a send-off and we really appreciated her being there to make sure we did get off as planned.

Yes indeed, this was the start of another great Cub odyssey, but for various reasons, there would be only four of us this year. Be that as it may, it sure did feel great to again be headed off to parts unknown with three of my sisters.

During the next few minutes, our fuel tanks were filled and amid much joking and merrymaking, our humanoids managed to make the planned trip known to everyone. It was a very ambitious plan that would require at least twelve or thirteen days to complete—with very little time for goofing off. The program called for making Kitty Hawk, North Carolina, in three days; then back to Gadsden by way of the Blue Ridge Mountains and Tennessee Valley during the next four days, to attend their annual J-3 Cub and Short Wing Piper Fly-in. After that we were to be on our way to Plains to visit our good friends, Tom and Martine Peterson who had a fantastic grass airport (Peterson Field). Then we were to just drift southward—arriving home sometime within two weeks after our departure day—today.

Mind you, this was the first time that my sisters and I had heard of this plan. We looked at each other and wondered if our humanoids really knew what they were taking on—what with that stalled weather front sitting directly over the area we were planning to fly in for the next week. Oh well, we knew we would be well cared for with no unnecessary chances taken and we would be in the air together. *Come on, gang, let's get going.*

During the past several months, many humanoids from other areas had heard about our little adventure last year and had invited us to be sure and stop and see them if we ever ventured into their area. It was for this reason that we had to get to St. Simons Island, Georgia, by this evening. EAA Chapter 905 members had invited us to spend the night with them at their clubhouse on McKinnon Airport. Our humanoids were to be very thankful for that invitation before tonight was over!

Off and running—I should say flying—from Kissimmee, we were in our old familiar "loose formation," with me in the lead, 474 on my left wing; 726 off my right wing and good ol' 885 still in the slot. I can never get over how great it feels just to be in the air with some of my sisters. It really tickles my ribs.

Our plan of action for today would take us to Palatka, and Keystone Heights, Florida, as well as St. Marys, Georgia, before our final destination of St. Simons Island. About forty-five minutes north of Kissimmee, we had our first encounter with something that would continue to bug us off and on for the entire trip—low visibility. It only lasted for about thirty miles, but it would have to be in the area of the real tall tower west of DeLand, Florida. There were times when I could just barely make out my sisters on either side of me. Of course I never could see 885 at my six o'clock position. (The weather forecast had been a good one for most of the day—this just happened to be a little low stuff that had not burned off.) My big concern was that stupid tower. Our altitude was well below the top of the thing and I certainly did not want to lead any one of my sisters into it, so we kept edging to the east until we knew we were well clear. Naturally, after passing the area of the tower, the visibility cleared very nicely and we were soon on the ramp at Palatka. None of us had seen the tower. We did not know it at the time, but that little patch of weather was just a very small sample of things to come!

The flying time from Palatka to Keystone Heights is only thirty minutes, but we Cubs only have an energy reservoir that will hold twelve gallons. This, coupled with the fact that we did not have or were not using those newfangled radio things, required a few extra stops. But who cared—we all loved to make landings and takeoffs! By making the stop at Keystone Heights, we would be able to make our next leg with ease. We wanted this to be a quick stop because it was getting very hot and those mean old black clouds that do a lot of crying were starting to take shape.

Come on, Sis, we know it is hot, but come on and start! Seven-two-six had decided to give her humanoid a workout. Her little Continental was hot and just wanted to cool off for a while. Lyle, my humanoid, took pity on Leighton and shut me down while he went over to help him get 726 purring again. *Aha, Lyle—big mistake, turning me off like that. I told you it was hot and we all really would like to cool off for a little while—so now is my chance.*

About thirty minutes later, after I had completely worn out Paul, Jim, Leighton, and Lyle—yes, all of our humanoids—my sisters and I decided that we had rested long enough and I might as well let those big 65 Continental horses go back to work. So with one last pull on my prop, we soon were ready to get back into the sky. Maybe we should not have done what we did, but it really was very hot and it was good to cool off for a little while.

The remainder of the day's flying was great. The weather was fairly good and we all enjoyed just being together in the air. After the stop at St. Marys, we found ourselves in the pattern at St. Simons Island under overcast and threatening skies. After landing, Chapter 905's clubhouse was very easy to find and soon we were all tied down nearby on the edge of the ramp. By this time the weather office had issued a severe thunderstorm warning for the airport area so everyone was making sure that all was secure—just in case. Thank goodness the storm never got onto the airport, although it did do a lot of rumbling.

As promised, Larry Williams, a member of EAA Chapter 905, was there to meet us with all sorts of helpful information as well as the key to the clubhouse and an invitation to attend a hangar party/dinner that was soon to be in progress. By this time it had started to rain. That is when our so-called barnstormer humanoids chickened out and decided to sleep in the clubhouse instead of their tents. Big deal—they get a dry place to sleep and *we* have to stay out here in the rain! All of us wished I had made them work harder back at Keystone.

Sunday June 5, our second day out, dawned very dreary and damp, with a low overcast and poor visibility. We were now in the area where the aforementioned stationary front is having its effect. From here on until we were back into central Florida we would be pestered by this weather mass. There certainly would be no early start this morning and we were expected to attend a cookout, in our honor, at Country Squire Airport, near Rock Hill, South Carolina, early this afternoon. All of us Cubs hoped our humanoids didn't try to push this weather. None of us felt that they would, but we had all heard wild tales about experienced humanoids with bad cases of get-there-itis.

Finally about mid-morning, we found ourselves lined up in our normal loose formation ready for takeoff. From here the weather did not look really good, but we decided to give it a try anyway. Once in the air, there was no joking or playing around as we must all concentrate on what was going on. The ceiling was about 800 feet and the visibility was variable from three to four miles. Our course line was quite easy to follow as it was the Atlantic Coast and we were headed for Hilton Head, South Carolina. There would be no frivolous gyrations or side trips on this leg as we needed to stick close together to make sure none of us drifted out of sight.

We do not see anything of Savannah, Georgia, as we passed by, but within ten more miles, the weather started to clear and by the time we had traveled the short distance to Hilton Head, the Weather gods had given us at least 1,500 broken and more than ten miles visibility. Fantastic, now we could relax and enjoy life again.

Quickly replenishing our go-juice supply, Hilton Head colored us gone. Now it was a beeline north to Orangeburg, South Carolina, for some more fuel. *Come on gang, we have a cookout to attend.*

Oh, what a beautiful grass runway they had at Orangeburg! This was the first time we had been able to put our little fat tires on grass since leaving home! My, it did feel good.The airports we had found thus far had not been taking care of their grass areas very well and I was not about to lead my sisters into something that was going to cause them to stub their toes. Well, face it, I was not exactly thrilled about doing myself any harm either. Orangeburg was another quick stop and we were outta-there.

Our humanoids could almost taste the good food and we were getting pretty excited ourselves as we made the mad dash north

881 over Columbia, South Carolina. Credit, Leighton Hunter.

under the Columbia, South Carolina, Class C airspace—north along U.S. Highway 77 to the shopping mall at the south edge of Rock Hill, then made a sharp left turn and we were lined up on a long final to runway 27 at Country Squire Airport. Yes, we are going to make the fly-in/cookout after all. *Hot dang, y'all anyway!*

EAA Chapter #961, and its chief cook and bottle washer, Tom Lempicke, really outdid themselves for us. (By the way, Tom also owns this great little grass airport and he and his lovely wife really knew how to make a quartet of Cubs and their humanoids feel welcome.) As my sisters and I made a low pass down the runway and returned for our landings the thought occurred to us that these folks really were glad to see us. It seemed the whole chapter was on hand to welcome us and take our pictures as our little fat wheels kissed the new-mown grass and rolled to the place of honor that they had waiting.

Country Squire Airport, South Carolina.

After eating their fill of some of the best barbecue ribs (Tom's specialty) they had ever tasted and spending some time enjoying the hospitality of the group, it was decided the time had come to introduce some folks to the joys of flying in Cubs. Four-seven-four and 885 had the honor and privilege of showing some first-timers what it was like to fly in a real airplane. From the big grins displayed on the faces of these new friends, I would say they did a very good job of strutting their stuff.

By the time 474 and 885 were back on the ground, someone or something had agitated a couple of grumpy clouds and they were now flashing fire and grumbling all over the western horizon. All hands went to work and very soon the remainder of the cookout equipment had been cleared and the four of us were pushed into the protective arms of Tom's personal hangar. It was a bit snug, but it sure felt good when we heard the first big drops of rain start pounding on the roof. (We did not know it now, but this would not be the last time for us to spend the night tucked inside, close together!)

Although we were in out of the storm, it was a bit disappointing because our humanoids would not be sleeping under our wings again tonight. That one thing had been something we had all looked forward to doing, but with this weather, we could understand why it would not happen. No, instead our humanoids would be sleeping in the home of our hosts. Maybe tomorrow night.

Getting tucked into Tom's personal hangar.

None of us slept well that night. It continued to rain off and on and occasionally a flash of lightning would light up the country-side. We could see through the windows that we had a lot to be thankful for by being in this nice cozy hangar. Finally we drifted off into a fitful sleep—each one of us wondering what tomorrow would bring—after all, we did have a long way to go and needed good weather to do it.

Hey 881, can you see anything out your window? That was 726 calling from her position along the back wall.

Nope, I can't see a thing, was my reply. Eight-eight-five and 474 both chimed in with, *We can't see anything either.*

This was the gist of our conversation as daylight descended on our location the morning of the third day, June 6, 1994. Finally, at about 9:00 A.M., our humanoids opened the big doors to our little nest and guess what? We still couldn't see a thing!

Again, the stalled front was playing with us. This time the fog was so thick that you could almost cut it with a knife. This was not good at all because if we are going to keep our planned program in operation, we really should get to Kitty Hawk today. Obviously, many phone calls were made to Flight Service and much discussion went on between our humanoids during the next couple of hours. At about 11:30 A.M. we kissed the Country Squire runway good-bye, made our final farewell salute flyby and headed east.

Even though the weather was not all that bad (five to six miles visibility), we had picked a highway and railroad track as our iron compass for this leg of our journey to Albemerle, North Carolina, just in case. As it turned out, it was a good choice because before we had completed the sixty-eight-mile trip we had to abandon that idea too. We were within thirty miles of our destination when all of a sudden it was detour time. Another one of those pesky angry clouds with fire and water coming out of it loomed out of the gloom directly in our path. A quick ninety-degree turn to our left kept us clear of the really bad stuff.

As you know, we Cubs were made to be flown by our pilot who watches landmarks on the ground 99 percent of the time. The other 1 percent we expected him to use our compass if there were few landmarks to follow or if visibility should go bad to the point where it was difficult to see those landmarks any distance away. This latter situation was where we were at this time and due to complacency on the part of my humanoid, my compass was at least twenty degrees out of calibration. Furthermore, he had not recognized this fact and would not do so until four days later when things really turned sour.

It was pure dumb luck on the part of my humanoid that he had me pointed in the correct direction and held that heading long enough for me to show him Stanly County Airport, at Albemarle. For several minutes he had flubbed around trying to orientate our location using the information from my erroneous compass. He never did really find himself and my sisters were dutifully following us in our meandering. I really wished I could have screamed at him, "Compass error, compass error, compass error," but this was one problem he would have to find for himself. Even 474, 885, and 726 saw a problem, but they said nothing.

Anyway, now safely on the ramp, we watched helplessly as the rain clouds and fog moved in and out. There were even times when the sun would peek through, but it never lasted more than a very few minutes. Many calls were made to Flight Service, checking on the weather in *all* directions, but they brought nothing but discouraging words. One minute it was "give up Kitty Hawk and head west to the mountains and eventually Gadsden." The next minute it was "forget the mountains and Gadsden and continue eastward." Talk about frustration and disappointment. Wow!

Finally, about 3:00 P.M., after much agonizing it became clear that it was very doubtful that we could proceed in any direction until the following morning—maybe. Now it again was obvious that our tents-under-wings program would not happen even tonight—not with all the rain that was falling off and on. This being our third disappointing night in a row is very disgusting and we are all beginning to use very harsh words when talking about this stupid stalled front!

Knowing that our humanoids were going to be in a nice dry motel while we spent the night out in the rain was a turnoff for us. I guess we should have known that we were truly loved, because after the decision was made to not fight the weather any longer, our humanoids started to search for a dry place for us before any thinking of a motel for themselves.

All of the normal hangar spaces were filled to capacity. However, Aviall, Inc., a major turbine engine overhaul company, had a beautiful hangar where they put the big corporate jets and turbo-props while they are working on them. This company was quite busy, but the hangar was empty at this time due to the fact that everything they were overhauling had been shipped in on trucks. I guess our forlorn appearance as we waited in the rain had its effect, because when L. D. Blake, the service manager, was asked if there might be room in his hangar for us, he welcomed us with open arms.

Once again, the four of us were tucked in neatly along one wall of this beautiful big hangar. I must admit that our bright yellow coats with those bold black lightning bolts, under the glow of the bright lights, did make an impressive sight—especially in a setting that is normally reserved for much more sophisticated members of the family. Immediately many cameras were brought forward and much merriment was made about what the board of directors would say when they saw what type of equipment L. D. was installing turbine engines in now. It was great fun posing for all of this photography while the rain pounded on the roof.

Not wishing to give up just yet, our humanoids continued to stay with us—just in case. In order to pass the time, each of them started to give us a gentle rubdown and general inspection. That was when 474 was able to point out that she had a slight breathing problem. The small crack that had developed in the rubber fitting between an intake pipe and the cylinder intake header was found and a search for a new fitting started immediately. None were to be found on the airport, so one was ordered for delivery by 10:30 the next morning. It would take less than ten minutes to make her as good as new—just as soon as we get the new part.

With this new development, a place to sleep was found for our humanoids and we four sisters settled down for another cozy night together, thankful that we were again in a nice dry, safe, place out of the storms. We had only been able to travel sixty-eight miles today and we knew everyone was going through some serious throes of frustration and disappointment. We had lost one full day of travel. This would make completion of the original plan almost impossible. Maybe the morning would bring good weather and we could be on our way. Again—this was wistful dreaming on our part.

Obviously sometime during the night at the "No-Tell-Motel," as our humanoids called it, they had held a big powwow, because when they awakened us the next morning, there was a more relaxed air about them. Their conversation indicated that we were now going to be operating by Plan B.

Thus, because of the weather and the loss of travel time we would forget about the trip through the mountains and to Gadsden. Instead, after Kitty Hawk—if we ever got there—we would make a leisurely trip to Plains for a couple of days and then drift on home. However, that mean ol' stalled front was still with us—so only time would tell.

The weather had improved enough so that we could follow the roads and the weatherman had promised good weather east of Raleigh-Durham, North Carolina, by the time 474 was completely healed with the installation of her new part. Our friends at Aviall, Inc. requested a low pass, which we were glad to give them as we departed under still-threatening skies. Everyone felt better now that the weather had improved somewhat and we had the promise of good conditions ahead.

We were not out of the woods yet. Even though the leg to Silver City, North Carolina, was not any problem, the next leg to Raleigh East (Knightdale, North Carolina) did present its own little problems. Not only did we have the worst weather of the day (it was moderate rain and fog) while flying under the Class C air space at Raleigh-Durham, we were below the level of some of those needles of death, as I call them, that poked up along our route in the same area. On top of that, my humanoid still had not recognized the fact that I was sick with a bad compass-ache and it was only by luck he was finding our position. Boy, was he dense!

As forecast, we found rapidly improving conditions after departing Raleigh East. Within a short time we were back into our type of flying—almost clear skies and visibility of at least eight to ten miles. We began to relax again and really started enjoying ourselves. You know—a little side trip here and there and an occasional wiggle of the tail now and then. At last we were back doing what we like to do best—fun flying.

Five-thirty in the afternoon found us all parked around the self-service gas pump on Dare County Airport, Manteo, North Carolina, less than ten miles south of First Flight Airport. The last two legs of the day—we had made a stop at Everetts, North Carolina, for some more go-juice—had been perfect. Besides that, it now looked like we would have tents under our wings tonight. What a great way to end our fourth day out, June 7, 1994.

Well, I was a little premature on that last statement. We were soon to find that we now had a bureaucratic problem! While the four of us were sipping refreshing essence of 100-octane, the airport administrator, Tim Gaylord, drove up in his truck to welcome us to his field. (We were soon to learn that Tim was one of the finest gentlemen you will ever meet—anywhere!) He could see that we were all excited about being here, going to the Wright Monument, using the grass along the side of his runways and having our favorite humanoids camped under our wings. We could hardly keep our tails from wagging.

Tim was almost equally excited about having the four of us on his airport; however, there was a little problem with some of our plans. First of all he suggested that even though the grass looked good, we should not land on it as there were hidden holes that could do us bodily harm. Even the designated grass runway was not fit for use. (OK, we wouldn't use the grass—no big deal.) Next, and we already knew this, First Flight Airport and the monument grounds are a federal park and no camping was allowed anywhere on that facility. Fact is you cannot leave an airplane parked on the ramp longer than twenty-four hours. It is a federal offense if you do. Then he also had to inform us that there was a county ordinance that prohibited any camping on *his* airport property. "We are trying to get that rule changed and hope to have it done within a few months. However," Tim continued, "I am not about to throw four beautiful specimens as you off of this field. If you happen to find yourselves tied down on the grass over there along the taxiway and four tents happen to sprout up over there along that tree line (indicating a nice grass area about 200 yards from our tie-down location) I am sure my security personnel will never say anything to you." With that he wished us well and said he would see us later.

OK, we could live with that. It wouldn't be as much fun, but what the heck—we could still see each other—and it wasn't raining—at this time, anyway!

Seven-two-six's humanoid went off to see if he could rent a car for ground transportation, while the rest of them proceeded to secure us in the recommended grass area.

Before all of this was complete, Tim came back to discuss a little proposition that he hoped we would be interested in accepting. It seems that an antique/classic aircraft fly-in was being planned for sometime in the spring of 1995 at the Wright Monument and Park. Tim had called the park ranger and told him about us four Cubs parked on his airport. Between the two of them, they had decided that maybe we would like to make some formation flybys of the monument, being subjects for a professional photographer to obtain pictures to be used in and on a publication being developed to advertise the coming event.

If the four of us could have done wingovers tied to the ground, we would have done them when we heard our humanoids agree to the idea. It was very difficult to contain ourselves as we listened to directions to meet the photographer on First Flight Airport at 11:00 A.M. the next morning. Also the fact that we would be there when the park opened at 9:00 A.M. did not exactly make us unhappy either. This made all of the weather and disappointment that we had encountered the past few days all worthwhile.

Much joy and happiness was shared between us Cubs as we watched our humanoids pitch their tents along the tree line. It would have been better if we could have been there with them, but just to see them joking with each other instead of worrying about the weather made life worthwhile. As soon as the campsite was in order, they drove off in search of something to eat, and we sisters drifted off to sleep with visions of a wonderful day tomorrow, dancing in our spinners.[1]

After a few rain showers during the night, dawn came on the wings of more low gray clouds and reduced visibility. Why in the heck did that stupid front continue to stick around? Didn't it know that today was supposed to be the day? Well, it was trying—the clouds weren't as thick as they have been every morning in the past and by the time our humanoids had gotten themselves in gear they had managed to break up pretty good so—it was fun time again. *This is the big one, gang. We're going to where it all started— Kill Devil Hills and Kitty Hawk. Let's get going.*

All of you descendents of the Wright Flyer take notice. If you have never visited the Wright Brothers National Memorial, you have missed one of the most impressive and meaningful destinations of your life. My sisters and I found ourselves changed, somehow, after our encounter with the revered grounds and area surrounding the place where the very first one of our kind took flight. It is a must-see place.

The distance from Dare County to the brothers' memorial is not far, so we flew an in-trail formation to the site. It was a federal park, so altitude restrictions applied and we certainly did not want to have any violations—especially at this location. When the monument first came into view, we all felt chills run up and down our longerons. We circled in awe of what lay below us. We had not discussed nor planned it, but to our surprise, as we orbited over this hallowed ground, we had positioned ourselves exactly ninety degrees to each other. I must say, we felt it was indeed a fitting salute to the ones who had made it possible for us to be alive today. After a couple of circuits, we broke out into the right-hand pattern for landing to the south at First Flight Airport.

It was just shortly after 9:00 A.M. on June 8, the fifth day of this adventure, when our Continentals quieted down on the ramp. We were parked where we could easily see the monument. For several minutes, we just sat there completely submerged in our own thoughts as we surveyed our surroundings. This is where it all

The monument honoring the Wright Brothers, Wilbur and Orville.

started. The park rangers knew we were coming and two of them were on hand to greet us and whisk our humanoids off on a private, personal, conducted tour of the monument and grounds. Of course, they also had to meet with the chief ranger, because he had some instructions regarding our photographic flyby.

The weather continued to improve and before long the clouds decided to give us some relief and allow the sun to shine through some rather large holes. The wind had picked up quite a bit—directly across the runway, which is located in one of those tree canyons. It was becoming very clear to us why the Wright Brothers had chosen this place to do all of their experimenting. Mother Nature had really created quite the natural wind tunnel that they needed to test their gliders and to make that first powered flight.

We really enjoyed our wait for the arrival of our 11:00 A.M. date with the photographer. Time went very fast because we quickly

For a bit of perspective, this is how the monument looks from above.

became friends with a fleet of Cessnas that lived with and worked for Kitty Hawk Aero Tours. This group of hard-working cousins were being flown by the young pilots whom our humanoids had met on the beach the night before. Since rain was forecast again tonight, Duke, their chief pilot, insisted that we should spend the night in his hangar back on Dare County Airport. Besides, he had another little project that he wanted us to help him complete. (More on that later.)

As the appointment time approached, our humanoids were brought back to us by Darryl, the park ranger who had been their escort for the morning. Very shortly, our friend Tim, from Dare County Airport, came driving in with Jim Lee of Jim's Camera House, our own professional photographer. During the briefing that followed, it became very clear that we were going to do some rather low flying in very close proximity of the monument. (All of this had been cleared with the powers in charge.) Another necessity was that we had to be able to communicate with the photographer in order to meet his needs as to our position in flight near the monument.

Even though the rules of this entire adventure would not allow the use of any electronic devices, neither 885 nor 726 were mute. They both had those fancy hand-held things if they were really

Part of the Six-Pack in a passing salute. Credit, Jim's Camera House.

needed. In the interest of efficiency, it was needed at this time. The decision was made for 726 to lead—she could talk to the photographer—and the rest of us would fall in behind her in the best diamond formation that we could possibly create. So, it was with much pride that the four of us taxied out for this unforgettable chapter of our lives.

As mentioned earlier, the wind had become quite strong—especially for us featherweight Cubs. Once airborne, we formed up in our best formation discipline and 726 led us close to the monument for the first pass. With the strong gusty wind blowing, it was quite rough, but we managed to stay in our flight positions with little difficulty. We were too busy to look, but later photographs would prove the fact that as we came into the area, all guests touring the grounds were looking at us rather than the monument. One more pass and 726 was told that was enough and we made our way back to First Flight Airport for the landing on the runway at the bottom of that tree canyon, with that strong, gusty, ninety-degree crosswind blowing.

It was with much greater pride that we came taxiing back to the ramp after our little show, as many of the guests waved to us from the side of the ramp. Even though I held my spinner high, I was very embarrassed about my condition. You see, my humanoid had worked my tailwheel steering springs so hard during the landing that one of them had broken. One of the most humiliating experiences you can possibly endure is to have your tailwheel repaired with safety wire while many humanoids watch! It was a terrible situation.

Our newfound friends at Kitty Hawk Aero Tours made several phone calls, and a new spring was soon on its way to us. It was to be delivered no later than 10:30 A.M. the next morning, which would allow us to be on our way to Plains by eleven o'clock. That was the plan anyway. It didn't work.

While our humanoids returned to their tour of the museum and grounds, including the spot where the first four flights took place, we basked in the beauty of our surroundings and enjoyed being eyed and talked about by many of the humanoids who were visiting this place where powered flight was born. Many of them had seen our performance during the picture-taking passes and thought we were part of a show that was put on for their enjoyment by park management—we did not tell them differently. This was indeed a very relaxed afternoon and all went fine until another one of those angry black clouds moved across the sky and dumped buckets of water on us. Somehow I am beginning to feel that even the clouds are tired of this front staying around so long. Wouldn't it ever go away?

Evening was rapidly approaching by the time it had stopped raining, and we were soon back in the air, headed for Dare County. As mentioned earlier, Duke had invited us to spend the night in his hangar and soon we were tucked in, snug and dry, with some of the Cessnas and a Waco UPF-7 that were used in the tour operations. It was then that we learned of the details of the project for which he needed our help.

Weather permitting, and we all were begging for it to be good, he wanted to get some pictures of his pilots standing beside us as if we were the type of equipment they flew in their operation. If he had these pictures, he could have a lot of fun with any new pilot applicant who wanted to work in his organization—knowing full well very few, if any, would have any such experience. Fact is, he admitted that neither he nor any of his present pilots had ever flown in a Cub, let alone being qualified to fly a conventional gear airplane. Eight-eight-five insisted that she would make sure that Duke flew in a "real yellow and black Piper Cub" before we charged off the next morning.

Yes, we heard the rain on the hangar roof again during the night. Morning light revealed low clouds and reduced visibility again. Even though the morning of June 9, the sixth day into our adventure, did not bring good weather, it was flyable. As it was, we could not leave until I had the new spring put on my tailwheel and it might be as late as 10:30 before it was delivered. There was plenty of time for the picture taking and 885 had ample time to demonstrate the joys of Cub flying. From the expression on the face of her subject, I know she did an excellent job.

The latest promised delivery time of 10:30 had come and gone—no new spring! It was now past 11:00 A.M., the weather is very good for Cub flying and we even had a tailwind if we could just get going. Where the heck was that delivery van with my steering springs? We were tired of the wait and it was a long way to Plains—time to get going. Finally my humanoid went to the nearest hardware store and purchased a couple of springs that worked just fine—thank you. At last we were airborne. (Those approved springs that had been ordered finally found me at home over a week later.)

It was a crime how the government has gobbled up the air space south and west of Dare County. It has hogged the area with more restricted areas than it could possibly use all the time. Well, be that as it may, government is there and for this reason we had to thread the needle between some of these areas. The weather was very good now, compared to what we had been flying through, so there really was no problem. It was during this close-tolerance operation that my humanoid finally noticed that I just might have a compass-ache. He did note the fact that it was reading about twenty degrees off, but he immediately blamed it on the wind drift. He was really being a Dilbert about this problem, but at least he had noticed there may be one. He would learn it is a fact later—the hard way.

We fought with those military restricted areas all the way to New Bern, North Carolina. What a waste of valuable airspace.

On the ramp at New Bern, 885 admitted that she had been using her hand-held on occasion around the more active airports. She usually just listened, but this time she had talked to one of our distant relatives as we made our arrival. It seems that Mr. Beechcraft Baron was charging toward the airport from the east and we were coming from the north. He announced he was six miles out and wanted to know if any traffic was in the area. Eight-eight-five felt the smart thing to do would be to tell him that there were four of us about three miles north of the airport entering downwind for landing to the north. Mr. Baron admitted that he did not have us in sight; however, he was going to proceed with his planned right turn to the runway. (Normal traffic is left turns.) Mr. Baron next announced that he was now three miles out on a right-base leg. With that 885 came to our rescue by stating that there were four Cubs in the pattern. One was just turning base to final; number two was on base; number three was turning downwind to base, and number four was still on downwind. With that Mr. Baron replied in his friendly voice, "Well, I guess I'm number five in that case, and I now have all of you in sight."

Poor fellow—we had him outnumbered.

Our energy supply was quickly replenished and the Flight Service station on the field was paid a quick visit. Even though our present weather was quite good, ol' grumpy stalled front was still with us. At the present time we were flying in a pocket of fairly nice conditions, but less favorable weather was not far away. The nice airport at Elizabethtown, North Carolina, was still in that bubble of decent, flyable, weather and if we did not wait too long, we would be OK. Once again, we were back in the air really enjoying life to the fullest, winging our way ever closer to Peterson Field at Plains.

Due to our late start, we felt that Elizabethtown was as far as we needed to go for this day. What a great choice we have made for this overnight. Tom Roberts, owner of Roberts' Aviation Company, met us at the gas pump. Even though the grass along the runway was not suitable for landing, he had a great place for us to nestle in for the night. This would be the first night since leaving home that we were able to have tents under our wings. At last. Tom also had ground transportation that he gladly let our humanoids use to go into town.

One thing that I have forgotten to mention is that at every airport where our humanoids have not been in a private home or motel, the airport managers have allowed them to have a key to the office where they could have the use of a nice hot shower and Elizabethtown was no different. Tom even had a better deal for them when he included a nice lounge with a big color TV for them to view. This was barnstorming?

Even though an overcast sky blocked out the stars, this was without a doubt the most tranquil setting we had had this whole trip. Here we were, four sisters with our favorite tents close by, sitting on a very peaceful little airport away from the hurly-burly of the big city. Before we all turned in for the night, a dawn patrol flight was planned for the next morning. Since one of these had not been possible so far on this trip, we all drifted off to sleep with grand dreams of what the first light of morning would bring.

Darn, wouldn't you know it. When is that dumb ol' front going to give up? Maybe it would never move—ever. These were the thoughts going through our timing gears when we caught the first indication of light on the morning of June 10, our seventh day since leaving home. As it grew lighter, it was obvious that we had an obscured sky with less than two miles visibility. Again, the dawn patrol was grounded.

Our humanoids are pretty strong willed, so by the time there was legal light, they determined that there was at least three miles visibility and the dawn patrol would fly. They had been robbed of the pleasures of our early frolics in the air each morning thus far, and they were not going to be deprived of those pleasures again. No way. Their positive thinking must have worked, because as we lifted off, we really could see three miles—barely.

This morning's patrol was fun, but it certainly did not nearly live up to past such adventures. We were very reluctant to venture far from our campsite, because things could become a little critical if we were not careful. This flight lasted only thirty minutes, during which Elizabethtown would know of our presence. (This was proven when our humanoids, dressed in their Cub T-shirts, were having breakfast at the local eatery. They were asked if they knew anything about the four little airplanes that were flying around earlier.) Now very much refreshed and back at our campsite, it became a waiting game for the weather to clear enough for us to continue our trek toward Plains.

It is interesting to note the attitude of different towns and communities toward what should be their most prized possession—the local airport. The little town of Elizabethtown should be and is very proud of its excellent facility. This was demonstrated very graphically to us just as the weather decided to let us depart. We were in the final stages of loading when a gentleman in a business suit arrived on the scene along with Tom, our host for the past night. This businessman was the chairman of the airport authority. Learning of the presence of the four of us on his airport, he took time off from his busy work schedule just to come and extend to us a heartfelt welcome to the area. He extended a sincere invitation for us to stay as long and fly as much as we desired. He also wanted us to know that we were welcome to come back anytime in the future. (Try to find that quality in most of your elected airport officials.) We tried our best to thank this real friend of general aviation with our best formation as we lifted off on the next leg of this weather-hampered adventure.

Mullins, North Carolina, was chosen as our next destination for two reasons. First of all there was a good road and railroad system that we could follow, and it was the next logical place to stop and check the weather further down the line. Let's face it, the low ceilings, the fog, the haze, the rain, and all the rest of the lousy elements were beginning to take their toll. It was still fun, but it could be a lot more "funner."

We were not excited or encouraged from the bits of information we picked up from the conversation between our humanoids as they prepared to mount up again here at Mullins. It was obvious that this segment to Orangeburg (yes, we were there on June 5th, and were now going back because of the nice grass runway) would be flyable but there would be areas of rain and such stuff. Checkpoints would be farther apart also, so there was going to have to be some dead-reckoning done this time. Oh! Oh! We may be in trouble because my humanoid still has not realized that my compass is not feeling well. *He still thinks his problem is with the wind. Hey, gang, watch us closely on this one.*

On the wing once again, my compass was indicating 240 degrees, the desired computed heading. Almost immediately, 726 started to drift away to the right. This was not unusual for her. She often took little side trips because her increased speed allowed her to catch up with no problem. However, this time she continued to get farther and farther away from us to the right and was not making any effort to get back in line. Four-seven-four and 885 were sticking with me, even though they felt all was not as it should be.

About twenty minutes into the flight, my humanoid realized that he might be a little misplaced. He could see that 726 was almost out of sight now, and the things on the ground did not match what was printed on the chart. I could tell he was beginning to have a little concern; after all, 474 and 885 were right there with us. A small town came into view and he soon found himself at least seven miles south of track. Now he was wondering what went wrong—after all, my compass has stayed on or very near 240 degrees. Then it hit him. He remembered a couple of days back when I got him to notice that I had this compass-ache and was indicating a twenty-degree west deviation, which he blamed on the wind! Thank goodness, he had finally gotten the message.

A quick heading alteration was made and we were soon back on track with 726. This little maneuver was accomplished just in time because very shortly we entered an area of light rain and very poor visibility. My how the drops of water did sting as they impaled themselves onto our leading edges and prop blades. We hated flying in this stuff, especially when we could not see very far ahead and no checkpoints were visible. I just hoped my aching compass wasn't forgotten again.

Within twenty minutes, we came to a beautiful interstate highway that would lead us the rest of the way to Orangeburg. What a relief to find ourselves very near the spot on that road that had been planned before departing from Mullins. Now it was just a matter of staying with the super-slab, avoiding all the towers, and flying out of this @#%*# miserable rain and fog. Another twenty minutes of very annoying climatic conditions put us into an area of improvement, and by the time we entered the pattern for landing on the grass at Orangeburg, the sun was making a very strong effort to shine on our parade.

As mentioned earlier, the fact that all of this frustration with the elements and disappointment of not being able to fly as we liked, was starting to tell on all of us. Now gathered around the gas pump on the ramp, it was very obvious that we all were getting a little weary of fighting with this constant weather problem. As we reflected on the last hour or so of what was supposed to be fun, we agreed it had not been fun at all and we were wondering just when our humanoids were going to call a halt to this foolishness. Enough was enough.

When called, Flight Service advised that the present weather on toward Plains was pretty good, but we could expect to find an occasional area of rain and low clouds along the way. Those conditions could be expected to stay around for the rest of the day, and if we wanted better flying weather we had best head south— to Florida. At that point, 474 stated very bluntly, "I'm going home! Now! From here!"

Thank goodness, she had enough compression to stand up and say what she was feeling. There was no doubt about it, we all were becoming very irritated with the situation and just maybe she had the right idea—maybe we *should* go home. We certainly had no desire to fly another segment like the one just completed. No sir! That was not Cub environment.

After a brief board of directors meeting, it was decided that since it was only thirty-five miles further, it was in the general direction of Plains *or* home, and the weather was good in that direction, we would terminate today's journey at Allendale, South Carolina. It was further agreed that after the weather check the following morning a decision would be made regarding continuing this adventure or going home. All of us hoped for the best, but expected the worst. It had not been good for a week, so why change now?

It was very hot and muggy, with scattered to broken clouds above, when we found ourselves secured to the ramp at Allendale. We would have to settle with staying on the ramp again tonight. This arrangement was all right because the tents could be pitched directly behind us on the grass.

Four-seven-four and 885 were wondering what was wrong when they saw the tents go up quickly behind 726 and myself and none appeared behind them. What they did not know was their humanoids were playing it cool and staying in the air conditioned office with a plan to erect their tents after the temperature dropped a few degrees. Later in the evening, this was proven to be a very, very smart maneuver on their part.

After about an hour of relaxation, our humanoids gathered close by and were obviously getting ready to conduct some sort of ceremony. The next thing we knew, a small fire erupted in their vicinity and several cheers were heard coming from the group. Just what is going on? Have they tumbled their gyros or what?

It turned out, they were just venting their frustrations. As we all knew, the past few days had been very hectic, what with fighting the weather and all. Also, this entire time had been flown within the confines of the Charlotte Sectional Chart and, if all went well, we would be moving to a new chart very quickly after departure in the morning. With the prospects of using another sectional, 885's humanoid decided to burn his Charlotte chart—it had brought us nothing but problems and maybe the new chart would bring an end to this lousy weather. Besides that, he had used the chart so much it was completely worn out and it was due to expire in a few days anyway!

By the time this little ritual was over, it was again time to find something to eat. We Cubs had to chuckle as we watched our four friends—our humanoids—drive off in that old pickup truck with two of them in the back shouting directions to the two in the cab, who were paying absolutely no attention to their orders. Not one of us visualized what was going to happen to us within the next eighty minutes.

No one saw it coming. It seemed to just materialize out of nowhere. At first it was just your average small run-of-the-mill cloud with an emotional problem. It did not seem to be moving, and the longer it stuck around, the larger it grew and the more it cried. Within a very short time, we were enduring the hardest downpour in our memory. It seemed as if someone had opened the floodgates of a great dam in the sky—and it would not let up. Finally after about thirty minutes, it decided it had created enough problems in this one area and moved further to the east. Even the local Cessnas, tied on the ramp with us, commented that it was the most rain in such a short time that they had seen in several years.

We were soaked through and through. It had rained so hard that water had been forced into our cockpits through the skylights and any other small opening it could find. Eight-eight-five came through in much better shape than the rest of us because she was wearing the rain cape that her humanoid always covered her skylight with anytime she was parked where the possibility of getting wet existed. Try as she did, the wind was just too much for 726, and she could not keep her door closed—it was really "wet city" for her. Thank goodness none of us suffered any real damage, but it really wasn't very comfortable sitting out here soaked to the longerons.

Yes, things were really a mess. The whole area, including the ramp, resembled a full-blown lake. Even the two tents that had been erected on higher ground appeared to be strange-looking watercraft anchored out in this newly formed body of water. Obviously, the two eager campers who erected their tents now had a *real* problem. Too bad they had not been as smart as the other two campers who still had not set up their quarters for the night. Well, things don't look very good for them either as all possible areas for such activities were now under water. Even our little fat donuts were sitting in water.

Our humanoids were not the most happy enthusiastic barnstormers when they returned and surveyed the new lake-front property in which we were parked. Even though a light rain was still falling, the first order of business was to start drying us out. Bath towels, normally used by humans, were put to good use drying our instrument panels, seats and other vital organs. The floating tents and their damp contents were put inside the hangar to dry as much as possible. As they worked, our humanoids held another board of directors meeting at which it was decided that the Weather gods had indeed won this long struggle and we would go home the next day, weather permitting, of course.

By the time things had settled down again, we were quite a scattered group. The two humanoids with the dry sleeping bags bedded down in the operations office of the FBO. The two with the damp sleeping bags went back to town to another one of those No-Tell-Motel establishments. Even we four Cubs were parked with two of us on one side of the ramp and the other two on the opposite side—definitely not our normal precision display team positions. This was not the way we wanted to spend what was to be our last night out.

After being kept awake most of the night by the flashing and rumbling of some very angry giants, it came as no surprise to find low ceilings and reduced visibility again as the dark shadows of night were pushed away by the first light of June 11, the last day of this somewhat disappointing adventure. Since they had closed the floodgates upstairs, the "lake" had almost vanished into the normal drainage holding areas. Once again, there would be no dawn patrol and since we were going to be headed home, our humanoids really were taking their time getting under way.

A phone call was made to our friends, Tom and Martine, at Peterson Field in Plains, to tell them that we would not make it as planned. That call further convinced us that we should head on home because that destination had zero/zero conditions and no one knew when it would clear. The next call was made to the man with the crystal ball at Flight Service, and he confirmed that if we headed south, we would eventually get away from this pesky system that had been raining on our parade for the past week. We should be finding much better weather once we were past Savannah, and by the time Brunswick, Georgia, was in our prop wash, it should be real Cub weather.

By mid-morning, our spinners were all headed south. It was a bittersweet departure because we were cutting our little odyssey short by at least three days. However, the thought of leaving all of these undesirable atmospheric conditions, especially those sting-ing water drops hitting our leading edges, helped ease the pain. We were not out of the woods yet, and there were a couple of times during our dash for Hilton Head when we really questioned the sanity of our humanoids, because we should have turned back.

The nice boost we got from the Wind Gods as we headed down the coast past Savannah produced the much-improved conditions as forecast. Soon we were able to relax and enjoy being in the air together absorbing the sights. Our ground speed was now almost ninety miles per hour. Wow—look out Concorde!

Mid-afternoon found us on the ramp at Leesburg, Florida, af-ter once again stopping at St. Marys and Keystone Heights to re-plenish our energy supplies. This would be the place for the start of the breakup of our little foursome. For the last time this trip, we lifted off the runway in our trademark formation. After departing the pattern, we bid 474 farewell as she rocked her wings and headed home to Clinch Lake. As she drifted away into the distance, we heard her call back, *No rain for next year.*

It was just the three of us now. Eight-eight-five had continu-ally flown in the slot position for the past eight days, so it was with great joy she went to the front of our V, leading us to her home at Plant City. (Yes, we needed to stop there, too, because, as men-tioned before, our twelve-gallon tanks do not make for long legs.) She would be safely tucked into her dormitory before 726 and I headed for Venice.

One hour after saying good-bye to 885, sister 726 and I were being pushed into our own homes on Venice Airport. We found it interesting to note that during the last three hours in the air we had encountered the best flying weather of the entire trip—including the first day when leaving home. It did feel good to know that all of us would have a nice dry place to sleep tonight if it should rain!

Speaking of sleep, I was ready for it. None of us got very much the last night due to the constant light show and occasional dripping water. While waiting for the Sandcub to come, my mind drifted back to all that had taken place during the past few days. Yes, we had been very frustrated and disappointed in not being able to do all that was planned. Maybe this venture had been too Herculean to begin with as it left little time to just goof off and have fun. In order to do everything, we had to keep moving very much on a schedule, and the weather certainly prevented that from happening. Don't get me wrong, we had fun—lots of it, but still there was pressure to make the next event.

Something else that we would do differently next time is we will either *not go* if there was a stalled weather system in our path or we would get through it as quickly as possible and not continue to try to play in the area beneath it. Our day at Kitty Hawk made all the problems encountered worthwhile. What a fantastic moment in all of our lives. Many other fond memories were made with the aid of the great humanoids that we encountered along the way. Their helpfulness, compassion, and hospitality will be remembered forever. We thank each one of them for all that they did.

[1]While our Cubs were taking a well-deserved rest near our campsite at the Dare County Airport in Manteo, North Carolina, Paul, Jim, Leighton and I headed into town looking for a place to eat. Paul and Jim were in the back seat, Leighton was driving, and I was riding shotgun as we drove away looking for a nice seafood restaurant that we had been told about. As we left the airport, my internal compass became completely confused and I was 180 degrees out of sync. I had questioned Leighton's sanity when he insisted on continuing in the direction he was going when I knew we were proceeding back inland—not toward the ocean. Just because we did find the establishment we had been told about, I was still firmly convinced we had gone west instead of east.

It was quite dark under overcast skies by the time we had finished eating. As we returned to the main road, Leighton challenged me as to how sure I was that we had not proceeded toward the ocean beach. I was so sure that I bet him ten bucks he was lost. If I had known my geography, I would have known that he was correct because the road sign indicated Nags Head straight ahead and that nice little town was definitely on the Atlantic Ocean Beach. Needless to say, Paul and Jim kept quiet—knowing full well I was wrong.

Soon, we were parked near a wide path that led down to the water's edge and we proceeded to the beach. I was still not convinced because we had flown over Albemarle Sound when we arrived earlier in the day, and my internal system was still telling me that this was that body of water before us. A group of young adults were having a party on the beach, but we did not want to bother them to clear up our dispute.

On the way back to the car, we met a young couple and Leighton asked them to tell us the name of the body of water behind us. Of course the answer was the Atlantic Ocean. I had to pay up on the spot.

As we were laughing about my confusion and stupid wager, the masculine half of this nice young couple exclaimed, "I know you—you are part of the Cub Six-Pack. We saw you tieing down at the airport this afternoon." What a pleasant surprise to find someone this far from home who had read about the Cub Six-Pack trip of a year ago in Touch-'n-Go Florida.

As it develops, this young couple were two of the pilots who fly for Kitty Hawk Aero Tours out of First Flight Airport, and they had taxied past us while we were tieing down our Cubs at Dare County Airport. They quickly invited us to join them with the above-mentioned group of young people on the beach. This entire group of fine young people were pilots who flew for the two competing tour operations at First Flight. It was a delight for us "old crows" to be talking with these young eagles. What a fine group of young ladies and gentlemen they are and we wished them well.

Only Two of Us This Time

Perturbed? You're darn right I'm perturbed! After all, late in March I was given a nice cleaning—I anticipated going to Sun-'n-Fun in April, but didn't. Two days ago, my front control stick was removed which led me to believe I was going to be leaving on one of those great barnstormer trips, but no! All I did today was haul my adopted brother's (the big Stearman) parachutes to Air Adventures at Clewiston Airglades Airport to be repacked. And to top that off, my humanoid didn't even replace my control stick when we got back to Venice. I'm not just perturbed, I'm downright angry. I'll get even with him—I'll develop an oil leak or maybe a flat cylinder or tire—anything to let him know that I do not like being led to believe we were going to have some real fun and then fail to do any of those exciting adventures, which are always preceded by cleaning and/or front control stick removal.

These were my thoughts as I tried to go to sleep on the night of May 9, 1995. How disgusted I was with my humanoid that evening!

I should have known better than to have those unkind thoughts. First of all, I would never do anything to make him unhappy with me. Thus no oil leaks or flats on purpose. After all, two wrongs do not make a right. Second, on Monday, May 15th, my oil was being changed and it still had at least eight hours of time left before the normal change time arrived. (This was a good sign.) To make matters even better, the following day various camping items were being trial fitted into my front seat, which explained why the control stick had not been replaced when we got back with the parachutes. Then the frosting on the cake came well before dawn on the morning of May 17, when I found all the necessary equipment for another barnstormer trip being loaded into my front seat. The final confirmation that another great trip was in store occurred when my older sister's (NC-22726) humanoid, Leighton Hunter, appeared out of the darkness with a load of camping equipment. His announcement that 726 would be ready to fly by the first legal light made my oil pump jump with joy, because at that time, I knew we were on the verge of another great Cub adventure with some of our sisters.

Sure enough, as the sun cracked the eastern horizon, 726 and I waved good-bye to our friends tied down on the ramp at Venice airport and pointed our spinners north. We did not know where we were headed, but both of us knew it was going to be fun no matter where we found ourselves during the next few days. We did hope that there would be more than just the two of us, but due to circumstances beyond our control, we were to discover that there would be no others to join us on this trip. Well, what the heck, we could have fun anyway.

While on the ground at Tampa North Airport, waiting for some early morning fog to go away and also to get our fuel tanks filled, the sectional charts were brought out and we listened intently while Lyle and Leighton discussed the mission for the day. It was obvious by now that the ultimate goal for this day was to visit our friends Tom and Martine Peterson, who own and operate the finest little grass airport in Georgia, near Plains. We also learned that our itinerary would be to Pensacola, Florida, on Thursday, May 18; Quincy, Florida, on Friday, May 19, and then we would play it by ear after that, arriving home sometime on Monday, May 22. Remembering the Herculean trip we had undertaken a year earlier, 726 and I heaved a sigh of relief as we knew this would be much more relaxed than had been the case at that time. Yes, this one was really going to be fun.

Within an hour, we were back in the air, winging our way northward. Next stop would be Cross City. This was not our first choice of destinations, but due to a problem with fuel availability at Perry, Florida, a stop at Cross City was mandatory. There were two reasons for our feeling about this particular port of call. One is the fact that its fueling nozzle was much too large to be used on our fuel tanks. It was more suitable for filling large aircraft such as the big twins or even DC-3 type aircraft. Why they insisted on using this large unit I have never figured out, as it is a very simple operation to replace the oversized fitting with one that is suitable for all to use. This is the only place in all of our travels that we have encountered such a large gas hose.

The second reason is the fact that in our travels, we have also found the cost of a gallon of fuel at this location seems to be considerably more than other locations of the same quality. I guess they know what they must charge, but these two problems do tend to send those like us to other destinations when it is possible to do so. Maybe that is the intent and purpose of their way of thinking. If it is—well, it really works.

Aside from having to follow a couple of Cesssna 150s making Boeing 747 approaches to the airport at Thomasville, the leg to that fair city was uneventful. Seven-two-six led part of the time and on occasion I moved to the front. She was the first to land at Thomasville and when I followed her to the ramp, she parked herself on the grass at least 100 yards from the gas pump. I could not understand the *why* of this action, but I followed along and parked beside her. Inquiring about the wisdom of doing this little act, she politely informed me that the grass was much cooler. Besides that, the gas truck could bring us our needed refreshments. I had to agree that the grass was much cooler and more comfortable, but that gas truck contained J-A-fuel. She knew as well as I that anything put into our energy source tanks from that truck was sure to give both of us a very severe case of indigestion. I was going to suggest that she needed glasses, because she admitted that she had not seen the sign on the side of the truck.

After our humanoids had put in a leisurely half hour of consuming refreshments and chatting with other of the same species, we were moved across the ramp to the gas pumps where we, too, were treated to a refreshing drink of 100- LL avgas. It sure is nice to be able to make such a slow-paced journey. No pressures, no weather problems, nothing—just good ol' fun flying.

Once again, back into the air. This time 726 was in the lead, but she was drifting off in the wrong direction so I took it upon myself to turn on course toward Plains and forget about where she might be going. (As it turned out, she wanted to go in the correct direction, but her humanoid was fiddling with some sort of music playing device and was not paying any attention to where they were headed until he spotted me well to the right of their position.) *Pay attention, girl, we have got to stay out of that Class D airspace at Albany, Georgia, on this leg.*

By the time we had come within concern range of Albany, 726 had gotten her humanoid under control and they were doing a very good job of leading us. The afternoon sun had warmed the surface sufficiently to produce some thermal activity and that, coupled with the southerly wind, made our ride rather swift, although I must admit a little bumpy.

With Peterson Field in sight, 726 started into a very slow descent with me slightly behind to her right. We needed to announce our arrival to our friends and the best way to do that was to make a low pass down the runway, which, I might add, passed directly in front of their home and office. (The bumps made it too uncomfortable for me to be as close to 726 as I liked for this type of arrival, but still I was in close enough for our friends to get the idea.) Our low pass completed, we broke formation and were soon rolling our donut tires on that soft green grass runway. Within a very short time, Tom and Martine had extended their warm greeting to us and we were tied securely to the grass ramp with our humanoids' tents erected neatly beneath our wings. It was almost 4:00 P.M. and now all we had to do was relax and wait for Petecraft Aviation to close its doors for the day at 6:00 P.M. That's when Tom and Martine could join our humanoids for dinner at Mom's, their favorite restaurant located in the town of Preston.

The sun was just about ready to say good-bye when the happy foursome returned from their dinner of grilled quail, and all the trimmings, including sweet potato pie and some of the best home-brewed lemonade you would ever taste. ("Mom" sure did know how to cook!) One of the things that our humanoids wanted to do on this trip was to make as many sunset and dawn patrol flights as possible and if they were to be legal tonight, they needed to get crackin'. We were quickly untied, and with Martine in my front seat, we were off and flying.

The beautiful red and orange sunset in the western sky with the golden ripe wheat and green rows of peanuts in the fields below made us realize what a good life we were living. The wind had subsided and the thermals had all gone to sleep so the air was smooth as silk. It really doesn't get much better than this. This is why we were created! All I could say is those creatures and things that cannot or will not fly have no idea of what they are missing. I was so thankful that I was a Cub and have a humanoid who loves to fly as much as I do. We could have flown for hours this evening, but darkness came much too quickly and we soon found ourselves again tied next to those nice little tents, waiting for the morning, which we were certain would bring a beautiful dawn patrol as well as another great day of flying to Pensacola.

The moon and stars shown brightly in the crystal clear sky almost all night and the tranquillity of the setting had convinced us that the coming day was going to be the best ever for Cub flying. Much to our chagrin, at about 4:30 A.M. the moon and stars disappeared as if someone had turned them off with a switch. Shortly thereafter, a light breeze from the southwest brought in reduced visibility. When our dawn patrol time arrived, the ceiling had lowered to less than 200 feet and visibility was less than two miles. It certainly looked as if we were grounded for the day—even though the hour was early. Where all of this stuff had come from was a complete mystery to us because the last weather report/forecast that we had seen was for beautiful weather on May 18, 1995.

With spirits as low as the clouds, Leighton and Lyle left in the Peterson's pickup truck, headed for breakfast at Granny's Restaurant in Americas. At the moment, it looked like we were going to be putting in a very long day stuck here on the ground. However, they hadn't been gone more than one-half hour when the breeze started to pick up and within another one-half hour, there was at least a twenty mph wind blowing from the southwest. Even though this wind would be directly on our nose, if we were to proceed toward our destination for the day, it was moving the fog away with visibility already up to at least seven miles. Even the ceiling had moved up so that by the time our humanoids returned from Granny's, we could legally go flying.

The present weather and forecasts for all points to and including Pensacola were checked in minute detail. No matter how you looked at it, things did not look good. Well, actually the ceiling and visibility indicators were not all that bad, but the long-range forecast for this day's destination predicted that if we did in fact make Pensacola, our chances of returning to Quincy the next day were very doubtful. On top of all of that, with that very strong wind blowing directly on our noses as we proceeded toward the southwest, our estimated three-hour trip was going to be considerably longer.

Our humanoids were in quite a tizzy because they wanted to visit the Naval Aviation Museum at Pensacola Naval Air Station, as well as attend the annual EAA Chapter 445 Fly-in at Quincy, Florida, on Saturday, May 20th. All forecasts indicated this would not be possible. Finally, they decided to proceed to Quincy and see what developed at that point. They even considered renting a car and driving from Quincy to Pensacola if that was the only way to make it work. (When 726 and I heard of that plan, we decided there was no way that would happen. We wanted to go to Pensacola, too.)

The very strong wind blowing in our faces made for some interesting flight planning. Our slow cruising speed, coupled with only twelve gallons of fuel, made it critical to find a suitable gas stop within our range. It was obvious that we could not proceed directly toward Pensacola—energy replenishing facilities were not close enough together—another reason to proceed direct to Quincy. Thus we were soon airborne, this time headed for Camilla, Georgia.

It was mandatory for us two Cubs to come up with some way to convince our humanoids that we could make Pensacola, and gamble on the weather forecast being wrong about not being able to leave there the following day. After all, weather forecasting is not an exact science. What it would be or how it would work, we had no way of knowing.

The further south we flew, the stronger the wind became and the more the ceiling and visibility improved. When our Continentals had stopped ticking over at the fuel pumps at Camillia, our humanoids made no comment, but each pulled out his section charts that would take them to Pensacola and headed for the office. Yes, our flight into better weather had convinced them to proceed with the original plan. Even though the wind was much stronger now than before, both 726 and I knew we had succeeded in our plot to press on.

Knowing full well that from this point westward we would be flying almost directly into the wind, some very serious flight planning was in order. With an anticipated ground speed of forty-five to fifty miles per hour, our fuel stops needed to be quite close together. After much searching, our humanoids came to the conclusion that we could make Ferguson Field on the southwest side of Pensacola by letting us place our wheels on the ground at Marianna and Crestview, Florida, where we could replenish our energy supply. The only problem that we could see with this plan was the fact that the wind would be directly across the runway at Crestview. That really did not create much concern as we knew we could land *across* the runway in the event it was too strong to handle with a normal crosswind operation.

As we happily launched we were headed directly into the teeth of the very brisk wind that had decided to grace us with its presence. Yes, it was quite bumpy and, yes, even the loaded gravel trucks traveling on the gravel roads were moving faster than our speed. It would be a long and rough ride, but we were flying and that erased many little defects. Just being in the air with one of my sisters made it all worthwhile and the slow speed and bumps were soon forgotten.

From the time we could see the large Marianna, Florida, airport at a distance of at least fifteen miles away, it took almost twenty minutes flying time to reach the traffic pattern. One of their main runways was almost into the wind so we landed on it. (There did not seem to be any good grass available that we could use.) The taxi trip from the runway to the ramp seemed to take forever. It was such a long way to go and we Cubs do not do too well on the ground in high wind. However, we did eventually find ourselves tied down on the ramp waiting for the fuel truck to arrive.

With our new supply of essence of 100 LL on board, we were ready to be on our way again. Because it was such a long way from the ramp to the runway, Lyle asked the young lady who was in charge if she objected to our taking off from the edge of the ramp. She had no problem with the idea and shortly thereafter 726 and I bounded into the air from the ramp in front of her office. It was interesting to note that we also had quite an audience watching our little performance. I guess they had never seen a *real* airplane fly before.

The further west we ventured, the stronger the wind blew and the rougher the ride became. By the time we were in the pattern at

Crestview, there were some real bumps below our 1,000-foot cruising altitude. Yes, there was still a ninety-degree crosswind when we landed, but still not more than we could handle. (I must say we were getting very proficient at those one-wheel landings.) We rocked enthusiastically in our tie-down ropes as the gas truck refilled our little reservoirs. I was glad we were tied down, because otherwise I was sure both of us would have been going our merry way with the wind.

Westbound from Crestview, we are entering the never-never land of military restricted airspace. Just like the area south of Kitty Hawk, this is an area of overkill by the military in its greedy grasp of airspace. (In our two days of flying in this area, we only saw two other aircraft in the air. I guess it was too windy for most of them.)

From the time that our humanoids had come up with the plan of flying to the Naval Air Museum (we were going to fly to within four miles of the Pensacola Naval Air Station), many had told us we could not do that without using a radio. Fact is, some had been willing to bet hard-earned money that it was impossible to do! True, there are a couple of very close tolerance "keyholes" around restricted and Class C airspace, but it could be done and we were going to do it. So there. And, I might add, we did it, too.

After a quick phone call to the good folks at Ferguson Field to confirm their 500-foot pattern altitude as well as to check on their wind conditions, we were again headed directly into our little resistor, the wind, riding the bumps and making an honest ground speed of forty-five to fifty miles per hour. Staying at about 1,000 feet to avoid the upper layers, we threaded our way through the three-mile gap between restricted area R-2915A and the core of NAS Whiting Class C airspace. Then it is to the north of the core of Pensacola Regional Class C airspace, around the west of same, and descending to below 700 feet into that little niche that NAS Pensacola Class C airspace has so begrudgingly given to Ferguson Field. After making one circle to confirm the wind situation, the beautiful grass, which serves as one of the runways at Ferguson Field, was caressing our fat little tires. Yes indeed, we had flown to and landed within four miles of the Pensacola Naval Air Station without using a radio to talk to anyone or for navigation purposes—the only way to fly.

Ferguson Field was nestled among some rather tall trees and thus was pretty well shielded from the wind. When Mr. Ferguson himself learned that we two Cubs wanted to park where we could have tents under our wings, he rolled out the red carpet and suggested we could park anyplace that suited us on his nice grass parking area. The entire area was well protected from the wind and soon our cozy little campsite was erected on the corner of the ramp nearest to the runway. Even under the slightly threatening sky, we were looking forward to another night of tranquillity with our humanoids sleeping in their tents under our wings. Oh yes, the

Our campsite at Ferguson Field.

sunset flight was canceled due to the inconvenience caused by all of that restricted airspace and the high wind and bumps that were still playing around in the air.

Now that our home for the night had been erected, it was time for Leighton and Lyle to start making plans for the next day. The first need to be satisfied was transportation so that they could get to the museum the next morning. Ferguson Field was rather isolated and it was determined that a rental car would be the best way to go. (And these guys claim to be barnstorming?) Once the car was delivered, our intrepid humanoids did something we would not have believed if we had not seen them do it.

This had been a rather hot and sticky day and everyone needed a bath. The only suitable water hose available for this shower was not located in a very secluded spot and we did not like the possibility of someone calling the authorities and reporting a couple of crazy, naked humanoids running around on the airport. Thus the suggestion was made that maybe a cheap motel room should be rented for the express purpose of taking a shower. The next thing we knew, our two humanoids were driving off to find someplace to make this wild idea happen. We wondered if we should let them go because who knew what next they might decide to do.

Evidently things worked out well during the shower expedition because about three hours later our barnstormers returned after renting a room, having their showers, and then finding a great place to eat. Yes, they even had the room key with them so they could return the next morning for another shower before checking out of the motel. Can you imagine what the motel people thought when they cleaned that room the next day and found the bed had not been slept in, but all of the bath towels had been used?

Remember the inclement weather that had been forecast for the Pensacola area and we had gambled on it not being there? By first light on Friday morning, May 19, we knew we had lost the bet. It had not started raining yet, but from all indications, it would before too long. There was very little dew formation on the tents, so they were soon dismantled and placed inside our cockpits, along with sleeping bags etc., so that everything would stay dry if it should decide to rain. Actually we were all laughing about that idea as both 726 and I leak like crazy if we are left out in a major downpour. (Oh well, the camping equipment will absorb most of the water and keep our vital parts dry.) Anyway, as soon as this was accomplished and our tie-down ropes rechecked, our best friends departed for their morning shower and a tour of the Naval Aviation Museum.[2] We did not know when they would be back; however we did know that everyone wanted to be in Quincy by night—weather permitting.

While our humanoids were visiting the museum, 726 and I did get our top surfaces washed off with a little rain that fell during the passage of a frontal system. As soon as this system went through, the clouds started to break up and the wind *really* started to blow. We watched it closely because at the present time it was still blowing from west to east and that was the direction in which we wanted it to remain. Yes, if we waited long enough, we could follow that front all the way to Quincy.

About two thirty in the afternoon, we found ourselves being reloaded in preparation for departure for Ferguson Field, bound for the EAA Chapter 445 Annual Fly-in, which is held on the airport at Quincy each year. The original plan had been to arrive at that function the night before it started in order to enjoy the camaraderie of those putting on the program. (We also had a little barnstormer trick under our instrument panels that we wanted to try out. More on that later.) So far we were exactly on schedule.

A call was made to Flight Service to check on the weather, and the same response we had been receiving for the past two days came again, however with a little different twist. First of all, their "computer was down" and they did not have any current weather available. (The unusual twist.) Second, as usual, "VFR flight is not recommended at this time," due to rain showers associated with the front preceding us along our route of flight. I swear, if we had stayed on the ground each time we were told that "VFR is not recommended" we would have never left home, let alone complete a great trip like we are now conducting. Our humanoids informed the briefer that he had completed his legal duty by telling us not to fly, but we were going to fly anyway. I feel that this standard phrase "VFR not recommended" is a lot like the "wolf" cry of the little boy in the children's parable. Eventually no one listens.

Even though it was relatively calm on the ground behind all of those trees, we could hear the wind blowing and saw the tops of the trees really swaying. The wind was blowing exactly ninety degrees to the runway, but in the right direction once we were airborne and out of this congested/restricted airspace. A quick check with ATIS at Pensacola Regional Airport confirmed that the wind was out of the west at twenty-four knots (twenty-eight mph) with gusts to thirty-one knots (thirty-six mph). Yes, indeed, it would be a pretty rough ride once we got out of this tree canyon in which our departure runway was nestled. True, both 726 and I would be flying and no doubt destroy ourselves if left to our own devices in that kind of wind, but neither of us were worried as we knew our beloved humanoids were very experienced and could handle us with loving care and protection. *Come on, gang, time's awastin'. Let's go fly!*

Lined up on the runway, looking at the swaying trees, did bring about a recheck for security of the tie-downs on the camping equipment and a second check of seat belts. Only one way from here and that is up and out! All sixty-five horses were running at full speed as we charged ahead on our takeoff roll. Very quickly our wings did their thing and took all of the weight off of our wheels as we continued to gain speed in ground effect in order to be able to cope with the sudden gusts and turbulence we knew would be waiting for us as we cleared the tops of the trees. We were not disappointed. Even before we had cleared the last remaining trees, the full force of that crosswind hit us broadside and we found ourselves being slammed into a forty-five-degree crab angle in order to compensate for this mass of fast-moving air. Thank goodness our humanoids have had considerable experience in working with such situations. Otherwise I would have preferred staying tied to that nice soft grass from which we had just departed.

Again, we weren't disappointed about the anticipated turbulence at the low altitude we were required to fly to miss all of that restricted airspace we must now avoid as we retrace our flight of yesterday afternoon. Many times the tie-downs and seat belts held everything securely in their places as we bounced along our way.

The ceiling and visibility was almost unlimited and, after we passed the Class C airspace of NAS Whiting, we scrambled to 3,000 feet where the bumps were relatively small. We could see the trailing edge of the weather system that passed during the morning, but it should be no factor. Now wait a minute on that one—a quick check of our ground speed told us that we were doing slightly more than 100 miles per hour over the ground. Wow! At this rate, we just might catch up with that weather and have to wait it out again. We would work on that problem if it should arise. In the meantime, 726 is having a hard time containing herself. Since she is a little faster on her prop than I am, she wanted to set some sort of speed record. However, being the good sister she is, she slowed down so we could travel together.

There was no doubt in our minds that with this tailwind we could have flown nonstop from Ferguson Field to Quincy with no problem. However, due to the fact that this was a pleasure trip with the purpose of visiting some different airports in search of relatives, *and* we were rapidly catching the aforementioned weather, it was decided to follow the original plan of stopping at De Funiak Springs, for a little refreshment.

The wind had not diminished by the time we entered the pattern for landing at De Funiak. The airport was not protected by trees, which made for a bit of a challenge during the landing, parking and departure at this short pause in our journey. I will never know the reason, but my humanoid kept my speed at least ten to fifteen mph too fast during our first approach and landing attempt. I guess he thought he was still flying a 747, considering how fast we had covered the last 100 miles. Anyway, there was no way on earth I could possibly land with as much airspeed as he was making me carry over the runway. Thus, it was a go-around. How embarrassing when I looked back and saw my sister, turning off at the first intersection on her first approach. Be that as it was, the next time around, we landed on the taxiway directly into the wind. Goodness, what will he get me into next? He knows better.

We could not be left alone on the fueling ramp as the wind would surely have blown us to parts unknown. Even with large chocks behind our 800x4 donuts, there were times when I thought we would actually jump over them—completely out of control. Trying to get to the runway safely, without humanoids walking along holding our wing struts and keeping us securely on the ground, would be impossible. Maybe we should not have stopped here after all.

Obviously, the FBO owner realized our problem because he gladly gave us permission to make our takeoffs from where we were parked—across the narrow ramp, directly into the wind. Thus after a quick run-up and another traffic check, our trusty sixty-five steeds jerked us into the air in less than 100 feet of ground roll. With a wing-wave of thank you to those on the ground, we were once again back safely in the air. (Even though it was a little windy and bumpy, it sure was fun to be able to show off our abilities once in a while. We also noted that not another moving aircraft had been sighted so far today.)

Our stop at De Funiak Springs had allowed the weather to move further to the east. Now as we proceeded along at our 100 mph clip, it would appear it was dissipating almost as fast as we are catching up to it. In the pattern at Quincy, we experienced a few drops of rain on our windshields as the clouds moved further along their way. Our journey from Ferguson to Quincy had been conducted under a clear sky most of the way. The only real clouds we had encountered were a few scattered here and there—even those few raindrops had fallen from a little cloud that seemed to have gotten lost from the pack.

Touchdown at Quincy was just before six o'clock in the evening and we had completed the entire trip in under two hours flight time. Not bad for a couple of old ladies.

Quincy. Ahhhh yeeesssss. Each time we Cubs venture out on a little trip like this, there is always at least one port of call that really makes our day and this time it has to be Quincy. Even as we circled in preparation for landing, we could tell this was something very special. The massive, well-manicured grass area along the side of the runway and ramp were enough to give us chills, in anticipation of having our wheels caressed by such soft green velvet. Even with the strong crosswind, the landing was everything we expected. Such bliss. And that was just the start.

The smiling, waving, figure that greeted us as we rolled to a stop was none other than Dennis Mathews, proprietor of Panther Aero, Inc., the FBO located on this great little airport. One thing about this man, he definitely was there to help and please his customers. During the entire time that we spent on his airport, we never saw anything but a smile on his face and an offer to help and make everyone welcome and comfortable in his actions. The world needs many more humanoids like this fine gentleman. When he was appraised of our desire to have tents under our wings for the duration of the fly-in, he enthusiastically waved us toward a nice grass area located at the edge of a heavily forested area along the north side of his grass ramp, less than 100 yards from the center of activity.

What a beautiful campsite. Our many winged relatives would be operating in the 180 degrees to our front and a nice thick virgin forest area was in the 180 degrees to our back. Again, down here on the ground behind all of the trees, we were well protected from that rush of air that had brought us to this lovely spot so quickly. It was awfully hard to find it much better than we have it here—isolated, but yet close to where the action was happening.

While our tie-down anchors were being screwed into the ground, Dennis Mathews walked over to extend a very warm welcome and to apologize for the fact that he did not have a gas truck and we would have to taxi over to his fuel pump to replenish our

Our campsite at Quincy, Florida.

energy supply. Seven-two-six and I were very glad to hear one of our humanoids explain to him not to worry, because we would be flying again this evening as well as the next morning. At that time we would stop at the gas pumps before returning to our campsite. *Hot dang, you all! It's another sunset/dawn patrol night!*

By the time Dennis returned to his office, he made sure we had everything that we needed, that we knew where all of those facilities that humanoids require were located, and he gave our humanoids a key to the office just in case they needed it.

While the tents were being erected near our wings, two more fine gentlemen came over to admire my sister and me as we prepared for the evening. I say that because even though they did say hello to our humanoids, they spent considerable time looking at our attributes before engaging them in any meaningful conversation. However, I will have to admit that these two gentlemen, Berry

Sherrill (chairman of EAA Chapter 445) and Steve Borona (EAA Chapter 445 newsletter editor) really came over to personally welcome us to their fly-in. They also wanted to extend an invitation to Leighton and Lyle to join them at a potluck dinner in the office building. Our two hungry humanoids quickly accepted that invitation and were on their way. Good grief, for camping barnstormers, these two characters sure live high on the hog when it comes to eating!

The wind had subsided to a light breeze and the sun was sinking very low in the western sky when our two friends returned from their feast. We knew what was going to happen now, as each one of them went directly to our tie-down ropes and removed them. Yes, we were headed for another sunset flight. I wished we could do this every night.

As mentioned earlier, we had an idea about doing something that real barnstormers did during their heyday. Whenever possible, they would make low passes over their town of performance to invite people out to the field where they were located. In other words, they were trying to drum up business. We had said nothing to anyone—nor would we—but that was the purpose of this evening's flight and the one at dawn tomorrow morning. The only thing that we were missing were leaflets to throw out advertising our services. I guess it was a good thing that we did not have them, as no doubt we would have been arrested for littering.

Seven-two-six was leading and I was flying very tight on her right wing as we made our formation takeoff in front of our gracious hosts. Above the tree line, it was still a little bumpy as the wind had not died down, but that didn't matter, we were here to have fun and try our experiment. For the next twenty minutes, our little formation circled around over the metropolis of Quincy. Nothing fancy—just a couple of Cubs doing what they do best—giving their humanoids pure unadulterated pleasure and joy. By now, it was rapidly approaching the end of legal twilight time when those of us without navigation lights must be on the ground. One more pass in front of our hosts and it was back to the campsite.

The stars were shining brightly and the night sounds had taken over completely by the time our humanoids returned from hangar-flying on the porch of the office building, with their new friends from EAA Chapter 445. As they fell asleep, their deep breathing was barely audible to my sister and me as we stood guard over our domain. It was very difficult to express our feelings as we basked in the tranquillity of our location. The star-filled sky enhanced the beauty of contrast between the dense forest behind us and the open expanse of grass to our front, eagerly awaiting the arrival of our relatives on the morrow. Soon, we, too, have succumbed to the quietness of the world and drifted off to sleep.

The eastern sky was quite bright, heralding the arrival of the morning sun, when our humanoids finally began to come to life. We were becoming a bit concerned, because we knew the last half of our experiment must be conducted during the dawn patrol and we needed to get going.

The rush of air pushed the droplets of early morning dew from our wings as they lifted us into the sun-streaked sky that was the beginning of May 20. Tucked in close to my sister, I could see these sparkling diamonds leaving her trailing edges as they reflected the early rays of the rising sun. Again I thought to myself, it really doesn't get any better than this. What a shame this moment cannot be shared with everyone who ever dreamed of flying. It was just too beautiful to. . . . Enough of that, it was time to get on with the program!

Our little formation made its way through the silk smooth air over the area of this earth known as Quincy, Florida. The extremely smooth ride made it possible for me to move in very close to 726. Fact is, I could almost read her tachometer, but not quite. We leisurely drifted around above the many inhabitants nestled in their homes below. Yes, we were at legal altitude and since we did not make much noise, I was certain we did not disturb anyone who was still sleeping, but all those who looked up knew something was happening. After about twenty-five minutes of this very enjoyable activity, we returned to the airport to give those preparing the pancakes for the fly-in breakfast another flyby salute.

Having completed the last half of our experiment, we returned to our campsite in anticipation of watching the events of the day and waiting for the results of our work. By mid-morning, many of our cousins were arriving. There were all sorts of them. One Aeronca 7AC "Champ" was on its maiden flight after having spent the past eleven years being restored. Boy, was he glad to be back in the air! There were homebuilts, antiques, classics, warbirds,

Spam cans, one sailplane, and even one hot air balloon in attendance. Even a large number of four-wheeled ground-borne vehicles filled the parking spaces for such types. Each vehicle dis-
gorged at least one or two humanoids, sometimes many more.

Breakfast was served until almost noon, at which time a lunch-
serving establishment was put into operation for the remainder of
the day. One trailer did a bang-up business selling soft drinks by
the large cupful. About mid-afternoon, the spot-landing contest
took place and we all had a great time watching each contestant
trying to outdo his or her opponents. Sis and I did not get involved
in such, we just enjoy watching the fun. However, if the need ever
arose, I am sure we could put our little fat tires on any spot, at any
place. In fact, when our humanoids registered our attendance, the
person in charge was concerned about whether we would enter
the spot-landing competition. He figured if we did, we would have
to be put into our own category and not compete with the others.
When he learned that we just wanted to watch, he seemed relieved.

All day long there was much hangar-flying and airplane-comparing conducted. Many, many buddy rides were given and the
EAA Young Eagles program was in full swing to give young humanoids a chance to experience the thrill and joy of flight, which
only our kind can give them. It was a fantastic day and we heard
no complaints from anyone at anytime.

Oh, I almost forgot! When the winners of the contests were
being honored, we were presented the award for having traveled
the furthest distance. It is a very nice wall plaque and we will
treasure it forever. When it was presented, I had to tell them that
my sister, NC-22726, would have to be declared the winner because her hangar was located about eighty feet further away than
my cozy hangar home. As has happened before, we all laughed
about the situation and Sis and I agreed to share the plaque equally.
This was the first time they had ever had a tie for this award.

It was very sad to witness, but by late afternoon, the grounds
were again back to what they had been the day before—void of
our many relatives and friends. Almost everyone had departed for
their homes. As we watched them soar into the sky, we could tell
that not a single one of them really wanted this day to end, but it
must. Our trip was not over yet, so Sis and I still had a few more
days of adventure before we, too, would have to return home.

Later in the evening while listening to the officials talk about what had just happened, we learned that they were sure there had been fifty-five or more of our relatives present. All in all, they felt it had been a very successful fly-in. One thing they were a little surprised to see was the large number of drive-in attendees.

Yes! Yes! Yes! Our little experiment had worked. Again, we did not say anything about what we had done, but we do like to think that our appearance in the sky the evening before and the early morning of the event really did help. If it did, it is just our way of saying thank you to EAA Chapter 445, for its great hospitality. After all, we are barnstorming and that is the way barnstormers advertise their wares.

As a closing gesture on this great day of fun and camaraderie, 726 and I were again in the air, in formation, over the inhabitants of Quincy. Just a way of saying thank you for coming out to see us. We hope to see you again someday." Upon landing, our humanoids were escorted to a great eatery in the area by Steve Borona and his lovely wife, Susan. When they returned from stuffing themselves, we found ourselves being prepared for the next day's early morning departure. We hated to do it, but we had to be moving on also.

Hey, what was going on? The sun was well above the horizon and our humanoids were still in their sleeping bags. We thought we were going to be on our way early.

As it turned out, we all had so much fun the day before, none of us really wanted to depart. This being Sunday, we were pretty sure that some of our new friends would be returning just to "hang out." Sure enough, by the time Leighton and Lyle had gotten themselves awake and finished a breakfast of eat-what-you-brought, several of them had entered the traffic pattern and were now parked near by. Our early morning departure turned out to be an almost-noon takeoff. Yes, indeed, we were really enjoying our stay at Quincy.

The destination for today was literally up in the air. We knew we would be up in the air, but where we came back to earth was anybody's guess. Finally, a decision was made to proceed to Live Oak, Florida. We could follow the interstate highway and not have to worry about precise navigation. Once we made it to Live Oak, we could pick another place to visit—if that was what we wanted to do. The weather is perfect for Cub flying and we are enjoying life to the fullest. (This is the only way to fly! No time schedule and no real destination, just drifting along, enjoying life.)

After making sure we had drunk our fill of essence of 100 LL, our humanoids took their charts, books, and plotters to the chairs beneath the large oak tree near the Live Oak airport's administration building. We could see that they were just relaxing, but also engrossed in conversation about where we should go next. We knew it was too early to make camp for the night and no way did we want to miss out on this great Cub weather either.

The reason our sister NC-25885 (Jim Sprigg) of Dade City, Florida, did not join us on this little adventure was because she was very busy supervising the construction of her new home located a mile or so west of Trilby, Florida. She has chosen to call her new home Cub Haven and it will be published on the new Jacksonville Sectional Chart. Even though construction was not completed, we decided to go that direction and check it out. Since 885 had no idea we were coming, an attempt was made to contact her humanoid. No luck. Nobody at home and no answering machine—if you can imagine that. This did not discourage us and we were soon on our way to Williston, Florida, where we would try to call her again.

"You guys really make me mad. I'm really ticked off at you because you have those beautiful yellow airplanes and I want one. Nobody should be having as much fun as you must be having." That is how our humanoids were greeted as they opened our doors on the ramp at Williston. Of course, this gentleman was smiling as he made his statements, and he sure did look at us with loving eyes. We were bringing back memories to someone who had learned to fly in one of our brothers or sisters many years ago. It made our day to hear him reminisce about his flight of long ago, in the safety of one of our long-lost family members. There once were thousands like him, but the numbers are dwindling and to find his kind today is quite a rarity. They are worth listening to as they remember.

We waited patiently on the ramp while our humanoids once again tried to contact 885's humanoid. They had decided if he could not be contacted, we would figure out some other destination for the remainder of this beautiful day.

Luck was with us and soon an arrangement was made to meet Jim at the Zephyrhills airport. We would be flying directly over 885's new home and Jim insisted that we should land there and spend the night. It sounded like a great idea, until we discovered that 885 herself had not landed on her new runway. Thus, we declined the invitation because that is her new home and she must be the first to make those three wheel tracks in her nice soft grass. No, we would take a look as we flew past, maybe even make a low pass, but it was her new home and *she* must make that first landing. We would land at Zephyrhills.

The sign on the door said that the airport would be open until 6:00 P.M. Here it was 5:45 P.M. and the door was locked tight and nobody could be found. That was the situation that existed when we parked on the FBO ramp at Zephyrhills on May 21. Since there was no one to tell them they could not do it, Leighton and Lyle picked a spot near the hangar to pitch their tents because the grass at our tie-down site was not in very good condition. As they carried their tents to the area, Jim and his family came driving in to escort our barnstormers on a personal tour of 885's new home as well as take them to a restaurant for something to eat. Since one of those recently developed grumpy old clouds had started dropping a few little water particles, the decision was made not to erect the tents until returning from their tour. Very wise, not because of the raindrops, but because of political problems.

To this day, we do not know if we were welcome on the Zephyrhills airport or if we were just tolerated. Darkness was rapidly approaching when our humanoids returned from their grand tour. As they prepared to erect their tents near the previously mentioned hangar, the owner of the FBO, who happened to live nearby but was not home earlier, approached and very politely announced that he preferred they not place their sleeping quarters on that particular piece of real estate. He further suggested that he was pretty sure that camping was not allowed at any location on the airport, but that was sometimes uncertain as well, because it seemed to change with the feeling of the police officer on patrol at the time.

Not to be detoured, our intrepid humanoids suggested they would camp on city property over near the airport administration building. Besides, the rest room facilities were located in that area. Thus, with permission to leave us tied in the grass on the FBO's property, the two tents were soon erected at least 200 yards away in plain view of anyone who would want to look in that direction. Even in the darkness, they were visible to the naked eye.

I must say our humanoids were a little intimidated because as they were about to leave our sides with their final load of sleeping bags, etc., a police car rounded the curve less than fifty yards from our location. If that officer had been looking, there was no way he or she could have missed us, as the headlights of their vehicle shown fully into our faces. This caused our brave "lawbreakers" to stop their activities and wait and watch. (See, I told you they were unsure of their position about being welcome on the airport.)

As they watched, the police car turned into a small parking area at the opposite end of the building from where the questionable tents were standing and turned all visible light off. All that could be seen was the silhouette of an officer standing beside the vehicle. All movement around us stopped. After all, neither Leighton nor Lyle really wanted to have any trouble with the law, but on the other hand, neither wanted to go to a motel for the night either. We had no problem with our location—we were Cubs and this is where we belonged.

Five minutes passed—nothing moved. Then suddenly, what appeared to be a civilian small car rounded the curve and proceeded to park beside the police cruiser, and it, too, turned all visible lights off. Interesting to say the least. Our humanoids continued to watch and wait. Another five minutes and still no movement. Finally, in frustration, Lyle suggested that they would just quietly walk over to the tents and if they were stopped, they would plead ignorance.

Walking to their tents under the cover of darkness took our humanoids, with their load of sleeping bags, within fifty yards of the vehicles in question. They did not try to hide, but on the other hand, they did not make any effort to make themselves seen. Within another five minutes, both cars departed and our fugitives from justice were soon sound asleep in their possibly illegal campsite.

One of three things happened. Either there was false information about being able to camp on the airport at Zephyrhills, or the patrol person did not see us, *or* did see us but wanted no part of what was going on as he/she was involved in a little clandestine meeting. Who knows. Our humanoids like to pretend it was the latter because as they were sitting under our wing eating breakfast the next morning, an attractive young blond lady driving one of the city trucks waved very enthusiastically to us as she drove around the aforementioned curve. Anyway, I doubt if we ever return to Zephyrhills with plans to have tents under our wings at night. We like to feel more at ease than we did last night.

From here it was a short seventy or eighty minutes of flight to home, which meant our little adventure for this year was coming to an end. As usual, we hated to see this portion of the trip materialize. However, if you look at it as we must—if this trip never ended, we could never start out on another journey in the future. Thus, at about 11:00 A.M., on May 22, with me in the lead, we announced to all of our friends that we were home as we made a low pass up runway 04 of the Venice airport. We repeated the pattern followed by our wheels kissing the sweet soft grass of home. This brought us to the final curtain of this, our latest adventure. It had been another fun trip and we both will relive it many times as we relax in the solitude of our T-hangar homes. The last landing of this outing was no different than all of the other last landings, we hated to see them happen, but then, what the heck, we'll do it again next year.

[2] I would like to emphasize the Naval Aviation Museum is a *must-see* attraction for anyone interested in airplanes and aviation. I am not a great fan of military aviation, but this is one facility that I will return to visit someday in the future. I highly recommend one of the guided tours, which takes almost two hours to complete. Leighton and I spent over four hours just looking around and still did not see nearly all there was to be seen. I'm not sure you could see it all and really absorb everything there is to learn in a full day. It is fantastic!

There was even one of 881's brothers on display in the museum. We all know that the U.S. Army used Piper J-3 Cubs, calling them L-4s. The U.S. Navy used them as well, designating them as NE-1s. The Navy had 230 NE-1s, none of which were built under a normal Navy contract. No, the Navy just took over Piper's stock of J-3C-65s and the ones on the production line. These airplanes were in "Cub Yellow" and some of them even had the Cub Bear logo on their tail, just as 881 does. Of course, the color yellow fit very nicely into the Navy's training fleet as that was the standard color of the Navy primary trainers (Yellow Perils). It never ceases to amaze me how versatile the lowly Piper J-3C Cub has been throughout its history.

The Winning Card Was at Thomasville

The clock indicated 11:00 A.M. when our throttles moved forward at the start of our takeoff roll on the morning of Friday, October 13, 1995. Yes, that's right—Friday the 13th! But we were not the least bit superstitious! We made a quick turn to the north and bid good-bye to our friends tied to the ramp at the Venice airport. My sister, J-3 Cub, NC-22726 (humanoid Leighton Hunter) and I, J-3 Cub, NC-87881 (humanoid Lyle Wheeler) were off on a three-day adventure to the twenty-eighth Annual Thomasville, Georgia, Fly-in, which was held on October 13, 14, and 15. Seven-two-six and I had received a special invitation to attend this year as they were highlighting Piper Cubs from 1938 through 1960. Also included were Aeroncas from 1945 through 1960.

The weather was beautiful—finally the rains had stopped—and with the light breezes blowing everything was right with our world. Our loads for this trip were a little different than in the past. Since my humanoid had invited a close friend, Ray Olcott, to ride with him, my maximum gross weight had been reached long before all of the essential camping gear had been loaded. Thus, my good ol' reliable sister, 726, came to the rescue by converting herself into a freighter and transporting the equipment and supplies for this three-day camping and fun-filled trip.

Four-thirty in the afternoon found us being directed to our parking/camping spot at the Thomasville airport. We had covered the distance from Venice to Thomasville in just four and one-half hours of flying time—five and one-half total elapsed time. Yes, we needed to make a couple of stops en route. One was at Crystal

River and the other, due to our limited range and the fact that Perry did not have fuel at this time, was made at that dreaded big nozzled place, Cross City. My how I wish they would make an effort to correct that problem!

We were not the first to arrive at Thomasville. Our arrival brought the J-3 population up to eight at the time. Our camping spots were adjacent to the main taxiway to the runways. It was great just watching the activity while waiting for the next event we knew would be coming up for us—the sunset flight. Our human-oids soon had their tents erected on our taxiway side so they, too, could enjoy the action without even getting out of bed!

While waiting for the long evening shadows to arrive, our hu-manoids were off hangar-flying with others and sister 726 and I "ramp flew" with our long-lost brothers, sisters and cousins as they either rocked gently in their tie-downs or taxied past on their way to or from parking. We discovered our sister NC-70209 (hu-manoid Dennis Garrett) parked a few spaces away. It was really nice talking with her as we had not seen each other since the Cub Six-Pack flew to Gadsden more than two years earlier.

About twenty minutes before the sun sank below the horizon, our humanoids returned. Nothing was said, but we knew what was about to happen as our tie-down ropes were removed. Much to our surprise, most all other flying had come to a complete stand-still. That was soon to change also. When others observed our tight formation takeoff into the sunset, they could not resist the call of the tranquil skies. Two-zero-nine did not fly and she re-marked that it was rather humorous to watch others come to life when we flew past. Many fully believed that if we had not taken to the air, no one would have flown that evening. It was a good thing that we did, because that was the last sunset flight possible and no dawn patrol could be made because of the weather.

Again snugly tied in our campsite, our humanoids were off to finish the evening with a delightful meal of several kinds of Italian pasta dishes. Obviously, they really pigged out from all of the complaints we heard about eating too much when they returned a couple of hours later.

As the sky grew dark, a large multicolored hot air balloon rose to the end of its tether line about 100 yards to our south. The roar from her burner directed all to look in her direction and the bright glow created by the flame from the burning gas caused all who observed her to admire her unmatched beauty. She was making an ascent and descent at the rate of one every ten minutes or so. She was giving humanoids a chance to experience her charm—all for *free*. All who made the short flight were duly impressed. Even those of us who could not partake appreciated her generosity.

Another very interesting and educational demonstration was taking place just a few yards further to the south of the balloon. An aviation museum from Valdosta, Georgia, was operating a completely restored aerial searchlight from World War II. This long shaft of blue-white light was dancing all over the darkened sky. I had never seen nor did I know that they could change the focal length of the lens to make that shaft of light do interesting things. Occasionally, we would find ourselves caught in the intense light beam and we then knew why these lights were so effective when used as a defensive tool in locating intruders high in the sky at night.

Eventually, all was quiet as the humanoid population either headed for dreamland in their tents and campers, or made the journey to a motel/hotel in town. No matter where their bed may be for the night, all were holding great anticipation for the big main event the next day. The stars in the heavens were in their places and we Cubs and our relatives were now able to relax and enjoy the tranquillity and joy of just being together here on the Thomasville airport. Oh yes, there were a couple of very rude campers who insisted on operating their noisy generators so that they could have air conditioned motor homes. It did not seem to matter that they were disturbing the peace and silence that many of us have come to expect when camping overnight in such a location as this. There should be a law against having those things on the airplane side of the boundary fence!

As the night wore on, a cloud deck started moving into the area, and by daylight the ceiling and visibility were much too low for any thought of a dawn patrol. Besides preventing that operation, it also eliminated the mass balloon performance we had anticipated. This did not dampen the spirits of those in attendance as they consumed large quantities of food at the breakfast buffet. Again, you could hear complaints of such good food and so much overeating! By mid- to late-morning, the clouds had broken up, the sun was shining, and a great day at the fly-in was well under way.

New arrivals, including homebuilts and antiques, were soon being parked and various venders were showing and selling their wares. A new WACO and an AT-6 were busy selling rides. Ultralights were buzzing around. Many buddy rides were being given, and the model airplane builders and pilots were really strutting their stuff. In short, everyone was really having fun. All this time, the traditional pot of boiling peanuts was bubbling away full blast for all to enjoy. Of course, lunchtime arrived and with it came one of the best southern fish-fry meals that could be imagined. Activities planned for the afternoon included a poker run, a spot-landing contest, aircraft judging, and an awards meeting just before the evening meal.

The briefing for the poker run was called for 1:30 P.M. sharp. At that time, ten aircraft, including myself and 726, were on the list. *Hot dang, you all! I have never done one of these before and I can hardly wait!* It was also a first for 726. The pot was worth $150. Pretty good return for the five dollars invested—if you win! Even though the course was designed for J-3 Cubs, we two were the only J-3s who took part in the game. There was one J-5 Cub and one Super Cub. The other six players were much bigger, faster, and newer. Each of us was dealt one card at Thomasville and then it was off and running! Oh yes, we were playing with two decks of cards, which made it more difficult to obtain a winning hand.

At Thomasville, the first card was drawn. Seven-two-six drew a three of diamonds. I drew the ten of clubs. Then it was into the air headed for our first stop of the circuit—Cairo, Georgia. What fun it was to arrive there more or less in a bunch. Of course this was the last place we were so close together as our faster and younger relatives were soon well ahead of us. The second stop put us four slower Cubs in the pattern together, and by the time we made the third pickup even the J-5 and Super Cub had left us behind. Not far, mind you, but still behind!

At Cairo, Georgia, 726 drew the queen of hearts while my card was the four of spades. Next stop was Camilla. Here 726 picked eight of clubs and the eight of hearts fell into my hand. At this point it didn't look like either one of us was doing very well at our first game of poker. Moultrie produced an interesting card for

726—the three of hearts. (How about that—two of a kind!) My hand was no better than before, when the six of clubs showed up on the draw. Then it was back into the air for the return to Thomasville where the fifth and final card would be drawn. With the cards that I was holding, there was no way that I could even show, let alone place. However, 726 did have a chance—she was holding two threes. Not much of a hand, but still possible.

As mentioned earlier, we J-3s were bringing up the rear and everyone was waiting for us as we came in for our final draw. Nuts—mine was the two of spades! No big bucks there! The final draw of the game fell to 726 and she came up with the second three of diamonds. Now she had three of a kind and it beat all others. She had won on three of a kind—threes! The winning card was in Thomasville. The 150 bucks were hers.

But wait a minute—726's humanoid knew that there had only been ten playing the game at $5 each. That would mean there was only $50 paid into the pot. Knowing something about the expenses that go into putting on a fly-in like this, he returned $100 of the winnings saying that he would gladly take the players' money, but would not take any money that belongs to those sponsoring the fly-in. Needless to say, 726's actions were appreciated.

The next order of business was to be the spot-landing contest. However, on our little poker-run venture, we had encountered some very low and wet clouds and when the 4:30 spot-landing time arrived, these clouds had found their way to our nice little event at Thomasville. All activities came to a screeching halt. Airplanes were re-tied and tents were secured in anticipation of the approaching cold front. As the dark clouds passed overhead, a light wind blew and a gentle rain fell. The wind soon subsided but the light rain continued. Just enough to make everything, not protected, wet—just enough to cancel the rest of the flying events for the day. Furthermore, since it would be too wet to have the awards presentation outside, it was decided to have this event in the hangar during the evening meal.

Speaking of the evening meal—it had been in preparation all afternoon. Those big chunks of pork had been slowly cooking over the barbecue grill for hours. The aroma was enough to drive any hungry humanoid crazy while he waited for dinner to be served. At last it was time to eat and everyone gorged themselves with

881 returns to Thomasville during poker run. Credit, Leighton Hunter.

some of the finest pork barbecue this side of the Mason-Dixon line. It must have been good because when our humanoids returned, they were still complaining about the food being too good and they had again stuffed themselves. My, I hoped we could get into the air for the homeward-bound trip, considering all the extra weight they are adding to themselves!

Very nice plaques were passed out for the most beautiful of various members of our relatives during the awards program. Much to our surprise, sister 726 and I were awarded the plaque for the furthest distance. Once again, I had to admit that she actually won the prize because she lives in a hangar located about eighty feet further south than I do. It really isn't as bad as I make it sound, because we do share the awards.

The light rain continued to fall off and on for the rest of the evening so the time was spent in just good companionship. Finally, as the last light blinked off in the tents surrounding us, we drifted off to sleep with fond memories of what had taken place during this fun-filled day.

During the night, the rain stopped and a fairly brisk wind from the north picked up. The temperature dropped about twenty degrees from the night before, too. By dawn, it was pretty obvious that the sky was clear and if that cold front kept moving we would have a great ride back home to Venice. After another delicious breakfast, the tents were taken down and we were packed, ready to depart. The call to Flight Service produced the same reaction that always seems to happen when you ask for a VFR briefing for no-radio Cubs flying at 2,000 feet or less at an airspeed of seventy mph or less. A useful briefing was not available. Our humanoids are very experienced in the art of aerial navigation so the lack of a good briefing did not seem to matter much. They knew there was a tailwind to help us along our way and with the passing of the cold front yesterday, the weather should be good. If not, we would go as far as possible—land, and wait it out. Very simple.

The distance from Thomasville to Cross City was about 100 miles. It was only sixty more miles beyond Cross City to Crystal River. However, we Cubs and our twelve-gallon energy supply tanks do not have very long legs. But on the other hand with this tailwind maybe—just maybe—we could make Crystal River and not need to stop at that miserable big nozzle place—Cross City. If we made Cross City in just over an hour, we would have enough remaining to reach Crystal River—only time can tell.

The little hand on the clock was just past the nine and the big hand was pointing at the six when our little formation waved so long to our friends and relatives on the ground at Thomasville. Yes, indeed, we did have a very nice tailwind pushing us along on toward home. By the time our dreaded big nozzle airport came into view, it was obvious that we could easily make Crystal River. What a relief! Thus as the elapsed time stopwatch clicked to two hours exactly, our little Continentals became silent on the ramp at Crystal River.

After drinking our fill of essences of 100 LL, we were once again headed south. This time, the challenge of making it all the way home without having to stop again presents itself. If this wind continued, and from all indications it should—or even increase—

there was no reason why we should not be able to make it. Well, we would have to see how long it would take us to reach Vandenberg Airport. If that took an hour or less, there would be no problem.

Sure enough, the wind did increase and there was no need to even consider the possibility of making the Vandenberg stop. Thus when we were parked in front of our hangar homes at Venice, the stopwatch indicated another one hour and forty-five minutes of flying. Total flying time from Thomasville to Venice, Florida, *three hours and forty-five minutes* block to block. Not bad for a couple of old Cubs!

Once again, being owned by a couple of humanoids who love to fly sure makes our life worthwhile. Thanks to them, we were again able to attend a fantastic grassroots fly-in and thoroughly enjoyed every minute of the adventure. On that October weekend, no matter what you were looking for, be it good companionship, good hangar-flying, good food, or good "plane" fun, the winning card was in Thomasville!

Journey Back to Our Roots

Our little fat tires kissed the soft grass beside runway 04 at our hometown airport just as the sun was sinking into the Gulf of Mexico, heralding the end of June 30, 1996. My leading edges were spattered with bugs and industrial dirt and exhaust stains covered the lower right side of my fuselage. My tummy was streaked with oil vapor, and traces of the good earth from my birthplace had taken up residence on my tail spring—but I was one extremely contented Cub. You see, one of my sisters and I had just returned from an eight-day journey "back home" to our birthplace—Lock Haven, Pennsylvania.

We had talked for a long while about someday going home and decided the Sentimental Journey to Lock Haven this year was the time to do it. Ray Olcott would accompany us, riding in my rear seat. This particular humanoid has been quite a regular passenger with me over the past months, but that is another story for another time.

Not much had been said, but Sis and I knew something was in the wind when we found ourselves being cleaned and serviced, even though it wasn't time for such things to happen. Her front control stick had been removed, but mine was still in place. This confused us because we knew space had to be available for camping equipment and personal items needed for long trips. However as time passed, we pieced together a plan of operation from bits of conversation overheard as our humanoids bantered back and forth.

This trip would be different. All sleeping under our wings would be done at Lock Haven; thus, the camping equipment would be

Pack mule 726 and her humanoid, Leighton Hunter.
Credit, Petecraft Aviation Services, Inc.

shipped prior to our departure. Ray would be riding in my rear seat, and 726 would be carrying the luggage in her front seat. We did not like the idea, but all overnights en route would be spent tied alone on the airport ramps while our humanoids went to motels. This was done in the interest of being able to depart at an earlier morning hour and flying much later in the evening. Another change about this trip was it would be the first we had made in many years in which it was planned to arrive at our destination as soon as possible. Not the most desirable way to travel for us Cubs, but it would have to do this time. At least we would have tents under our wings once we got back to our birthplace.

Under way at last.

The weather over the entire state of Florida had been rather unsettled for the past several days and the morning of Saturday, June 22, 1996, was no different. Flight Service advised our humanoids that we could expect increasing thundershowers throughout the day until we were well into Georgia. Even though we were ready and willing to be airborne sooner, our humanoids goofed around and we lost a good forty-five minutes of precious flying time before finally bidding adieu to the soft grass of Venice Municipal Airport and pointing our spinners northward.

In less than twenty minutes, the rays of the early morning sunrise were making a beautiful rainbow off our left wings as they bounced off the raindrops falling from a gentle shower that was rapidly developing over Sarasota Bay. Visibility was very good as we hurried toward Zephyrhills, our first renourishment stop. As always, it was such a good feeling to be airborne with one of my sisters, headed off on another great adventure with our two beloved humanoids and their friend, Ray.

Entering the pattern at Zephyrhills, we saw another nice yellow Cub waiting patiently on the ramp near the refueling island. At first we did not recognize her, but as we got closer we could see that it was NC-25885. Our spars quivered with joy as we anticipated her joining us on this journey back home. She and her humanoid, Jim Sprigg, had traveled with us in the past and to have them join us on this trip would be perfect.

After warm greetings to and by all, our energy supply was soon replenished from the self-service system. No fuss no muss—just insert your credit card and pump your fuel. I like the system very much—when it works! But this very system was to let us down on our return!

Due to our delayed departure from Venice, 885 had been waiting more than thirty minutes for our arrival. Much to our disappointment, we were soon to learn that she would not be accompanying us on this new adventure we were undertaking. No, she had just come to greet us as we passed through this first fuel stop. However, we would be able to enjoy her company for a short flight as she would lead us to her new private landing strip—Cub Haven—about seventeen miles north of Zephyrhills.

It was pretty obvious that some of those nice puffy clouds in the area were becoming a bit irritated and were going to create problems for us if we tarried long, so the three of us were soon back in the air, winging our way northward. Within minutes, Cub Haven came into view. Eight-eighty-five circled overhead while 726 and I made our low pass down her runway past her new home. Pulling up at the north end of this beautiful grass runway, we met our sister, 885, head on, gave her a farewell wing-rock and headed north. Next stop—Keystone Heights.

As we proceeded on our way, we observed an occasional sad little cloud shedding a few tears. Peering back toward the south, we could tell things were not improving behind us. However, the weather soothsayers must have been correct in their predictions of better weather to the north as that was exactly what was happening—our "not bad" conditions were getting better as we traveled.

Keystone airport came into view on schedule. By the time we had shut down at the gas pump, we had added another one hour and fifty-four minutes to our log books. Now that we were rapidly leaving the area of disturbed weather, there was not the sense of urgency that had been present at our first fuel stop.

As our little twelve-gallon energy supply tanks were being refilled, some of the local humanoids gathered around to admire our "plumage" and stare in disbelief at our sparse instrument panels which contain a tachometer, an airspeed indicator, a nonsensitive altimeter, an oil temperature gauge, an oil pressure gauge, and the all important compass. Even our gas gauge, which is nothing more than a wire stuck into a cork protruding from our gas tank cap, brings about many interesting comments. At almost every stop made on any trip we take, most observers cannot believe that we Cubs could cover such great distances with a compass, watch, chart, plotter, and a humanoid's finger or thumb as our only navigation equipment. That is bad enough, but when they cannot find any type of radio, except an emergency locator beacon, it really blows their mind! Many declare it cannot be done. Well, it can be done, because we do it all of the time, folks, and this trip was over 1,100 miles in each direction!

Anyway, after listening to several versions of how best to avoid restricted airspace R-2903A located just north of the airport, our humanoids thanked everyone for their help and once again the two of us pointed our noses north, this time toward St. Marys, our next proposed R & R stop. I say "proposed" because if all went as we hoped, maybe we would be able to extend this leg further up the line. That decision would have to come later as we had no idea what the wind would do to us over the next eighty miles.

Seven-two-six and I decided that we would take turns leading. After all, I do get tired of always being the one to take the heat if we should wander off course once in a while. Thus, 726 was in the lead as we swung past the west side of area R-2903A, above Starke, Florida, and followed the railroad to Baldwin, where a slight adjustment of heading to the left took us around the Whitehouse NAS traffic area, followed by a slight right turn directly to the vicinity of St. Marys. Since we were cruising at less than 1,000 feet altitude, we were below the top layer of the Jacksonville International Airport Class C airspace. There was absolutely no reason to concern ourselves about talking to them. Fact was, at our altitude and with as little "sheet metal" as we are carrying, I doubted very much if their radar could even see us!

About fifteen miles southwest of St. Marys, we snuggled up close while our humanoids communicated via hand signals. Shortly, the decision was made that we both have enough go-juice to continue to Malcolm McKinnon Field on St. Simons Island. Things were really looking good. The weather was great, and we actually had picked up a slight tailwind. Fantastic!

While Leighton and Lyle were seeing to our needs and deciding where we should make our next stop, Ray was doing what he does best—telling everyone about the Sun-'n-Fun Fly-in at Lakeland. He had brought along a large supply of decals advertising the 1997 program to give away. I just hoped he rations them enough to be able to spread them evenly over the whole 2,200-mile trip! There was an EAA clubhouse on the ramp at McKinnon and this being Saturday afternoon, there was a large gathering of members. Thus, Ray had quite an audience for his sales pitch. This was the same clubhouse in which our humanoids slept two years ago while the Six-Pack Minus Two spent the night tied on the ramp in the rain. We never did forgive them for that!

Onward to Walterboro

Having consumed our fill of essence of benzene and with Beaufort, South Carolina, as our next destination, we were soon back into the air. It was my turn to lead on this leg. Our route took us to Hilton Head where a slight heading change to the left would take us direct to Beaufort. Just keep the water on the right side and the land on the left side. Should be easy!

As forecast, the weather remained perfect as we proceeded up the coast. The visibility was very good and we felt very few bumps.

Being her normal self, 726 decided to do a little extra sight-seeing on this leg and she descended to a comfortable level above the deserted surface. She had a ball following the beach for several miles, watching her shadow race along the sandy shoreline. Even I had great fun riding along at a somewhat higher elevation, watching her frolicking among the natural wonders of the local environment.

Approaching Savannah Beach, Georgia, we put a respectable amount of air below us as we passed over a more congested part of the world. It was interesting to see the *huge* floating marina being built for the Olympic games on Wassaw Sound. (We wondered what they expect that structure to do when the first hurricane passes through the area!) Then it was over the jetties into South Carolina airspace. The beautiful homes, yachts, and airport of Hilton Head passed beneath our wings and soon the clock indicated we should be over Beaufort County airport.

The clock said we should be there, but where the heck is it? Boy I can just hear it now—all the heat about getting lost on a piece-of-cake navigation leg! It was not a happy sight in my cockpit. Lyle had told Ray to keep a watch out for the airport and he was almost ready to start a square search. Where could it be? Ray yelled out something about a road but no airport. About this time, Sis, who had been flying about one-fourth mile to my left peeled off to her left and started down. Lo and behold, she found the airport and it was exactly where it should have been! In my efforts to avoid the controlled airspace around Beaufort MCAS, I had flown about three miles too far to the east. At our low altitude, finding a small airport among winding roads and waterways did present a slight problem—if your humanoid is not on his toes. Obviously, mine was not! Yes, I would take a little ribbing on this one!

The original plan was to spend the night at Beaufort, but after consulting the airport directory and finding that places for humanoids to stay were far and few between (oh for the joys of a tent under our wings) it was decided to proceed another forty miles up the road to Walterboro, South Carolina, where motels, restaurants and airport facilities were more readily available. Beaufort would have been a great place to pitch a tent for the night, but that was not the plan.

The leg to Walterboro was short, but good landmarks are almost nonexistent.

Thus dead-reckoning would have to be the primary mode of navigation. Thank goodness 726 would be leading this time. I could relax. Besides, I was not sure anyone in the group would trust me after getting misplaced on the easy leg we had just flown!

Off and flying again I discovered a problem that soon got my humanoid's attention. Flying a true course of 357 degrees with five degree west variation, plus five degrees of west deviation and no wind should have made my compass read 007 degrees. However, I found that in order to keep on the same course as Sis, my compass read about 300 degrees at times and 015 degrees at times with everything in between at other times. I knew my humanoid could hold me on course better than that—it was very obvious that I had developed a bad case of compass-ache again. I had gotten Lyle's attention, but we would just have to live with the problem until we got to Lock Haven.

Over the years, we have learned to be very observant when approaching airports that indicate skydiving in the area. Two very real hazards exist if care is not taken. One is that humanoids are actually falling out of the sky, and no one wants to get in their path. Once their chutes open, they are quite easy to find. The other problem is one of our cousins, the airplane that has launched these great adventurers into their earthward journey. I do not understand what has possessed these members of our family to do the things they do! Almost without exception, once they have unloaded their cargo at altitude you will find them coming down at a very rapid rate and landing on the first available runway, no matter what the wind or traffic. I know they are in a hurry to get back on the ground for another load of jumpers, but why they never fly a normal traffic pattern I will never know. More than once we had been on final approach to an airport when all of a sudden here comes Mr. Jump Plane from some other direction, landing either in front of us or on another runway that intersects the normal pattern runway.

Walterboro was no different. Turning downwind for runway 35, we were a little surprised to find Mr. Cessna in a very steep spiraling descent from well above our pattern altitude direct to the runway. We Cubs have no problem with making 360s over the airport, but I sure hope we are always able to find that unusual dive bomber approach so that we can stay out of the way. I know Mr. Cessna was no doubt on the radio—yakking all the way down about his location and intentions—but that still does not eliminate the requirements of obeying normal pattern rules and courtesy. But what the heck, no damage was done and we were all here to have a good time and *nothing* was going to prevent Sis and me from enjoying our little journey!

We Cubs are so quiet that it is very easy for us to make an arrival and no one will know we are there until someone walks into the office. This arrival was of that type. Only the humanoids preparing to jump out of Mr. Cessna knew we were in the area and they certainly were not interested in finding out if we needed anything. After being parked in front of the gas pump, our humanoids walked over to the office. Entering this nice air-conditioned establishment was the beginning of a very delightful encounter with Lloyd, "Mr. Walterboro Airport" himself.

Lloyd will tell you that he came from California many, many years ago and he has been around and working on the Walterboro airport for ages. I'm not sure he remembers when he went to work at this nice facility. As soon as he found out that we needed fuel and wanted to spend the night on his airport, he could hardly wait to get with the business of taking care of our needs. Our humanoids made it clear that they would put the gas in our fuel tanks and make sure we were securely tucked in for the night if Lloyd would just tell them where he wanted us. With that, he gave them the key to the gas pumps so that refueling could get started while he made some phone calls trying to locate a nice room (with transportation) for them.

Ray stayed in the office helping arrange motel accommodations while Lyle and Leighton proceeded to take care of our needs. By the time 726 and I were securely tied down on the ramp next to our cousin, Cessna 172, dressed in his county sheriff uniform, Lloyd was out there with us wanting to know if we needed anything else. Yes, we did. We sure would like to have some chocks for our little fat tires, just in case a strong wind came up. Even though we were securely tied down, we like the added security of something to keep us from rolling. In a flash, Lloyd went in his personal car to locate the requested restraint. He must have searched every nook and cranny on that airport before returning with the necessary wooden members.

Meanwhile, this fine gentleman had made arrangements for our humanoids to bed down in a motel about six miles away. Since the humanoids at that place of business could not come and get them at that time, he had also arranged with a family of skydiving humanoids to transport our friends into town. The motel operator would gladly bring them back to us the next morning.

It was with much disappointment that we watched our three traveling companions disappear around the office building on their way to town. We really preferred having their tents under our wings, but that would come later. Now in the waning hours of the first day of this great adventure, my sister and I relaxed in the coolness of the gathering dusk, reflecting on the fun we had during the past seven hours and fifteen minutes of flying time. Venice airport might as well have been a million miles away as we drifted off to sleep while visions of our coming triumphant arrival at our birthplace danced in our cylinder heads.

Hey "Cuz"—Watch Out!

I was jarred out of my fitful sleep well before dawn on Sunday morning, June 23. That gosh-awful noise was coming from the sheriff, cousin 172, still tied beside us. Man oh man could he snore! It didn't seem to matter what position he was in, he could really snore. No need to think about going back to sleep with that racket going on so I might as well get up. The noise was not bothering Sis at all. She just slept away.

As the early light of dawn made its way into our world, it was very obvious that this morning was not going to be the most ideal for Cub flying. Heavy mist and haze blanketed the whole area and as it got lighter the temperature and dew point got closer together causing the threat of fog to became very real. By the time our humanoids had returned to rescue us from our bonds to the earth, visibility was down to three miles—if you looked real hard. However, the sun was making an honest effort to burn through as it pushed itself above the eastern horizon.

After much discussion, it was decided that if we followed Interstate 95 to Summerton, South Carolina, made a left turn up U.S. Route 15, we could find Sumter, South Carolina, without stumbling into any restricted areas or controlled airspace. No really tall towers or other obstructions could be found on the sectional and there were at least two alternate airports if things really got bad. Still, with a questionable three miles visibility, extreme caution was the rule. Flight Service had advised that all reporting points in the direction we wanted to go were giving VFR conditions—although marginal—and the forecast for the entire area was a constant improvement up to six or seven miles visibility. There were no clouds above so, in time, the sun should do its job and make things improve. Then we would soon be on our way.

By the time preflight inspections had been completed and engine start time had arrived, Mr. Walterboro Airport drove up to again ask if he could be of any assistance. He agreed that the visibility was three miles and wished us a pleasant trip with an invitation to return at any time. Yes, indeed, we would return. With service like he has given—who wouldn't!

Holding our takeoff heading for five minutes took us directly to I-95 and there was that 359-foot-high tower right where it should be. I was in the lead and I must admit trying to keep the road and 726 both in sight was a bit of a problem. The visibility was not as good as expected. By climbing above the dense layer of haze, we could stay in contact with the road and horizontal visibility did improve a little. Lyle was watching my compass very closely as well. That compass-ache, which developed yesterday, put him on alert and he finally figured out that as long as the vibration from my engine kept the card from sticking, the average deviation on northerly headings was ten degrees west. This rough calculation proved to be quite accurate as we proceeded onward to Lock Haven where repairs could be made.

As we proceeded along the interstate, the visibility continued to oscillate between "bad" and "not good" until Lake Marion slipped beneath our wings. Over the lake proper, there was considerable doubt about the wisdom of us being in the air as the added moisture of the lake surface created a thin layer of fog, which completely obscured the road. However, ahead a few miles we could see much improvement so we continued on our heading to Summerton. Within five minutes things started improving rapidly until the promised seven miles plus visibility prevailed in all directions.

Ahhhhh—this was Cub weather. Smooth air and relatively good visibility so that we can all enjoy the scenery. Now it was just a matter of following U.S. 15, staying out of restricted area R-6002, staying under the Class C airspace of Shaw AFB, and landing at our destination.

The Sumter airport was blessed with two runways. One was the standard paved slab with no personality at all. The other was a beautiful wide grass strip, which crossed the other runway and taxiway at mid-field. This was normal, but I wish to mention this configuration for a reason that will soon be clear. A quick check of the windsock and local traffic showed no wind and no aircraft moving at this time. Obviously, being Cubs, my sister and I desired to land on the grass so we entered left traffic for landing on runway 14. The surface was as soft and velvety as expected. Even though a little mowing would have made it better, we certainly were not complaining. It was the first grass landing area we had found since leaving Venice and it felt gooooooood!

Picture the above-mentioned runway layout. Also picture two bright yellow Cubs having just touched down on that beautiful grass and now rolling out, rapidly approaching that intersection of grass and paved taxiway. Got it? OK, now add to that picture a bright white-and-blue Cessna 172 merrily taxiing through that intersection on the paved taxiway without bothering to recognize the fact that two of his distant relatives—the two of us—had just landed on the runway he was crossing, which he did not bother to check *before crossing.* Very interesting picture—wouldn't you say? Anyway, we got stopped, he continued on—he never did see us. All is well that ends well.

It was interesting to hear the comments of the airport manager who witnessed the whole event. He apologized to us and made it clear that Mr. 172 would be informed that real airplanes *do* use the grass runway. Our humanoids made it clear that no harm had been done. We all make mistakes. Even though the manager thanked us for our patience, he promised to have a talk with Mr. Cessna when he returned to home base.

Onward to the Hills

Although five to seven miles visibility was good Cub weather, our humanoids were more accustomed to the twenty or twenty-five miles visibility back home in Florida. Thus, it was decided that after takeoff we would "hang a left" up U.S. 15 as far as Society Hill, South Carolina, where we would swing further left and follow U.S. 52 all the way to Albemarle, North Carolina, and Stanly County airport. Ahhhh yes—Stanly County—the Six-Pack Minus Two spent what seemed like a week there two years ago, waiting for the rain and fog to clear out!

Our energy source reservoirs were replenished and 726 was in the lead as we made our ever-impressive Cub formation departure from Sumter. (As a stranger humanoid remarked one day, "Man you really do haul out of here don't you?") What a relaxing way to see the countryside. Yes, the highway does meander a little, but at our ear-popping altitude of 1,200 MSL who cares—we were just enjoying the scenery as we did what we do best—fly low and slow. We wonder just how many of our cousins, zipping along at well over 100 knots, way up there in the sky 5,000 feet and above, can truly enjoy what they were seeing. Did they see the details of the farmers working their fields, that pasture full of cattle, the kids fishing the streams, or the many other things that God put on this earth for all to enjoy? It is a pity that more of the younger generation of humanoids have not been able to see this world as only we Cubs can show them. It's a real shame that large numbers of them will never know the beauty of this kind of flight.

Stanly County Airport came into view on schedule. Well, we were a little late, as this leg has taken us two hours. We would find that it was the longest of the whole trip. Very little had changed in the past two years, except the weather, and it was much better this time. While Leighton and Lyle tended to our needs, Ray had once again found an audience to whom he can "sell" Sun-'n-Fun. He had so much fun doing this that on occasion, just like his lovely humanoid wife, Jo, does, we have to tell him, "Say good-bye, Ray, we're leaving." He always does and we always do!

After the usual airport lunch of crackers and soda pop, our humanoids brought out the charts to decide where we should go next. Since it was my turn to lead, I sure hoped they made it an easy leg—considering my ailing compass.

Danville, Virginia, looked like a good destination. The direct route would be a good DR navigation leg in order to confirm the estimated ten-degree west deviation that Lyle had calculated. If that didn't work there were good roads within a few miles to the left of course that could be followed. Let's see, there were some really tall towers (2,649 feet msl) south of Greensboro, North Carolina, and we need to stay out of the Class C airspace around Piedmont Triad International Airport. No big deal if the visibility would just stay as good as it was now. All indications were that it would actually improve, so we were off and run . . . er . . . flying!

Fifteen minutes after takeoff, we crossed our first checkpoint, right on the money. This confirmed that my compass-ache was ten degrees west as estimated. This proven fact helped promote a much more relaxed atmosphere in my cockpit. The visibility improved to over fifteen miles, and in another ten minutes the first of the big tall towers was plainly visible. Nothing to do now but sit back, relax, and watch the countryside leisurely slip past below our wings. The only way to fly!

Again, our navigation must have been somewhere close to correct, because Danville came into sight at the proper place in the windshield and the numbers on the clock were the correct amount of time. As we entered the traffic pattern, we could see an alarming amount of activity on the approach end of runway 24. We couldn't make out what kind of aircraft they were, but at least four of them were in the air at one time chasing each other around in tight circles. Seemingly without cause, they would change directions and do all sorts of wild aerobatics. Obviously, it was a radio control model airplane event being held on the end of runway 24, which was marked closed. It was interesting to watch them as 726 and I maneuvered for landing on runway 20. We kept our eyes open because if one of them turned on us—man—we would be outta here!

While taking a short breather at Danville, it occurred to us that we were actually witnessing something that has almost become extinct in modern-day aviation. True, it was a modern-day family member (a Piper Warrior) that was performing this feat, but it sure brought back fond memories to 726 and me. We remembered the days when we were doing the very same activity from small grass runways scattered around the countryside. We could see that he was selling airplane rides! There was the banner hanging on the fence shouting to all who would listen AIRPLANE RIDES—FIVE DOLLARS. (In our day it was $1.50!) While we watched, our young brother must have taken at least six guests for an adventure into the realm of flight. They were not gone long, but those who were involved were having a ball. Talk about bringing back memories—wow!

With full fuel tanks, we are once again in the air with our spinners pointed north toward Lock Haven. Seven-two-six is in the lead as we enjoyed the tranquillity of being in the air together working our way toward Falwell Field at Lynchburg, Virginia. What a beautiful afternoon this day had become.

While reviewing the Falwell airport information, it was discovered that there was a very emphatic note stating that landings should be made on runway 28 and takeoffs should be made on runway 10. While planning this leg at Danville, we thought that must be some sort of wimpy rule established because someone did not like airplane noise over his house. However, after further study, we found that there was a 9.1 percent up-slope on runway 28 making the threshold 261 feet lower than the opposite end of the runway. It was also noted that one end of the runway was not visible from the other end. Besides that, the runway was only twenty-four feet wide with plenty of grass-covered clear area on each side. However, this grass was not suitable for landing or taking off. My humanoid had not seen anything that steep since flying the bush in Alaska many years ago. Now we understood the restrictions.

Sure enough, the runway was as advertised. After touchdown, it took almost half throttle to get up the runway to the taxiway into the ramp. You must remember that those expander tube brakes that we Cubs possess are not the best stopping devices ever invented. So, when we turned onto the curved taxiway that led to the ramp with its rather steep downhill slope, those binders really got a good workout. I am so glad they held because if they had not, I would not be here today telling this story. I do not remember when I worked so hard to keep from rolling too fast. Once on the ramp, things were pretty much on the level; however, we did feel more comfortable once those chocks were tucked around our little fat tires.

It was interesting to see our relatives who call this unusual airport home. There were a few relatives from the Piper family and about the same number of cousin Cessnas in the area. All were of the single-engine lineage. However, one big fellow by the name of Beech King Air also claimed this rather limited access facility as home.

The presence of such stately twin engine turboprop kinfolk living on such an unlikely airport brought about many questions. First of all, he explained that he operated as a charter aircraft from the Lynchburg Regional Airport, just over the hill about seven miles to the southwest.

Normally he did take off on runway 10 and land on runway 28 as we were doing. However, on occasion, he had done just the opposite when the wind had been very strong.

He did not carry much weight or fuel from Falwell Airport. He only slept and relaxed here and flew over to the big airport to take on fuel and payload for any trip he might be chartered for.

Yes, his V-one (abort/continue speed) is before starting his takeoff roll. Once he starts rolling, the takeoff will be completed—no stopping! He has the capability of doing that maneuver on one engine. (Hmph—no big deal—we Cubs do one engine takeoffs all the time!)

Another very interesting observation was the number of "clipped shirttails" from first solo humanoids hanging on the office walls. All I can say is that any humanoid who can attest to having soloed from this particular runway can be very proud of the fact that not only did they solo, but they also did it from a runway that many seasoned pilots will not venture onto if given a choice.

Bidding farewell to new friends, we headed up the taxiway from the ramp. This was quite an uphill pull, but once we reached the taxiway leading to the end of runway 10 my little Continental had to turn 2,000 rpm just to keep us moving. Man, that 9.1 percent slope became quite a reality now! No way could I get into the air going up this hill, especially with this load of humanoids and fuel! Once over the crest of the hill, we had about twenty yards of gentle uphill slope before reaching the end of the runway.

The completed run-up confirmed that all systems were go and I took a look at the runway as I moved into position. There was only fifty or sixty feet of runway visible. It just vanished over the top of the hill. We had been very observant as we taxied out, but the thought of an unseen aircraft landing on the other end of this runway crossed our mind. This really was not something to be concerned with, as any landing relative would be at least 200 feet below our takeoff point. Also with the high temperature and light breeze, they certainly would not be going around either. I also knew that due to my configuration my humanoid would be completely blind except for peripheral vision once we started our takeoff roll. I knew he could keep me straight, but this runway was only twenty-four feet wide. *Keep me straight, Lyle, keep me straight!*

Lined up in the center of the runway with all sixty-five horses pulling on the engine mount, we started our takeoff. I rolled true and shortly we were over the crest of the hill on the downward run with my tail wheel just barely off of the ground. As I knew would happen, in less time than it takes to say "it," the hill dropped away from my sneakers and we were back safely into the air. *Hey—this is really fun! I want to do this again! Maybe on the homeward trip—I hope!*

Since 726 was behind me this time, she really got an interesting display of unusual happenings. She, too, experienced the same sensations and concerns that I had during the takeoff, but she also had the advantage of watching and recording for posterity, via photographs, the sights of my leap into the air. Later, she would produce pictures of the "now you see the Cub, now you don't," "and now you do," sequence as I made my departure from that very unusual airport. Yes, we must return someday.

Shenandoah Valley Country

With this latest adventure behind us, we pressed onward toward the north, ever closer to the Blue Ridge Mountains. This eastern range of the Appalachian Mountain system extends all the way from southeastern Pennsylvania into northern Georgia. In Virginia, where we would be crossing this range, they were only twelve to fourteen miles wide and our humanoids had chosen the pass just south of Waynesboro, Virginia, to make the transition into the Shenandoah Valley. It seemed they did not want to overwork us by making us not climb too high for the crossing. Indeed, the pass they had chosen would allow us into the valley with an altitude of about 3,000 feet.

As we approached this gateway through the hills the landscape made a gradual change from low rolling hills to much steeper contours of small mountains. Due to the light flow of air from the east, the visibility became less and less as the haze layer piled against the slopes of the mountains. It was nothing to become alarmed about, but for those of us who are accustomed to more than fifteen miles of visibility it was something to think about. The closer we got to our "doorway," the thicker the haze became and by the time we were ready to fly through that gap in the hills, the visibility was down to three to five miles. Plenty low enough for us flatland Cubs!

As if by magic, someone turned the haze machine off and the visibility started to improve as we progressed into the Shenandoah Valley, over the downwind side of the range. By the time Waynesboro passed beneath our wings we could see at least ten miles and soon the visibility was almost unlimited. What a beautiful sight—the 4,000-foot-plus mountains thirty miles to our left and just off our right wing, the 3,000-foot high ridges we had just passed through. The late-afternoon sun enhanced the beauty of the many farms that lay below us in the valley. It made us wish we had enough fuel to stay in the air well past New Market, Virginia, our next stop.

After reviewing the airport book and calculating our ETA to be about 5:30 P.M., our humanoids decided Valor Field/Airport at New Market would be far enough to travel. This spot looked like a good place to end another very enjoyable day of playing in the sky and seeing many new sights. Besides, it would be an easy two-leg trip for the morrow and the latest weather report indicated no problems. (However, it really *was not* going to work that well!)

The runway at New Market was snuggled near a rapid-rising ridge to the northwest. This being the case, a right turn to final was required to runway 06, the active runway. It was great fun to have my nose pointed directly into the forest on the side of the hills and then at the last minute swing it around to the runway. This mountain flying was really a lot of fun if you used caution and common sense.

Once on the ground we proceeded directly to the gas pumps. The AOPA airport book indicated there was service until 7:30 P.M. on weekends. This being Sunday, service should be no problem. Right? Wrong! When our little Continentals had ceased their powerful roars, the silence was deafening. How peaceful and quiet. All

881 over the Shenandoah Valley of Virginia. Credit, Leighton Hunter.

that could be heard were the birds singing and the grass and leaves rustling in the breeze. It was perfect except for one thing—there did not seem to be anyone around and we needed a place to be secured for the night. We could get fuel the next morning.

Lo and behold, as luck would have it, a young attendant was found locking up the business for an early departure. This young man did not seem too eager to help at first, but when he was informed that we needed gas and a place to stay he came to life. A key was produced to unlock the fuel dispensing equipment, our humanoids were told where they could find tie-down ropes, and he would look in the phone book for a list of accommodations.

By the time 726 and I had our fill of 100-octane low-lead, the young man had made a list of three or four possible sleeping sites for our humanoids. Again the question was asked as to where we could be secured, because not one single tie-down rope could be seen anywhere. Lyle walked past us mumbling something about tall grass and weeds as he headed toward the area indicated as being our resting place. As his strides took him further into this never-never-land, I could not believe what I was seeing. The further he went, the taller the vegetation became until finally it entirely obscured both of his legs. At last, he turned around and shouted to us that there was *no way* he would put us in this jungle, even though the ropes were new.

As he waded back toward our location on the ramp, a sweet little 1946 BC-12D Taylorcraft (she was one of our first cousins) came rolling up. I heard Lyle telling her humanoid that we had planned to spend the night here, but after seeing where my sister and I would be resting he had decided we would be going further north. Ms. Taylorcraft agreed completely and admitted they had been trying to get something done about the sad condition of the grass areas on the airport for a long time, but nobody seemed interested in making the effort. With that, our bill was quickly paid and once again we were back in the air.

How sad it was in this day and age that such a great, little peaceful hometown airport as New Market was allowed to become so overgrown. Back when Sis and I were young, before paved all-weather runways, all grass areas on such a fine haven for the likes of us would be mowed and trimmed for all to use. Oh well, I guess that was the sign of the times. This younger generation of family members with their training wheels in front are only interested in using the hard, impersonal surfaces of pavement. What a pity they will never know the joys we have known. Well, enough of that!

As is often the case, a change of plans proved to be a blessing in disguise. This proved to be one of those times. Winchester, Virginia, was only another fifty miles northeast up the valley and offered everything we needed for a pleasant and safe overnight— since we again would not have tents under our wings.

The sun was riding quite low in the western sky as 726 led us onward. The elongating shadows increased the beauty and tranquillity of the rural landscape below our wings. The air was smooth as silk and it seemed that we could see forever. Passing over the patchwork of fields and occasional private landing area made us want to kiss each one with our fat little donuts and then pop back into the sky until we found the next one. The intoxication of flying in this environment makes us Cubs really glad we were created and given this leg to fly.

In our minds, Winchester came into view much too quickly. But then, the sun would soon be gone for the day and we did not have lights for safe and legal night operations. Our line of flight put us onto the base leg for runway thirty-two at Winchester Regional Airport, which in turn led us to the ramp of Winchester Aviation. These fine folks quickly arranged to have our energy tanks filled, pointed out tie-down spots, and had the nice people from the Budgetel Inn on their way to pick up our favorite humanoids. Sis and I would again have to spend the night alone on the ramp of a strange airport. Even though we could still see each other, we would be secured about fifty yards apart across the ramp. There were several of our cousins on the ramp with us so we would not be lonely.

An interesting sidelight was the fact that we were now less than sixty miles from our nation's capital. Maybe we should make a little side trip to the White House to visit Mr. Clinton. I wonder what would happen if we were to land on the Mall? We could, with ease, you know!

The Blocked Pass

Monday morning, June 24. Things were pretty quiet here on the ramp as we patiently waited for our humanoids to return from their night at the inn. It was a little fuzzy around the edges, but as the sun crept over the eastern horizon we could see that this was the dawning of another great day of flying—at least here in Winchester. We were in an especially happy mood this morning because we were within 160 miles of our birthplace, Lock Haven. Just under three hours of flying time and we would be back to our roots. We could hardly wait!

About 8:00 A.M., our jolly humanoids trooped across the ramp with their excess amount of luggage. You would have thought they were moving—even though they had shipped all of their camping gear ahead via UPS. As this mountain of cargo was being fitted into 726, who by this time thought she was a pack mule, we heard bits and pieces of conversation regarding the weather ahead. It seemed the good folks at the Budgetel Inn had installed the weather channel on the TV system and our dear friends had learned of possible severe thunderstorms approaching the entire area within the next twelve to fourteen hours. The plan of action now was to be under way as soon as possible and get us Cubs into a hangar in Lock Haven ahead of the storms.

It was sixty miles on a true course of 350 degrees to Bedford, Pennsylvania. En route we passed over the northwest corner of Virginia, the panhandle of Maryland, and the foothills of the Allegheny Mountains where Bedford County Airport is nestled. It had been calculated that it would take us approximately one hour to traverse this distance. So, without further delay, it was flying time. Hooray. Hooray! We will be back in Lock Haven before noon!

I was in the lead on this leg so my ailing compass would once again be put to the test. As we proceeded up the course line, the visibility did not improve. As a matter of fact, it was slowly reducing from the seven miles (good for this part of the world) to something less. The compass error on this heading was a few degrees different from the deviation that Lyle had computed earlier in the trip. Thus, about twenty-five miles into this leg we found ourselves headed up the wrong valley. Sis recognized my error and continued in the proper direction. Finally, I realized that she knew where she was going and we were soon established on the proper line on the chart. (I sure will be glad to get my compass fixed!) Now that we once again knew where we were, the visibility continued its slow but sure reduction. By the time the runway at Bedford came into view, it was down to three or four miles at the most.

Even the humanoids operating the gas truck at Bun Air Aviation on the Bedford airport were commenting about the forecasted arrival of very bad weather. It was already getting rather dark in the northwest, but we were going to be traveling toward the northeast. Maybe we could stay ahead of it if we did not tarry long. Let's see—we would be following U.S. Highway 220 to Interstate 80, which would in turn take us to the road that went through the mountain pass about five miles west of Lock Haven. Also, there were several airports that would give us shelter if needed. Both 726 and I were very glad to see that our humanoids were thinking ahead. This could get tricky!

Being the oldest by eight years, 726 would be leading us on this final leg to Lock Haven. This had been decided way back in the planning stages of this little journey. She deserved the honor. After again demonstrating our famous Cub formation takeoff, we were on our way. Only ninety-eight miles left to go! *Hot dang! It won't be long now.*

It all sounded good and felt good. If only it looked good, too. We were soon to find out just how Mother Nature can adjust things to her way of thinking!

For the first twenty-five miles or so, there were no problems. Oh yes, the visibility was certainly nothing to write home about, but it was flyable. Shortly after passing over the town of Altoona, Pennsylvania, we could see rain and low ceilings starting to move over the ridge ahead and to our left. Soon we were flying into the stuff that we had been looking at. My, it was moving fast across our path! I personally wanted to hop over the ridge off our right wing into better weather, but 726 kept pressing onward. I wanted very much to stay with her, so I, too, continued. Finally just past the town of Tyrone, Pennsylvania, I observed a red light come out of the gloom and pass about one-eighth mile off my right wing. It was a radio tower located on top of the ridge. I guess a Higher Power was watching over us, too, because at that point a couple of bolts of lightning flashed to the ground a couple of miles in front of us and as if on cue, Sis and I made a synchronized sharp turn over the ridge to our right into that nicer weather I mentioned earlier.

Now safely in the next valley to the southeast of our original route, we once again turned toward our destination. This did not last long either, for within minutes that fast-moving block of mean-looking weather had jumped the same ridge and was now forcing us to move further to the southeast. We almost waited too long before making the decision to move further southeast as the top of our rudders must have been in the clouds as we crossed yet another ridge in search of better weather.

By this time, our humanoids have finally decided it was time to get us on the ground. Thank goodness! Even though we were once again in fair to good weather, that bad stuff was hot on our tails. Yes, our faster speed was moving us away from it, but we were not real sure exactly where we were. I'm not saying we were lost, I am suggesting that we seemed to be slightly "misplaced" at the present time. All hills and valleys looked the same. The visibility was not good enough to get a fix using the contour lines of the chart and there were no roads, railroads, or power lines in sight. All we could do was hold a compass heading—and I was not sure my compass was anywhere near correct going in this direction.

Another little problem that was rapidly showing its ugly head was the fact that within twenty or thirty miles on this heading we would be running out of chart! You see, our humanoids had been so cheap that they had not spent the extra fourteen dollars for the Washington and New York Sectional Charts that are needed to proceed further east. Bad decision. *Come on you guys. We Cubs were not made for this kind of flying! Do something to find us and get us on the ground.*

I was about one-half mile behind and to the right of 726 when Leighton and Lyle both spotted a small lake on the ground. Again as if we had been practicing the maneuver, on cue we made a synchronized turn directly to the lake. Once we could confirm the shape of the lake, it was an easy task to find ourselves about seventeen or eighteen miles west of the Mifflin County Airport. Without hesitation, we made a beeline for the airport. As we taxied to the ramp, the first large tears from that angry storm cloud splattered on our wings.

Naturally with the forecast of severe thunderstorms in the area, we wanted to get under cover if at all possible. As soon as the "swing-wing" bird (humanoids refer to it as a helicopter) that he was servicing had departed, the nice airport humanoid rushed over to the main hangar and opened the doors so that we could get in out of the weather. That big roll-up door had just finished closing when rain came down by the buckets. We really had not planned to be here at Mifflin County, but it sure was a lot better than being where we had just come from—in the air wishing we were someplace exactly like this place! The time was about 10:30 A.M.—the approximate time we thought we would be putting our sneakers on the ground at the place where we had been born. Obviously, those storms were moving much faster than forecast. They had forecast twelve to fourteen hours and here it was less than four hours later. Oh well, only about thirty-five miles to go and the day was still young. Might just as well relax and enjoy the sound of the rain on the roof.

The heavy downpour lasted for about fifteen or twenty minutes and then it seemed to be more of a drizzle that would come and go. We watched in fascination, through the windows of the hangar, as the surrounding hills would fade in and out as the scud raced along their contours. We could also see our humanoids as they waited in the office building across the way. Obviously, they were as eager to continue our journey as the two of us because they have developed a ritual of coming outside and gazing at the sky every few minutes. They might as well relax and enjoy the stay, because only Mother Nature would determine when we could depart.

Resting quietly over in the corner, near the window overlooking the four-wheeled vehicle parking area, was a distant relative of ours—a Schweizer 1-26—you know, the ones that fly without an engine. This pretty little wisp of an airframe was quite shy, but after a few minutes she began to come out of her shell and engage in conversation with us. She was soon bubbling over with enthusiasm, describing the events of a recent long weekend. It seems there had been a Soaring Society of America sanctioned sailplane meet held right here on her very own airport. (No wonder the grass landing areas were in such magnificent condition.) She could hardly contain herself as she told of the many contestants from all over the United States as well as several foreign countries. According to her account, the surrounding mountain ridges were ideal for ridge soaring most of the time. As she gleefully talked about her many adventures, she noticed one of her favorite humanoids drive into the parking lot. She was overjoyed to see him and very pleased to see that he was introducing himself to our three humanoid friends.

R. L. "Butch" Thompson was the humanoid Miss Schweizer looks upon with such admiration. Butch did indeed befriend our humanoids with all sorts of information about the joys of flying sailplanes. Actually Leighton is an avid supporter of the activity; however, he was content to fly 726 for the time being. It seemed that Butch resided in the valley about a fourth of the remaining distance to Lock Haven. He confirmed the fact that it was indeed instrument conditions in that direction and we might as well take it easy for a while. During that little interlude, he invited our humanoids to join him for lunch at the Honey Creek Inn, on the road that leads to Reedsville, Pennsylvania.

During the short drive to the inn, Butch disclosed that he was a retired airline pilot who moved to this area for the express purpose of flying sailplanes. He had a Maule aircraft, which he used to tow gliders and sailplanes into the air. He also described his own pride and joy, a German-built ASW-20. Our humanoids, especially Leighton, jumped at the opportunity when he offered to let them view his equipment after lunch.

The Honey Creek Inn was a very old establishment located—of all places—on the bank of Honey Creek. It seems that many, many years ago a beekeeper had a large number of beehives along the banks of the creek. A flood from some very heavy rains caused the hives to wash away leaving large quantities of honey floating on the surface of the creek—thus the name. Even though this restaurant was not owned by an Amish family, the owners boasted of some of the best authentic Amish cooking around. After sampling its menu, all agreed this had to be a true statement.

Now completely stuffed, this load of humanity returned to inspect Butch's flying machines. He had not exaggerated one bit about the ASW-20. What a fantastic piece of equipment it was and the trailer in which it was kept left many so-called luxury trailers weeping with envy. All agreed the engineering and technology that had been used in the development and construction was on the leading edge of the game.

A phone call was made to Flight Service at about 3:30 in the afternoon to check the weather into Lock Haven. Local conditions were not good, but Butch and a couple of other local humanoids who had dropped by, felt certain that we could continue our journey—if we flew through the correct valleys. Sure enough, the weather-briefer on the other end of the phone line confirmed we should be able to continue. However, he also advised that severe weather, in the form of thunderstorms, was approaching from the northwest at a very rapid rate which would bring some rather unpleasant changes.

This information caused some very fast-moving activity to take place. The hangar door was opened, our fuel tanks were filled quickly, and within ten minutes we bid farewell to our new friends. Even though it was my turn to take the lead, 726 did the honors for the same reasons as previously stated.

We have never doubted that local humanoids can always give you good information about their area. Thus, we took their advice by departing from runway 06, making a left turn over U.S. Route 322 and following the road through the valleys. This route would be a little further to Lock Haven, but considering the present weather situation, it was the best. Once in the air, we found it to be the only way to go because the clouds were almost sitting on top of the ridges. No question about it, we either flew in the valleys or stayed on the ground!

We had been told to follow route 322 until we saw the sports stadium at Penn State University in State College, Pennsylvania, then to turn right in order to follow Interstate 80 the rest of the way to Piper Memorial Airport. (Well, it would not lead us all the way as we would have to go through a pass in the ridge about five miles southwest of the airport.) The visibility was no more than three or four miles and checkpoints were not easy to spot—especially with the rain showers that were scattered here and there. By studying and flying the contour lines on their charts, our humanoids could see that a little time could be saved by making that last right turn as soon as we passed the ridge that formed the southeast wall of the valley containing I-80.

Due to the weather, this was not the most scenic or enjoyable flight of the trip, but all seemed to be going well. As far as I was concerned, all checkpoints were falling into place even if we could not see them very far away. Then all of a sudden, 726 made a sharp right turn up the wrong side of that last ridge. Even though Lyle knew he could not be heard, he started shouting, "Leighton, no. No. Not that one! The next one!" Since 726 is faster than I was, there was no way I could catch her. If she looked back and saw me following, she would continue, thinking she was going up the right valley.

In desperation, Lyle whipped me into a rather steep 720-degree turn hoping my wings would be seen and she would come back to where she belonged. The second time around, Sis could just barely be seen, still headed up the wrong valley. With that observation, we rolled out on course. I really hated to go off without her, but this weather was not conducive to chasing around in the hills. Oh well, she was a big girl and I felt sure we would see her later on the soft grass at Lock Haven.

Due to the rain, light fog, and low ceilings, we never did see the Penn State stadium. However, Interstate 80 slowly materialized out of the gloom. I did not like it, Ray did not like it, and Lyle really didn't like the situation into which we seemed to be progressing. The rain became steadier and the visibility certainly was not improving. Even the scud seemed to be getting heavier as it blew over the ridge to our left—from the very valley we needed to traverse into just five miles west of Piper Memorial Airport. Lyle kept repeating, "I don't like this Ray—I don't like this!" But we pressed on because we were getting so close to our goal. This is what accidents are made of and, if I, as a Cub, could have personally turned us around and found a place to land—I would have done it long before now! This is called get-there-itis and it tends to break airplanes and hurt humanoids.

This was dumb, dumb, dumb, dumb, stupid dumb!

Things really weren't good, but I did have a couple of alternate airports behind me, which I could reach provided the weather did not worsen. I wondered if 726 was finding the same weather I was. I had not seen her for the last twenty miles—not since she made that wrong turn.

Finally, I saw it—the road that went through the pass just west of Lock Haven! From here, it looked as if the pass was closed, but we needed to get a little closer. In the meantime, I had better take a quick look behind to make sure we can still turn around. Hey, what was that? There was 726 about two hundred yards off in my four o'clock position. Boy, was I glad to see her! (Later she would tell how she turned around looking for me and had seen my wings just as I rolled out on course back there where she had gone astray. She managed to take a couple of shortcuts and caught up with me as I approached this pass just ahead of us.) Feeling much better now that Sis was back with me, I once again turned my attention to the problem at hand. This time there was no doubt in my mind! No way could we negotiate that pass and get to Lock Haven. Mother Nature had won again. We needed to turn around and find a place to land.

As mentioned, there were two landing sites available to us as we retreated from our goal. Both were within twenty miles of our location. One was Bellefonte, Pennsylvania, and the other, University Park, Pennsylvania. Bellefonte was our first choice for two reasons. First, it was closest by about five miles and second, it was the smaller. However, at this point, we would take the first one we saw as the rain and lower clouds were moving into the areas that had been relatively good as we passed this way a few minutes earlier.

Our ground speed was still a stately sixty-five mph, but under these worsening conditions it seemed we were moving at a snail's pace. The sky was getting darker by the minute and occasionally we could see bright flashes of lightning ahead of us. (I began to wonder if we had indeed waited too long before turning back.) My, how that rain was stinging our leading edges. Even the nice finish was being eaten from our propellers as they were pounded by those drops of water falling from that angry cloud threatening our path of flight.

There it was—less than a mile away—the runway at Bellefonte. In these atmospheric conditions, that black surfaced runway sure was hard to find. Thank goodness for the white numbers on the ends of it. A landing on runway 07 allowed us to roll out to the end and make a quick turn to the ramp. By the time our trusty steeds (we each have sixty-five of them you know) had stopped at the fuel island we were about fifty feet from the office door. Our humanoids ran to the office, leaving us to sit here in the rain. I sure hoped they didn't forget us. What a drag!

There was no reason for us to feel that way because our present humanoids have never treated us in that manner, although others had in the past. Sure enough, in less than three minutes we were being moved to a nice cozy box hangar that was just large enough for both of us. The nice young gentleman who led us to our shelter was Jeff Elnitski. He and his father John J. Elnitski operated Pleasant Valley Aviation on Bellefonte Airport. I might add that they also own the airport.

What a pleasant welcome we have received here at Pleasant Valley Aviation. The Elnitski humanoids know and enjoy being with us older generation of flying machines. They both appreciate the likes of us and make it clear that we are always welcome to stop in at anytime. While Jeff was assisting our humanoids in making us comfortable, John was in the process of trying to find a place for our three friends to spend the night.

In due time, a van pulled up in front of our resting place and carted all of the luggage and our humanoids off to a hotel near the Penn State University campus. It was hard to visualize these three characters back in a college town! From all of the chatter we would later hear, it could be assumed they did have a very pleasant stay in town.

As the gray of the rainy evening turned to the dark of night, our thoughts returned to the events of the day. Yes, we had encountered some unwanted atmospheric phenomenon and we had been concerned about why we continued to press onward when it seemed to us we should be on the ground. But we both knew that our humanoids were very experienced and would do all in their power to protect us. For this reason we would, in turn, do all in our power to take care of them. Even though a bright flash of lightning followed by its roll of thunder occasionally jarred us from our thoughts, the steady drum of heavy rain on the roof over our wings soon lulled us into deep slumber. We hoped the next day would find us with tents under our wings on the nice soft grass of our birthplace.

Lock Haven at Last

From her position in front of me near the big door, 726 could peek through a small crack and watch the dawning of the new day—June 25. The reports of her observations were not good. It had stopped raining, but visibility did not look good. If we couldn't continue this morning, maybe we could get these nice humanoids at Pleasant Valley Aviation to swing my compass while we waited it out. That sounded like a fine idea, but the only compass rose available was located at another airport and if we could fly, we might as well proceed to our original destination, which was only thirty minutes away!

At about 9:30 A.M. the big hangar door rolled open and there stood our beloved humanoids. The sun was trying its best to burn off the fog and haze and it was obvious everyone was rarin' to go. Since it would take only about thirty minutes of flying time to finish this leg of our journey, preparations for departure were very relaxed with much time spent in conversation. I think we were giving the sun a little more time to cook the haze and fog. Finally at a little past 10:00 A.M., with 726 still in the lead, our wings lifted us back into the air and our spinners were once again pointed toward Lock Haven. Bellefonte and its kind hospitality will always be remembered. Someday, we will return.

Through the pass and over the town, and there it was—Piper Memorial Airport. The last time I saw this place was the morning of January 17, 1946, when I was a very excited three-day-old

Cub, departing on my way to my first home in the southwestern part of the United States. Really, not much had changed—except maybe the runway and parking areas. *There are the offices in that end of the building and—look over there—that is the main assembly building where I was created! And there!—that's where I got my first glimpse of the sky as I rolled into the great out-of-doors for the first time on January 14, 1946. Over fifty years ago, wow. That's where I left the ground for the very first time!* Sis is having much the same reaction; however, she is remembering way back to 1938 when she was born. That is over fifty-eight years ago. This is going to be one great gathering.

As we entered the right pattern for landing on runway 27, it was obvious that we were the first arrivals for the camping area in the Sentimental Journey compound. Turning final, we can see the beautiful grass runway that has been established on the south side of the main runway. Oops—there is a big yellow X at each end of the grass so I guess we are stuck with the hard surface. The grass must be too soft from all of the rain. We were to find out later that it was closed because the airport manager had decided we could not use it until the following day, the official opening day of the program.

Shortly after clearing the runway, we were met by Calvin "Cal" Arter in his golf cart. This fine humanoid serves on the Sentimental Journey board of directors and is president of the organization. He is also air operations chairman for the fly-in. We were honored to have him personally lead us to a very choice parking spot where we could spread our wings over our humanoids' tents. He also was taking care of all of the camping gear that had been shipped from Florida.

No, Lyle—not that way—please. Lyle, Lyle, hey. Not that way. Oh no. Darn, right through the mud. Darn. And now you have stopped in the mud and that newspaper reporter is taking our picture. I was tempted to use stronger language. The heavy rains over the past day had created a few mud holes in the campgrounds and Lyle, in his eagerness to stay in close formation with Sis as we moved to our parking spot, had put me through the largest one on the site. Now he had succeeded in stopping with my left sneaker buried at least three inches in mud. How embarrassing to be in this situation and have your picture taken for a newspaper story.

Yes, the picture was taken and the interview given before our humanoids had a chance to get out of our cockpits. And yes, the picture was used on the second page of the next morning's (Wednesday, June 26, 1996) issue of the Lock Haven newspaper—the *Express*. If only that reporter had waited a few minutes, I would have been pulled back out of the mud onto nice soft grass. Oh well, I have been known to operate out of some pretty muddy places in my day and this is nothing compared to that! I was not going to let a little mud spoil my fun so let's get on with the program.

It was now about 10:40 A.M. Within minutes, Cal had brought the shipping boxes containing the camping gear and they were now stacked neatly between the two of us. The sun was shining brightly and there was a brisk breeze blowing from the west drying the area where our humanoids would eventually erect their tents for our stay here at Sentimental Journey. While we were waiting for the drying process to take place, we might as well be doing other things. This was where we were born. There were so many things that we wanted to do and so little time to do them. *Come on gang, let's get crackin'!*

The journey from Venice to Lock Haven had taken nineteen hours and thirty minutes flying time. That plus the time we flew before departing Venice brought both of us to the oil changing time limit. Knowing in advance that this would be the case, Butch and several other humanoids we had met at Mifflin County had been asked about where we Cubs should be taken for this type of service. We knew from experience that not all FBOs look forward to having the likes of us on their ramps for service. Without exception, everyone suggested finding Al Bailey on Piper Memorial Airport. He would be no problem in locating as they were sure everyone at Lock Haven would know where to find him. They were correct, and, in short order, both 726 and I were on Bailey's Aircraft Services ramp with the life blood of our little Continentals being replaced.

With the blessing of Al, Leighton and Lyle also pitched in to make the operation go faster. I wanted the complete treatment—you know—oil changed, oil pressure screen checked, and compass recalibrated. Also, Al's helper discovered my primer line was cracked and so it was repaired. Since 726 only required a routine oil change, she was ready to return almost an hour before I was completed. Once everything was done, I quickly caught up with her at our assigned campsite, ready and eager to participate in the next flying adventure of the day.

By the time all of the little aches and pains were cared for, the mud hole was almost gone and the ground where our own little private camp would appear was nice and dry. Within minutes, it was a welcome sight to see three tents erected beside us in anticipation of at least three nights of pure relaxation and joy. As of now, we were the only campers in the area, but we knew others would be arriving—if not this evening, for sure the next day.

Our humanoids had been invited to attend a welcome party for early arrivals, which Cal hosts at his home in Mill Hall, Pennsylvania, each year. I don't know how our guys manage to do such things, but for barnstorming pilots, they sure do get involved in some mighty good food arrangements. It seems to happen every trip! The party did not start until 7:00 P.M. Free transportation to the event was available anytime for the asking, the sun was shining and it was only six o'clock. We all know what that means—flying time. We could get in at least thirty minutes—let's go!

Campsite at Sentimental Journey.

Our ropes were quickly untied and we were taxiing out for takeoff. I guess the airport manager had softened a bit because the Xs were gone and we swung onto that beautiful grass runway 27. Throttles were to the firewall as we blasted off past the Old Piper

Plant on our left. Soon we were in a right turn for a downwind departure to the east toward Williamsport, Pennsylvania. The wind was still rather brisk and the air was a little choppy as we played along the valley, but who cared. Soon Jersey Shore, Pennsylvania, airport came into view. It is more than 726 can take and she is overcome by the siren song of that grass runway and makes a quick touch-and-go, just to say she has been there. I knew then that before we started back to Florida, we would be exploring other ports-of-call nestled among these beautiful hills. But for now, due to what was now a head wind, we needed to make our way back to our campsite.

As soon as we were once again secured in our ropes, our humanoids departed for the party. We heard comments about a dawn patrol flight, but hey, our energy source reservoirs were almost dry and so we suggested that we not go anywhere before they were filled.

I have no idea what time our humanoids returned to camp. I know it was long after 726 and I had drifted into slumberland. It had been fun for us to sit in the quietness of the late evening here at our birthplace, and reminisce about what it had been like so many years ago on our birthdays. It really was good to be able to return and remember. Even though there were only two of us with tents now, we knew there were many more on the way. Very good weather was forecast for at least the next four days, which meant lots of fun flying and many hours of talking with relatives and friends.

Quick Trip to Towanda

The ground seemed to shake and the noise was deafening! Good grief—what was it? It seemed to be going directly through our humanoids' tents, which were erected between us! Those thoughts raced through our cylinder heads as the clouds of sleep were rudely and quickly chased from our frames. Once the slumber fog had dissipated, we realized it was the daily scheduled 4:30 A.M. westbound freight train that lumbers past on tracks located less than 1,000 feet south of our nesting place. No point in trying to go back to sleep because the anticipation of things to come was too exciting for that. We might just as well relax and watch the sunrise chase the dark shadows of night away to the west.

It was about 6:30 before our humanoids poked their heads out of their tents. By this time it was quite light and most of the early morning mist had evaporated from the surrounding hills. This was the official opening day of the Sentimental Journey Fly-in and we expected someone to be up bright and early awakening all of us to watch the hot air balloon flight scheduled for this time. Evidently something happened because neither event took place. Thus, we waited patiently for our humanoids to return from breakfast at one of the on-site eating establishments. As of now we had no idea what we would be doing today. We did know we would be flying—someplace.

In due time all were gathered at the campsite again and preparations were being made for another adventure this morning. What it would be we did not know. Dawn was long gone, so we knew we had missed dawn patrol. First order of business was to catch the roving fuel pump and replace our energy supply. When this truck pulled up, we discovered we would be filled with 80-octane aviation fuel. We had not had this in our tanks in years and it sure tasted good. We thought it was no longer available, but we were to find that the next four days of flying would be conducted using this great tasting liquid that we were originally designed to drink.

Fueling and preflight procedures completed, it was time to pull out the charts and pick a destination. It seemed that while attending the party at Cal's last evening, our humanoids had found a friend of theirs who needed some help in bringing his chariot to the event. His name was Rosco Morton, whom we have heard announcing the airshows and major events at both Sun-'n-Fun and Oshkosh every year. In the winter, he lives near Frostproof, and in the summer he resides north of Towanda, Pennsylvania. He owns a distant cousin, a Varga Kachina, which is kept at the airport at Towanda.

It had been decided that Leighton and 726 would transport him to pick up his conventionally geared steed and I would tag along so that Lyle and Ray could make the trip as well. Thus about 10:30 in the morning, we blasted off for an enjoyable journey of about sixty-five miles through the hills toward the northeast to visit another of the fine landing sites in this part of the country. Rosco carried his hand-held GPS but did not let Leighton see the ground speed readout because with the head wind we were making less than fifty-five mph and he didn't want to hurt his feelings. Heck, he should have known that we feel that is a good speed—considering how rough it was and the direction the wind was blowing!

Towanda-Bradford County airport was a delightful little place, which welcomes the likes of us on the ramp. We did use the paved runway as the grass needed mowing, which is not unusual when hard surface is available. Wandering around the main hangar, our humanoids found a Stearman and a Navy N3N being restored. The Stearman was being finished in the early Navy colors just like my adopted brother. Both of these aircraft were still several months away from flying again because finding parts had been a little difficult, but they will fly again. The little Varga was towed to the fuel island where we were all refueled and soon ready to depart. The Kachina would let us get a long headstart as he was much faster than us. As a matter of fact, we never saw him again until we were back on the ground at Lock Haven.

With tongue in cheek, 726 had been bugging me about my slow rate of climb with both Ray and Lyle included in my gross weight. She didn't exactly go up like a homesick angel when we left Lock Haven this morning when she, too, was carrying two humanoids. I had not said anything but she knew that I was well aware of her poor performance. I was about to really outdo her!

The temperature was rather warm and the twelve- to fifteen-knot breeze was coming over the ridge immediately on the left side and blowing ninety degrees across runway 05 as we departed Towanda for our return flight to Lock Haven. Since 726 now had only one humanoid with her, I knew she would literally jump into the air compared to my performance. Thus as we rolled down the runway, we both became airborne at about the same time and she indeed did rapidly outclimb me. The over-the-ridge air currents that further hindered my rate of climb—actually causing me to sink back into ground effect—came as no surprise either. However, as we made our right turn out into the valley she did something I will never understand—considering Leighton's experience with thermal soaring—she missed the benefit of the ridge. She turned directly down the middle of the valley, which allowed me to make a rather large radius turn that put me in the rising air near the downwind ridge of the valley. This maneuver allowed me to pick up rising air, which must have pushed my rate of climb to at least 1,500 feet per minute. Wheeeeee! Within seconds I was well above 726 and still climbing rapidly! *Hey, Sis, who is out-climbing whom now?* Yes, I was ridge soaring! All the rest of the way back to our campsite, I played with the ridges and managed to make the trip using at least 150 to 200 less rpm than I had used outbound. *Come on, Sis, this is fun!*

Approaching Piper Memorial Airport once again, we could see there had been and still was lots of activity going on. Many of our brothers and sisters were on the ground and many more were in the pattern for landing. Lots of cousins were also filling the transit area as well. Before our departure earlier in the day, each of us had been given a small yellow sheet of paper to put in our windshield so that the parking crew would know that we already had a place to park and they would not have to escort us. Soooo, after another soft landing on that beautiful grass, we taxied back to our campsite and settled in to watch the fun.

Long-Lost Almost-Twin

Since our camp was located within the most desirable camping area of the campus, the surrounding sites were almost full by the time we had returned from our little outing to Towanda. As we continued to get acquainted with those in our immediate vicinity, NC-87863 was discovered parked across the taxiway directly in front of me. Her humanoid came over to see me and we discovered that not only was her registration number eighteen numbers lower than mine, her serial number also was eighteen numbers lower. How about that! She was the closest relative I had seen in years! (I do wish Lyle had not lost the paper on which he wrote the name and address of her humanoid.) We tried to figure out if we were born on the same day (January 14, 1946) or if she had been born on the evening before (January 13, 1946). Her humanoid did not have a complete record of her life and she was having a memory problem so we never did figure it out. Oh well, it really didn't matter—it was just so good to see each other after all those years.

Most of the afternoon was spent in watching the arrival of friends and relatives. Our humanoids made a couple of quick turns through the exhibit area, but found life more exciting out with us among all of the airplanes. As the evening hours approached, the

Varga that we had retrieved during the morning invited Leighton to go for a ride. Of course he eagerly accepted the invitation, but failed to tell us when he would return. As the evening shadows grew longer, Lyle and Ray decided to take me for a little jaunt through the valley of the west branch of the Susquehanna River northwest of Lock Haven. *Sorry about that, 726, but since your humanoid was not here you would not be going this time!*

Off we went into the sinking sun in the western sky. The ceiling and visibility were almost as good as we have in Florida and the air was smooth as silk. Up the river we went, staying well below the ridge tops, well down inside the canyon. A close watch was kept for crossing power lines that were not marked on the chart. Great fun and unmatched beauty were experienced as we wove our way around the bends and twists of the river. By studying the contour lines on the chart, we could tell if the canyon was about to become too narrow to make a turn around. In due time it was decided to turn around after this next bend and head back toward the field. As we cleared ourselves to make sure that it was safe to make a sharp 180-degree turn, 726 was observed sitting about 100 yards off our four o'clock position. What a pleasant surprise. (We would later learn that Leighton was returning to the campsite when we took off and had expedited their departure in order to catch us. They had just throttled back from the chase when we saw them.)

What a beautiful sight. The bright yellow plumage of 726 flying close to that deep green background of forest covered hills with the setting sun shining through an occasional gap in the ridge. And to enhance the beauty even more, there was the river meandering through the valley a short distance below. In our haste to get airborne, none of us had brought a camera. What a shame. Too bad. Well, we will always have our personal memories to keep forever.

Since we had not taken on more fuel after returning from Towanda we felt it was time to return to camp. Besides that, the sun was almost below the horizon. As we came out of the valley over the city of Lock Haven, there was still enough time for a little side trip west of town. Returning to the field, I moved into close formation on 726 and we made one circuit around the fly-in and then entered the pattern for landing. It was interesting to note that prior to our little formation flight, not one other single formation flight had been observed. However, after that, it seemed there was some sort of formation in the air all of the time. I guess they just needed someone to break the ice.

Again secured in our cozy little campsite, Sis and I relaxed and enjoyed our fate while our humanoids happily headed off in search of something to eat. That really was no problem as the nightly "corn boil" was in full swing and there were at least six or eight establishments selling food less than 100 yards away. One thing they were going to have to watch on this trip was how much weight they might gain.

As the evening shadows grew deeper, the pleasant sounds of the nightly live band performance drifted our way. Each night a different band performed the music and sounds of years gone by. It was a soothing interlude of melodic tones that brought back memories—both good and bad. We were close enough to the stage that the volume was just right—not too loud and not too soft. Thank goodness they did not make that noise they call "rock music." Yes, I know some like it, but this crowd was from a whole different world.

By 10:30 P.M. our humanoids were tucked into their sleeping bags inside those nice little tents. Now we could really relax as we watched over them, waiting for the dawning of a new day, which we knew would bring a new adventure. I guess we would have to again endure the passage of that 4:30 A.M. westbound freight in the morning, but then, that wasn't too bad—it just gave the event more character. *Good night, dear friends—see you in the morning. Hey, thanks for bringing us home—this really is fun.*

And the curtain closed on another fantastic day—Wednesday, June 26.

Time to Explore

Thursday, right on cue, the cry of that lonesome whistle with the rumble of those big diesel engines in the background announced the coming of our 4:30 A.M. alarm clock. As it got closer, the rattle of steel wheels on steel rails was enough to make certain that all were awake. Minutes later it was gone and most were able to catch a few more Zs, but not us. We had too much left to do, with time growing shorter every minute.

Within an hour, it was light enough to see the heavy morning mist clinging to the hillsides. It was barely VFR at this time, but there was no doubt that it would soon dissipate when the warm sun's rays made contact with it. As we whiled away the time, we saw some activity taking place among the J-2s that were parked behind us. This special group of our older brothers and sisters was being spotlighted at this year's event so this early morning activity came as no surprise.

Those who thought they were going to sleep in this morning had a big awakening coming. The above-mentioned activity was NC-16745, one of the early J-2s assembled here, preparing for the dawn patrol flight, which he would fly each day. He was powered by a forty horsepower Continental, which had a very short exhaust stack on each of its four cylinders. This configuration created quite a clatter as he warmed his organs before taking off. As he added power to taxi out to the grass runway, those little stacks would pop and crack with authority. Once in the air, he came back over the campus making as much noise as possible. His humanoid would "jazz" his throttle as they passed overhead and on occasion close it to an idle and then shout loudly to those on the ground—announcing it was time to rise and shine. After a couple of circuits over the campers, 745 would return to his tie-downs where he patiently waited for the next morning. Oh yes, he flew several times during the day, but it seemed the flight he enjoyed the most was that daily dawn patrol.

Not one single complaint was heard about 745's early morning escapades. He was making "airplane noise" and everyone welcomed those beautiful sounds. Besides, everyone was now wide-awake to observe the hot air balloon as it departed the area. This morning's ascent was unusual. The heavy mist layer was still evident as the huge bubble of hot air started its climb. It was interesting to watch the layer of vapor engulf the round sphere while the sun's rays kept it plainly visible through the heavy vale as it climbed higher into the clear air above. Those who chose to get more shut-eye missed a very spectacular sight. Too bad!

The morning meal was completed and our tanks once more filled with good tasting 80-octane avgas. Obviously it was flying time again. *Hot dang, you all. Let's get going!* By now, it was a beautiful clear morning with a great forecast for the entire day. It was time to pull out the ol' charts and figure out where we should explore today. After a little perusing of the map, it was decided to go wherever our spinners took us. We knew we must avoid the controlled airspace around Williamsport and we also knew we really needed some sort of plan to make this program work. Quickly, a vision did develop. We would take off to the west; hang a left through the pass just west of town, follow Interstate 80 east to where it crossed the west branch of the Susquehanna River, hang a right and then follow the river to Sunbury, Pennsylvania. We would stay below the tops of the ridges and enjoy the sights.

What fun it was chasing each other through the valleys and around the hills. Little did we care that even the big trailer trucks on the interstate were overtaking us as our shadows playfully hopped along the ground. How lucky we were to have humanoids who enjoyed this type of pleasure as much as we did. We weren't even watching the clock, but in due time the bridge over the river came into view. A nice sweeping turn around to the south soon had us headed toward the grass runway at Sunbury.

726, somewhere over Pennsylvania. Credit, Ray Olcott.

I was in the lead and my humanoid discovered another landing site that he thought we should look into before ending this session of pure joy. Thus instead of landing at Sunbury, a nice gentle turn over the airport had me headed directly toward Danville, Pennsylvania, about ten miles up the Susquehanna River. It seemed that every state that we visit has a "Danville," but the landing field that served this one is something special.

There it was—located south of the river about three miles southwest of the town. Look at those runways! Runway 09/27 was 2140 by 350 feet and 15/33 was 2170 by 198 feet! Man—we could land crosswise on either one of them if need be! Following a Cherokee shooting touch-and-goes, we turned final for 09. Yes, the grass was as great as it appeared. What bliss to feel our little fat donuts kiss the velvet of that lush green surface. Even the taxi trip to the ramp was much like a golf green that was a little overgrown. Why can't we find more landing sites such as this around the country?

We were greeted with open arms even though we didn't need or purchase any services. These people were genuinely glad to see us and wanted us to feel welcome. While consuming cool drinks from the vending machine, our humanoids engaged in light conversation with the local personnel. At least forty-five minutes had passed when our little Continentals were propped back to life and we were soon climbing over the river, again headed for Sunbury.

The landing runway at Sunbury is on an island, which for all practical purposes sat in the middle of the intersection of the Susquehanna River and its west branch. Due to heavy rains that had been in the area a few days before, the river was very muddy and it was interesting to see it mixing with the clean water flowing in from the north. The real mixing action could only be seen from above and we had that opportunity as we approached for our landing.

Circling the field in preparation for our arrival, it was pretty obvious that this was not a beehive of activity. Our airport books indicated fuel was available and the facility was attended during daylight hours. Since our little twelve-gallon tanks were getting a little low and that nice grass runway had recently been trimmed, we thought what better place to make a quick stop for fuel. We were going to land here anyway, just to run our 800x4s along the grass. As we descended into the valley on final to runway 23, we could sense that our books might be wrong as there were no ground-bound vehicles visible.

The momentum from our landing roll took us directly to the tank trailer that served as a refueling island. The only sound that we could hear as our sixty-five horses came to a halt was the buzzing of insects. The smell of the new-mown grass was especially intoxicating for those of us who had spent many of our early years living and flying in some of the rural parts of this great country. How peaceful this place was and what a great location to pitch tents. We could enjoy the solitude and go flying at the least little whim. Not only that, the river was just a short walk in any direction. Well, that was not in the plan for today—maybe some other time.

Sunbury, Pennsylvania. Unusual fueling trailer, but no fuel avilable.

Ray, Leighton, and Lyle left us parked while they took a little stroll around the area. They made a quick tour of the office/hangar area (which looked like it had not been occupied for some time), then made a little side trip to the river bank and slowly ambled back to our resting place. With nothing better to do, our human-oids started taking photos of us after they had posed us to their liking. All of these activities must have required at least thirty minutes from the time we landed. Now it was time to find someplace where we could get a drink as we would need it in order to get back to our campsite on Piper Memorial. The charts were brought out and we very quickly decided to proceed another five miles down the river to Penn Valley Airport, just north of Selinsgrove, Pennsylvania. From all information our humanoids had, that landing site had everything we needed, and more.

The calm wind conditions and lack of any other traffic allowed 726 to lead us in a takeoff maneuver exactly opposite to our landing. It was fun to see the cloud of newly mown and drying grass go flying off as our propellers churned up the air during our run for the sky. Within minutes, we were in the vicinity of Penn Valley.

What a nice-looking site this was with its nice long runway and beautiful grass alongside. Everything looked just fine except for one little thing—actually two little things. Each end of the runway had a very bright white X strategically placed, indicating the runway was closed. I would say this would have been a good time for our intrepid humanoids to have checked NOTAMS before charging off half-cocked this morning.

Even with this new development, the situation was still well in hand as we had plenty of go-juice to get back to that beautiful grass at Danville Airport. As I have said many times before, our humanoids do take care of us by always having a way out if the original plan does not work. After meeting a couple of our relatives (a Piper PA-12 and a Luscombe) who were en route to Lock Haven, we were soon parked by the fuel pumps at Danville. Our hosts found our explanation for this return visit to be rather humorous as they could have told us what we had learned by visiting those two airports. (I personally am glad they did not tell us because we may not have visited those locations if we had known.) Now, as fuel started to flow into our tanks, what a pleasant surprise it was to find that once again we were getting a nice big cool drink of 80-octane avgas. Man, that red juice does go down smoothly!

A gentle breeze of five to ten mph was blowing on our noses as 726 led us back to Lock Haven. We proceeded in a modified straight line in order to see new sights and expedite our arrival. After all, it was now past lunchtime and our humanoids were thinking seriously about something to eat. Just a little over an hour after leaving Danville, we were once again relaxing in the heart of the activity at the old Piper plant. This would be our last flight for the day as our humanoids wanted to explore the activities of the fly-in now that it was fully operational. There would be no time for a sunset cruise as Jim Davidson of Davidson and Derion Insurance had invited our friends to have dinner with him. Again, these guys sure know how to "rough it like real barnstormers," don't they. Ha!

I guess they were getting tired, because the sky was barely dark enough to see the stars when all of our humanoids had returned and retired to their sleeping bags. The sandman soon did his "thing" as the notes of those lovely old tunes of the past drifted over us from the stage. We didn't even hear the band's grand finale.[3]

Unwelcome Conversation

By Friday morning, we had become accustomed to the freight train that came through our campsite on its lonely journey westward. That was just a warning to let us know that NC-16745, that little J-2 Cub with his "short stacked" forty-horsepower Continental, would soon be in the air proclaiming it was time for all to rise and shine—a delightful way to wake up each morning!

When our humanoids completed their daily ritual of showering, shaving, and filling their food blister, they gathered around us in what was the most serious conversation we had heard in days. They were in the process of deciding what we should do today and how we would break camp in preparation for departing for home tomorrow.

What were they thinking about? Departing for home? No way! This program was not over until Sunday afternoon and we were having too much fun to even think about going home! Besides that, we were already home—this was where we were born.

Responsible thinking and good common sense prevailed and a plan was soon formulated. We would go for one last tour of the area this morning. Upon our return, the remainder of the day would be spent enjoying all of the activities surrounding us, including watching the action-packed spot-landing contest. With the completion of that event around mid-afternoon, all of the tents and camping equipment were dismantled and made ready for shipment. Bob Mason, the humanoid in charge of parking all of us, loaned our humanoids his van and soon they were off to a grocery store—

yes, a grocery store—where their large boxes were left to be forwarded to Florida. Then, they proceeded to Mill Hall to check into their sleeping quarters for the night. Sis and I would spend our last night on these hallowed grounds of our birth without our humanoids. Really no problem, considering all the family members present.

With all of the off-campus details taken care of, our humanoids returned to give us one last drink of 80-octane avgas so we would be ready to depart at first light. The sun was very low on the western horizon by the time all preparations were completed and in order to savor what was left of the day, we all just relaxed, watched the joy experienced by others doing their fun flights, and chatted with our newfound friends and relatives. Finally, as the first major shadows of night crept upon us, our humanoids again took the borrowed van and headed for their beds at the motel. It was rather sad, but we all knew departure time had to come eventually. We still could look forward to that westbound train and the clatter of 745's wake-up song. We were confident our humanoids would not depart at first light.

Good-bye, See You Later

Saturday, June 29, dawned as the past three days had done—good weather with wispy mist and cloud layers hugging the mountainsides. It was obvious, too, that this condition would rapidly improve as the heat of the sun overcame the coolness of the ridges. Shortly after 6:00 A.M. our beloved humanoids parked their loaner van and soon we were being readied for departure. I guess we really are going to have to say good-bye.

In the midst of our preparations, Mr. Hot Air Balloon departed on his daily journey, only this time he would do something that he later would proclaim as a first in over 300 flights. As he rose into the early morning sunlight, we could tell there was very little wind above us. Fact is, it appeared as if there was no movement at all. Finally "ol' hot air" started drifting toward the northeast. Within ten or fifteen minutes, we observed him returning directly to his takeoff site as if he had control over the movements of the air currents. Close overhead, his humanoid shouted to his assistants on the ground to get another tank of fuel as he would land and start over again. Sure enough, he was able to put his basket in almost the same spot where, a few minutes before, he had departed. Quickly changing his fuel tank, he was airborne again. This time the air currents were taking him southwest along the ridge toward town. Shortly we, too, were in the air and passed him as he drifted serenely above the sleepy town of Lock Haven.

As we made our turn to pass through "the gap," which had welcomed us to Sentimental Journey a few short days earlier, we caught one last glimpse of our birthplace and said farewell. We had been home, but it was now time to direct our attention to the task at hand, making our way back to Venice, Florida. It had been decided that we would more or less proceed back south over the same route we had come. Since some of us needed to be back at work, we wanted to be in our hangars by Monday evening—if possible. A final destination for the day had not been determined. We had found it much more fun to let our mood and feelings dictate how far we journey in one day. You know—the way we Cubs are meant to travel cross-country.

Even though we were not really happy with it, we had more or less accepted the constant haze condition, which seemed to be ever-present in this part of the world. As we proceeded down the valley toward Bedford, the visibility fluctuated up and down like a yo-yo, between something very near four miles to about ten miles. To this day, we do not know what it was with Tyrone, but sure enough as we neared that little town, the whole weather pattern seemed to go to pot again. For about ten minutes, the haze and fog became so thick that it blocked out the sun and visibility came down to no more than three miles—if you looked real hard. The weather briefing before departure had not indicated anything like we had encountered, but we pressed onward. Sure enough, within another few miles, as we passed over the northeastern parts of Altoona, things had improved and by the time our little Continentals had stopped ticking over on the ramp at Bedford, the visibility was an honest six or seven miles.

There was no need to tarry in Bedford, so quickly our tanks were filled and 726 took the lead for the next leg to Winchester. Approaching the 2,300-foot-high ridge ten miles southeast of Bedford, we could see that the entire area on the other side seemed to be filled with white cotton. Hoping it was just a thick haze layer, Sis continued on over the top of the ridge, with me close behind.

What we found was definitely not thick haze. No, it was full-grown fog and low clouds. We were well on top but the other edge of this layer could not be seen. We knew that meant a quick 180 back to better conditions.

At this point, I was ready to proceed further south in an attempt to get around this stuff. There were airports scattered along that direction, which would provide an easy out if needed. But not dear ol' Sis—no she wanted to try to follow Interstate 70 through the hills and on into Winchester. So it was time to backtrack toward Bedford until we pick up the interstate and turn east.

Over the interstate, we once again approached the ridge. Lower and lower we descended until it was obvious we could not safely proceed in that direction, thanks to the thick clouds that now extended all the way to the ground. I guess my mental telepathy worked because once Sis completed her 180-degree turn, she took up a heading for Cumberland, Maryland. Within an hour, we were having our energy source reservoirs filled in preparation for the next leg south—wherever that might be!

Over the years, our humanoids found that the average Flight Service specialist has no idea how to give a briefing for a flight in a sixty-five horsepower, sixty-mile-per-hour, low-flying Cub. Oh they try, but it is way beyond their training and CYF (Cover Your Fanny) mentality. Soooooo—when it comes to preflight briefing, our friends always ask specific questions and make their decision from the answers they receive and Weather Channel broadcasts they manage to see.

This current call to Flight Service confirmed the weather was as had been forecast. All reporting points were "marginal VFR" until much later in the day. There were no real IFR conditions predicted, but "VFR is not recommended due to reduced visibility." So what else was new? We went through some of that stuff over Tyrone and tried to get over or under some more out of Bedford! We are going anyway and, I would bet, we would get through safely. That was how much we trusted our humanoids.

After studying the charts, a large, long, straight power transmission line was found that would lead us over the ridges to Interstate 81, about eight miles southwest of Winchester, in the heart of the Shenandoah Valley. At that point, we could follow the road back to either New Market, Bridgewater, or Shenandoah Valley airports in Virginia. Leighton and Lyle had arranged for hand signals to be used if upon arriving in the New Market area, they felt we had enough fuel, we would proceed further along our course. Also, the therapy that had been performed on my compass really worked and I was no longer reluctant to venture across sparsely marked landscape. *Ready? OK, let's go!*

As our power plants were being propped back to life, one of the airport employees called to advise us that there would be an airliner landing in a few minutes. Nice to know, but not-needed-to-know information. Ray suggested that maybe we should go to the edge of the ramp and wait until the airliner was on the ground.

Lyle almost came unglued. He informed Ray in no uncertain terms that we (Cubs) had every bit as much right on this airport and in this airspace as any airliner—even a Boeing 747! No, we were not going to wait! After all, the pilot flying that airliner put his/her pants on the same way we do—one leg at a time! I guess Lyle should know, since he had been the senior captain, flying 747s for a worldwide airline. With that we taxied out and were soon on our way again. (No airliner ever appeared.) It was my turn to lead on this leg of our journey.

Ray's Hungry Again

The power line, road, compass, watch, combination proved to be a very good system for navigating this segment. All things worked very well and by the time we crossed into the Shenandoah Valley, the visibility had finally stabilized at a respectable six or seven miles. Even the Wind Gods were helping a little as the light breeze blowing on our tails helped push us along. Approaching New Market, 726 snuggled in close again so that Leighton and Lyle could exchange hand signals, which confirmed we would proceed to Shenandoah Valley Airport.

Ray was very happy with this decision. For quite some time, he had been complaining about being hungry. Evidently the fruit and nuts (other than the humanoids) that 726 and I had on board were not what he wanted. By reading his airport guide, he discovered Shenandoah Valley Airport had a deli on the field. As far as he was concerned, deli is a synonym for sandwich. After hearing of the news of the availability of something good to eat, Leighton and Lyle also felt this was a wise choice of stops.

As was always the case, we Cubs took first priority everywhere we went. It was no different here as our needs were fulfilled before heading for the deli. In the light conversation with the gas truck humanoid, our gang was informed that the deli was not open on weekends. This is Saturday, folks—sorry about that! Now you guys know what it is like to have to continually drink 100-octane low lead instead of that real good 80-octane stuff. *I'm sorry, we couldn't feel too sad about your having to eat the normal FBO fare—vending machine cuisine. We found it rather funny.*

Actually we did feel a little sorry for our humanoids as we climbed back into the ever-improving sky on our way to Falwell (Lynchburg), Virginia. They were griping a little about the lack of a good deli sandwich to eat, but the charms of our flying ability soon had them soothed and literally enjoying the thought that maybe they will lose a little weight by not eating a big lunch.

Southbound Cubs

Once out of the mountains and over the eastern slopes, the visibility improved rapidly. The sky was clear and shortly we could see at least ten or fifteen miles. Nothing to do except enjoy the scenery and wait for Falwell Field to come into view. You might remember that was the airport that was built on the big hill. We wanted to return. Now, here we were, making it our next stop.

Knowing what to expect sure helped in the planning and execution of an approach and landing on a runway such as this. We knew that it would take lots of power to pull us to the turnoff after touchdown on runway 28, so we added power immediately after our tires kissed the asphalt, which made the climb to the ramp almost effortless. As we cleared the active, we observed one of our cousins, a Cessna 150, doing his run-up on the pad located at the crest of the hill. His presence suggested that we take a look at that point as we prepare to depart.

Refreshed with a new supply of 100-LL for us and more vending machine for our humanoids, we were once again turning 2,000 rpm to pull ourselves up the hill for departure. Instead of going all the way to the end, we turn onto the run-up pad where Cuz 150 had been parked. It was obvious this was a much more desirable point to start our takeoff roll as we could see down the hill from here.

Run-up completed. Good, all systems showed. Into position and off we 'goed.'

These words caused 881 to say, *Come on now—settle down. You guys, good grief!*

Sitting on the runway pointed downhill at this position really was much better than at the west end. With this big downhill run, we certainly did not need the full length for our launch into the wild blue. I was not nearly as blind as before and this full downhill run should be lots of fun. With full throttle and full forward stick, my tail jumped into the air. What an unusual feeling to be pitched way over, nose down, and still have my main gear on the ground. Even though it was not more than a glimpse before my wings pull us away from the hill, that short-lived view was interesting and fun. I wished we could have done it again, but we need to press onward—further south.

Hey, Where's the Service?

In the interest of exploring grass runways whenever possible, it was decided that with the slight tailwind we seemed to have at altitude (less than 1,000 feet) we could easily make Air Harbor Airport located just north of Greensboro, North Carolina. The book said they had a turf runway beside their paved strip. Fact is, it recommended that we use the grass because the pavement was in very rough shape. It also suggested landing on runway 09 and taking off on runway 27 due to a 1 percent slope. The printed information also stated the field was attended during daylight hours. Sounded like they had everything we needed and that slope was nothing compared to what we had just used. So, Air Harbor, here we come!

Entering the pattern, we can see that this Air Harbor facility is not one of the best kept establishments to be found around the countryside. There are two rows of hangars which appear to be occupied and a couple of cousin Cessnas tied in the grass. Even three or four four-wheeled vehicles are in their parking lot. Well, from all indications, there must be something going on down there even if it does look pretty beat up.

The grass runway was good considering the shape it was in and the paved slab was as bad as advertised. Arriving at the gas pump, we could see it was locked by a very large padlock. *Hey, gang, it is only 4:30 and darkness is still a long way off.* Further investigation proved the office was locked as well. Now what do we do? We really need fuel.

Lyle spotted a couple of humanoids walking toward their car and as he caught up to them, they just waved and drove away— even after he called to them to stop. Hmmm—I wondered why they are afraid of him? Not to be discouraged, he headed for one of the hangars where he could see someone working on our cousin, Cessna 172. As he got closer, that humanoid waved and got into his truck and started to drive away. This act irritated Lyle a little bit so he ran after the truck, caught up with it and banged on the fender.

Finally, getting the attention of someone, he asked how to get fuel for those pretty little yellow airplanes parked near the gas pump. Even though this humanoid owns the 172 he is working on, he claimed to have no idea as to how to get fuel. However, there was an old gentleman in the hangar who might know. He used to work here a long time ago. Hmmmm—very interesting— but stupid.

Nope, the older humanoid did not know how to open the lock, but at least he would talk to us and did suggest that the kids who run the place should be around somewhere. A search was started and finally one of those fancy sports cars came roaring in and discharged two individuals who claimed they were in charge. One tossed a key for the gas pump lock to us and then went inside to watch television. The other came out again with his camera and took pictures of us. He had never seen anything like us before and thought we were a bit odd. *Well, la-di-da! Take all the photos you want, fella, 'cause we are a bit special and there ain't many of us around any more!*

Tanks were filled again and we were outta here. Self-service is one thing, but the service here was really help-yourself-if-you-can. "We sure as heck ain't gonna do anything more than we have to and then only if you can find us," must be their motto. Not much wonder their airport was going to pot and business was bad. I seriously doubt if either Sis or I would ever return to this garden spot of I-couldn't-care-less. Nor would we ever recommend any of our relatives to stop there either. Next stop Rockingham, North Carolina.

It's Been a Long Hard Day

One hour and thirty minutes after getting away from a very bad experience we could see the Rockingham-Hamlet airport. Somehow, we had failed to see in the directory it had a beautiful 500 x 3,000-foot grass runway in addition to the paved one. When we saw that grass, there was no doubt in our minds where we would put our little fat tires. Sure enough, it was every bit as soft as it looked from the air. Ahhhh, how nice that felt after a long day of traveling. It had already been decided that we would spend the night. For Cubs, we had come quite a long way from Lock Haven to Rockingham in one day. Even though we were a bit tired, we had thoroughly enjoyed every minute of the eight hours and fifty-five minutes it had taken.

Approaching Doyle's Flying Service's ramp, we were met by a smiling young man who was eager to help with anything we might need. (What a change from the last stop!) When advised of our needs, he quickly got our fueling operation started and then went inside to make a quick phone call for reservations at a motel for our humanoids.

Before we had consumed our fill of essence of 100-LL, he returned with a station wagon and instructions on how to get to the motel. The next thing 726 and I knew, we were being gently moved to our tie-down spots and secured for the night. Within minutes, our friends bid us good-bye until morning and they were gone.

As the sun slipped below the western horizon and the cool evening air surrounded our weary frames, we were thankful for such a pleasant day as this. Yes, there had been a few times when the weather had been a bit undesirable, but what the heck, that was to be expected on a journey like this. Even though we were parked and secured on a ramp rather than in a hangar, we did not complain. These lovely small airports brought back memories of our younger days when we spent weeks without seeing the interior of any building. Very quickly the softness of the night sounds played their magic and we were sound asleep.

Mr. Walterboro Revisited

Shortly after sunrise on Sunday, the old station wagon rounded the hangars and stopped in the parking lot. Out stepped our favorite humanoids and as they lugged their baggage toward us, we could hear their friendly banter. It seemed that the early morning Weather Channel news/forecasts told of some very serious conditions to the north of us that were rapidly moving in our direction. From reports received, most all of Pennsylvania and the areas through which we flew yesterday had really been dumped on and the front was marching southward with gusto. Obviously we needed to be on our way.

Since the sun had not cleared the persistent early morning haze and fog, it was decided to stay pretty close to the railroad and highways, which eventually would lead us once again to Sumter. It was a wise decision as the visibility remained just barely legal for almost thirty minutes. Finally, after the water tank with SOCIETY HILL, S.C. painted on its side had passed under our wings, the sun came to our rescue and gradually increased the visibility to at least ten miles. Now we could relax and wait for that nice grass runway at Sumter to appear.

Right on schedule we found ourselves rolling out on that nice grass. It still needed a good trimming; however, there was no close encounter with Mr. Cessna 172 as had been the case a week earlier. The employees at the FBO remembered us and were eager to tend to our every need. Even though we felt welcome, our departure was very quick. This fine weather was conducive to being in the air, so there was no point in staying on the ground. Thus, after a quick hello/good-bye, 726 led us to a quick intersection takeoff and turned south toward Walterboro.

As she should be, 726 was quite concerned about navigating away from the Sumter area. Not only did we have to avoid the Class C airspace over Shaw AFB, there was also a row of tall towers to be cleared just east of our course. In addition, restricted area R-6002 could present an additional problem. She did fine until rounding the southeast quadrant of the arc forming the inner cylinder of the C airspace. At that point, due to too much interest in objects on the ground and not enough attention to her compass, she wandered off in the wrong direction. *So long, Sis, we'll see you later, I'm heading south!* By the time we had separated at least a mile, she realized her problem and hurried to catch us.

Leaving the final tower behind allowed us to better enjoy the panorama passing beneath our wings. Visibility was very good and we could see Lake Marion as well as the patchwork quilt covering the ground. All of these things had been missed going north due to poor conditions at the time.

Following Interstate 95 also presented an interesting little game to while away the time. At least 90 percent of the traffic was moving faster than we were going so it was rather unusual to come upon a vehicle motoring along at our exact speed. One such van was spotted and just for the fun of it, I put my shadow directly on top of it. It was really quite a challenge trying to stay in position when the object you are trying to fly formation with was at least 600 feet away, and while maintaining a constant watch for other traffic at your level. I wonder what comments, if any, were made by the occupants of that cubicle on wheels. They had to know I was there, because on occasion my shadow jumped ahead, behind, or to the side of them and then eventually returned to directly on them. This game lasted for a good ten minutes at which time more interesting sights were viewed.

We have found welcoming open arms waiting for us when we returned to places we passed through on our way north. It was as if we were returning to family. This feeling was even greater at Walterboro. Lloyd, Mr. Walterboro Airport, was genuinely happy to see us again. He wanted to know all about our adventures and, in the course of our conversation, declared that we were indeed part of his family now. He actually referred to us as "his boys." (I guess he was referring to our humanoids as the two of us Cubs are of another gender.) No matter, it was a very warm feeling to be accepted as an intimate member of an airport family so far from your real airport home.

Home from Here? You're Kidding!

Big corporate jets, fancy privately owned twins and singles, and other more well-to-do relatives are brought to mind when we hear someone mention Hilton Head, South Carolina. Having graced their ramp on a couple of times within the last two years, we Cubs remembered being welcome, however, not as warmly as others of "higher stature." On our northbound journey last week, we had been told about an additional new FBO, now in operation at the Hilton Head Airport, which had a completely different attitude toward the likes of us. So, with that in mind, we soon found ourselves headed in that direction.

Actually, the Hilton Head stop was mandatory, no matter what the situation may have been. With our little fuel tanks and our inability to operate into controlled airspace there were no other airports available within our safe-operating range in the direction we were flying. We knew—if we had just a hand-held radio, this would not be a problem. We like it better this way, thank you.

My compass had really proven itself, so without hesitation we took up a heading of about 170 degrees after leaving the pattern at Walterboro. This heading would carry us to a point well clear to the east of the Beaufort MCAS where we would alter heading to about 200 degrees. If our calculations were correct, in one hour we should find ourselves at Hilton Head. The weather was perfect now with almost unlimited visibility. Sure enough, by the time we made the course adjustment toward the south-southeast, our destination runway was in sight—at least twenty miles away.

Entering the ramp area, we could see all sorts of our relatives dressed in their expensive plumage. Some of them would never dream of lowering themselves to recognize the likes of us, but then I guess many families have that same problem. We soon spotted a young gentleman smiling broadly as he beckoned us toward his ramp. (It was pretty obvious who was the new kid on the block.) As he was effortlessly directing us into our parking spots, he also determined, through hand signals, that we required fuel. Before our sixty-five horses came to a standstill, a nice clean fuel truck was parked where it could fill both of our tanks without moving again. Before our humanoids could dismount, the fuel hose was being deployed and ladders were being readied to put fuel in our wings.

Hold the phone! Just a minute, please! Excellent service is great, but it must be done properly! Leighton and Lyle soon had the situation under control and convinced everyone concerned that they would put the fuel in our tanks. The fuelers were very eager to please and no problems with this self-fueling arrangement developed. They admitted they had never serviced the likes of us and were surprised that the gas was being pumped directly into our engines. No one had ever told them that some of us have our energy reservoirs located directly behind our firewall. One actually asked if the gas was being pumped into 726's engine. The nicest thing about this whole event was the fact that they were eager to learn and welcomed the chance to further their education about Cubs.

The FBO that made us feel as welcome and important as many of our jet-powered relatives already on their ramp was Carolina Air Center, Inc. Not only was their facility and service excellent, but their fuel prices were even lower than some of the lesser operations we have visited on this trip. During the short time it took to fill our tanks and pay the bill, our humanoids were invited to return at any time, with a promise that they could pitch their tents. They also had a complete change in attitude about bringing us back to this location. With an attitude and service that has been shown by Carolina Air Center, Inc., we felt right at home among all of our high society relatives on the ramp.

Thoughts once again turned toward our homeward journey, now that our operational needs had been met. Our eyebrows tended to rise when we heard words like "all the way," "tailwinds," "plenty of daylight," "nice weather" being dropped as our three friends searched for our next destination. (All the way from Rockingham to Venice in one day? In Cubs? Not likely!) Within minutes, our intrepid birdmen came up with a plan: to fly to St. Marys, Georgia, nonstop if possible, and then make our final decision at that point. If we could do this, and the weather still looked as good as it was now, we would continue our journey on to Venice, arriving just about sundown—provided the tailwind still wanted to help us a little. The possibility of it working would remain to be seen.

Once back in the air, after proudly taxiing out between a couple of our jet-powered cousins and waiting for another to land, we were winging our way along the Atlantic shoreline. I guess our thoughts were more on getting back home on this passage as neither of us made any side excursions to examine the beach at a lower altitude. In the vicinity of McKinnon Field, near Brunswick, Georgia, 726 closed in on my left wing and Leighton and Lyle once again exchanged hand signals, agreeing to proceed to St. Marys. Thus, one hour and fifty minutes after departing Hilton Head, we were trying to find someone to sell us fuel in St. Marys.

I do not know what has happened to the great service that once was available at these smaller airports. I guess our younger cousins, with all their bells and whistles, have overflown them for so long that now nobody cares. Maybe the likes of Sis and me have outlived our usefulness. Nope—after coming as far as we have on this trip, that definitely is not the case! Nope—I'm sure it is lack of interest!

Our airport books confirmed that this place was "open with the type of service we require available." As we sat looking at that big, locked, padlock on the fuel pump, the empty land vehicle parking lot, and the office with all of the blinds pulled, there was considerable doubt that we would be back in the air this afternoon. Nothing was moving and from all indications, everything was locked up tight and nothing would! Not to be discouraged, Leighton walked to the office door and gave it a try. Much to our surprise, it opened and there on the sofa, sound asleep with the television blasting away, was the young humanoid attendant. He was jolted awake by Leighton's friendly hello and rushed out to help us. (We could forgive him a little, when we thought of the time yesterday when all the attendant did was throw us a key.)

Refreshed once again, we were ready to fly by about 3:30 P.M. There was little doubt about the weather remaining good all the way and we still had about five hours of daylight remaining. *OK, gang, let's go home!*

Once again we retraced our route of just over a week ago. With the help of a little breeze working to our advantage, within one hour and ten minutes we found additional essence of 100-LL being administered to our tanks on the ramp at Keystone Heights.

Unwelcome at Zephyrhills?

It seemed that we were becoming more and more like the horse heading for the barn. The closer we got the faster we went. There really was no hurry, but the weather was beautiful, a slight tailwind was working for us, and we were having a ball doing what we do best—flying. Might as well keep going while all was right in our world. One last time we told Ray, "Say good-bye, Ray" and he hurried out to occupy my rear seat.

As the horse ranches and their attendant race tracks near Ocala slipped beneath our wings, we started to realize that we were rapidly approaching the end of another great adventure. This time in any journey always comes, and I hated it. But then, on the other hand, if the present "book" never closed, how could we ever open a new one? Yes, I guess it was a good thing. Little did we know that as we approached Zephyrhills, we had one last experience to take in before making that last leg home.

It was just after 6:00 P.M. when we idled up to the self-service pump at Zephyrhills. As on the northbound trip, we anticipated quickly filling our tanks and being on our way. But it was not to be on this occasion.

Much to our chagrin, the electricity to the facility was out. Nothing! Try as they did, our humanoids could not make the system work. Three local residents observed our predicament and made a valiant effort to help. They were of the opinion that since today had been a new employee's first day, he had turned the improper circuit breaker off when he went home. Several phone calls were made to the numbers listed and the only thing that answered was an answering machine. Well, that stupid thing knew even less about how to make the system work than we did!

Finally, one of the good Samaritans trying to help us drove over to the local FBO on the southwest corner of the field. This operator had the fuel we needed in his truck and it was thought he would be happy to fill our tanks. Boy, were we wrong. His comment was that the city was selling 100-LL and it was not his problem that we could not get fuel. No, he would not sell us any fuel even if we came over to his ramp for service. With that he advised us to take it up with the city and he closed his door.

Well, thank you, my friend. Maybe we can't get any fuel from you, but we do have some rather thirsty relatives who burn jet fuel and they will be told of your attitude. I am going to suggest that when they frequent your facility, they will be sure they have enough in their tanks to prevent disturbing your supply which you have to sell. I have never been treated this way in all my years.

This is the second time we have wondered if we were really welcome on the airport at Zephyrhills. We had camped here a year ago under some very confusing and doubtful conditions. Maybe we should start avoiding this place completely.

Our fuel remaining endurance was less than fifty minutes so we really were in a bind. Making a trip to the local automobile gas station was considered, but neither 726 nor I had the necessary FAA paperwork to burn auto gas. Now that we were this close to home, we really did not want to spend the night. What were we going to do? We needed energy-juice and time was running out.

Leighton to the rescue! He pulled out his cellular phone and very quickly called the good people at Plant City, Florida. Yes, they would be happy to sell us fuel if we could get there before seven o'clock—in just twenty minutes. They would wait for us to arrive, but please hurry.

Friendly Service and Then Home

Those friendly smiling faces that welcomed us to the Plant City ramp were really a pleasant sight. They seemed more than glad to see us and sell us what we needed even though to do so was going to make them work past their going-home time. Within a few short minutes, our tanks were filled for the last time on this trip. Just as quickly, our wings lifted us into the air and our noses were pointed south-southwest where, one hour later, the little round donuts kissed the soft green grass of home. Our flying time had been nine hours and fifty-five minutes. We are a bit tired, but boy has it been fun!

As was mentioned at the beginning of this little dissertation, I was rather dirty, and of course Sis was in no better condition. Actually, we weren't too bad considering we had spent more than forty-four hours flying across some of this great country during the past eight days. However, it did feel good to be back in our T-hangar homes again.

As we filed away the memories of this latest great adventure, we would remember the great times we had flying to all of those new places. The pleasures given and received as we winged our way across the miles can never be forgotten. However, my fondest memories of this journey will be the returning to my birthplace and Sentimental Journey '96.

But you know what? I'm wondering—where will we go next? Give me a bath and I'll be ready no matter where it may be!

[3]I need to add a few words about the meaning of this Sentimental Journey and what it was like to visit the Piper plant at Lock Haven where 881 was made. There is no air show at any time. (However, just spend some time seated along the runway and you will see one of the best "air shows" you have ever seen!) This annual gathering is more like a good old fashioned fly-in where everyone is laid-back and only interested in having a good time talking with old and new friends. Lots of impromptu flying and buddy rides are conducted at any time during the day as well as much airplane-comparing. Many forums and seminars regarding the

restoration, care, and feeding of those old fabric-covered Pipers are held and much educational information is distributed to any and all.

There are many vendors on the property hawking their wares, most of which are directly related to aircraft and aircraft owners/restorers/builders. One such company has reproduced the one-of-a-kind Piper Sky Skycycle from just a photograph. This full-size replica was flown several times each day and samples of the construction kits were on-site for viewing. Yes, there are people there ready to take orders for the kits, too. Good food is available from several nonprofit organizations as well as four or five other

William T. Piper Jr., retired president and CEO of Piper Aircraft.
Credit, Leighton Hunter.

for-profit establishments. We all feel the pricing of items at this event is very reasonable—not jacked up as we have found in some cases.

Many former Piper officials and employees are on campus also. The original test pilot of the Skycycle was on hand and took the opportunity to fly the nice reproduction. He had nothing but praise for the little airplane. We had the privilege of spending more than thirty minutes taking with William T. Piper Jr. on the porch of the administration building. What a delightful experience that was for all of us. We talked with Bill and Alice Fuchs who had been a husband-and-wife team that worked as production test pilots back in the days when the Cub was the ultimate in its field. Later, Alice developed the program that was used to train pilots who would fly the Piper Navajo and Cheyenne.

The history and historical individuals that abound at this event are unbelievable. Even more heartwarming is the fact that none of these celebrities are above taking time to chat with anyone at anytime. This whole event reminds me of those good ol' county fairs I attended as a kid. You know, where there are no strangers— everyone is a friend whether you actually know them or not.

One thing does concern us. As we look around, it is very obvious the mean age of the attendees of this event is quite high. We would venture to say that the average is well into the mid- fifties. Also the volunteers and officials doing the daily hard work must average well into the forties. The question we want to ask is what is going to happen to this fine gathering in a few years when all of we old duffers can no longer make it work? Maybe we are way off in our thinking, but it sure would be a shame to lose this fine program because not enough of the younger generation wants to perpetuate these fine old airplanes.

The Piper Museum, across the runway, is well worth visiting. Naturally, as any such facility in this stage of development, it is in temporary quarters. Many of its artifacts are not displayed for lack of space. However, the many items available for viewing make the ride to the other side of the field well worthwhile.

This event is one of those real fun things to do. No pressures of competition, no time schedule to meet, and no images to project. Just relax and enjoy the program for what it is—friends, both old and new, getting together to talk about and fly the most important machine in their lives—their airplanes. Leighton commented that he had never seen so many Cubs and other fabric-covered Pipers in one place at the same time. Yes, it is unusual, but that is why we are here just to enjoy all those lovable ol' fabric-covered Piper air- planes.

It's a Long River

Making Ready

Let's face it, mental telepathy is a rather unusual way to communicate and many humanoids do not believe it is possible. However, when we are in our T-hangar homes at the Venice airport, it is the only way that my older sister, NC-22726, and I can talk to each other. We have been having nightly discussions about when and where our humanoids, Leighton and Lyle, might be taking us on our next great adventure. Almost a year ago, we made the trip to Sentimental Journey held at our birthplace in Lock Haven, Pennsylvania. Since that time absolutely nothing has been mentioned about taking another trip. We are wondering just what has happened that such restraint has been imposed upon our activities, as we do indeed enjoy those outings with our humanoids. Could we have done something to discourage such adventures? Neither of us could think of anything that we had done.

The months since Sentimental Journey have slipped by very rapidly. In fact, since that joyous trip to our birthplace, 726 has not flown one minute. Part of the reason for that is because her mighty sixty-five horsepower Continental engine has been taken apart for a complete major overhaul, but that was several months ago. Now here it is the first week in May 1997, and all of a sudden Leighton and his favorite I.A., Dale Kraus, have been working late into the night putting her engine back together again. The test flight is imminent and there seems to be a big push to get all the necessary break-in time completed as soon as possible.

Even though I have been semi-active over the months, suddenly I find myself being cleaned and readied for something big.

Sis and I cannot understand what is going on as nothing has been said to us, nor in our presence, about anything other than routine flying in the immediate future. Our mental communication systems have been working overtime these past few nights, but nothing makes any sense at all. *Nothing*!

On the morning of Friday, May 9, 1997, my hangar doors were rolled open and there standing beside my humanoid was a very good friend, Ray Olcott. Now Ray has been occupying one of my seats almost every time I have flown recently and he seems to always be involved with any real long trips. Obviously, flying was not on their minds this morning as both quickly went to work giving me a new pair of 800 x 4 sneakers. Why they would be doing that, I had no idea, because my old ones seemed very comfortable to me even though they were worn a little and had a few bald spots on the tread. As it turned out, this changing of sneakers was a very good thing because the conversation that transpired between those two humanoids was very enlightening.

During the course of one of those goof-off breaks, between short periods of work, a stack of new sectional charts that measured over three inches high was produced by Lyle from the cab of his truck. The more those two humanoids thumbed through the charts, the more excited they became. Within minutes, it was very obvious to me that Sis and I were very shortly going to be departing on one very big adventure! We are going to fly to Lake Itasca, Minnesota (the headwaters of the Mississippi River), and then follow the river all the way as far south of New Orleans, Louisiana, as possible. Once again, it was to be a barnstorming-type trip with tents under our wings at night and no radios for navigation or communication. It was going to be another one of those good ol' days adventures. Even though I would have to wait until the stillness of night to talk to 726, I could hardly wait to tell her what I had learned. Whoopee! We are *really* flying this time!

Another surprise was forthcoming when, that night, Sis told me about a new GPS that she had caught a quick glimpse of that day. It seems that Leighton had purchased one and would be taking it with him on this trip; however, it would be used only as a "back up" for when things really got tough for dead reckoning and pilotage. You know, when the visibility is down to just barely marginal VFR. (Actually, that is *exactly* how the GPS was used on this trip. However, by the time it was over, even ol' diehard Lyle was convinced that a GPS would be nice to have on our next great adventure! It is about time he decided to use some of this modern technology. He can *always* turn it off when he doesn't want to use it anyway!)

After comparing notes of the day, 726 and I came to the conclusion that within a matter of days or possibly weeks, we would once again be in the air together doing what we enjoy doing most— flying to some far away place while at the same time giving our beloved humanoids the pure unadulterated pleasure they enjoy while flying cradled in the safety of our airframes. A Cub's life just does not get any better than ours.

During the next few days, our close attention to what was being said as we were being preened allowed us to learn further details of this latest proposed adventure. That stack of charts, mentioned earlier, consisted of twelve sectional charts as well as 5 Class B airspace charts. The total distance involved for this little journey was estimated to be somewhere around 4,000 miles— plus or minus a couple of hundred. This distance did not include any extra little side trips that we always venture into during our long cross-country excursions.

The time frame for this outing was determined to be the last week in May and the first week in June 1997. Let's see now— Hmmmm—that would be a total of sixteen days if we take advantage of all weekend days. Further calculations indicated we should require about fourteen days of actual travel time—considering planned extended stops and figuring we only cruise at sixty mph, block to block. I guess that gives us two whole days to take care of any delays due to weather. Let's see now—yep, the total flying time should be something around seventy or seventy-five hours. I guess that also means we need to plan on at least two oil changes if we depart with a fresh change already in our tanks. Yes, indeed, it should work. Besides, only 726's humanoid has to be back to work and he is the boss at his company so he should be able to take as long as he wants.

After more tweaking of ideas and plans, it was determined that Saturday morning, May 24, 1997, would be the start time for what now seemed to be quite a Herculean undertaking when looking at the whole big picture. Be that as it may, we are definitely going because my humanoid has been dreaming of this trip down the Mississippi in a Cub for more than twenty years. Thank goodness he waited for me to make it happen! Sis and I can hardly contain ourselves as we patiently wait for time to pass.

Fried Quail and Sweet Potato Pie at Mom's

Streaks of the early dawn were just beginning to paint the eastern horizon when the doors to our hangars were pushed open on the morning of May 24. Even though all three humanoids involved in this program had limited themselves to only three changes of clothing, 726 still resembled a pack mule by the time most all of the camping gear, food, and clothing was piled into her front seat. Even including Leighton, her takeoff gross weight was still well within legal limits although the volume of her load made it look as if she could not carry another ounce. My load consisted of Lyle and his three changes of clothing, Ray, and a few items of camping gear. I hoped these guys planned on doing laundry pretty often. It was obvious that I had enough room, but my gross weight was one-half pound over maximum takeoff weight with a full fuel tank.

This did not present a problem, because I would burn that much weight in fuel just getting to the end of the takeoff runway, thus making everything legal for the actual launch into the sky.

Shortly after 7:00 A.M. our throttles came forward, starting our takeoff roll from runway 13. Over the center of the field, we started our sweeping formation turn that pointed our spinners north. At last, we were once again doing what we loved to do most—flying—and headed for a brand-new adventure.

Residing on the Sun Coast of Florida, as we do, makes the first and last few legs of every journey north very repetitive. I guess we could not expect anything other than this, considering our residence is located on a peninsula. Anyway this first leg would be to Tampa North Airport where a fresh supply of go-juice awaited us. Although it was not clear, the weather certainly was nice with smooth air and very good visibility.

Seven-two-six was really feeling her oats. Her perfect rigging had always made her much faster than I can run, but with her newly overhauled engine, she was really on the go. Due to the fact that she needed to work her new power plant pretty hard in order to break it in properly, she was as much as ten to twelve mph faster than I was with my heavy load. She had no desire to race way ahead of me so she started a maneuver that would continue for at least three days until her little Continental had been run long enough so that it could be throttled back to less than 75 percent power for long periods of time without slowing the break-in process. She would race ahead of me until she had reached one-half to three-quarter mile ahead and then she would make a very lazy 360 degree turn, which would once again put her behind me as we proceeded along our course to our next destination. This maneuver would be completed two or three times each leg, depending on the distance between ports of call.

Tampa North Airport came into view right on schedule. As we entered downwind for landing, we spotted one of our sisters and occasional traveling companion, NC-25885, waiting on the ramp. She and her humanoid, Jim Sprigg, had traveled with us in the past and we had hoped that she would come along on this adventure as well. Much to our disappointment, this would not be the case. It seems she had made the trip from her home over to our first fuel stop just to wish us well on our long journey. We tried and tried to get her to join us for as far as Plains where we all had good friends who were waiting to see us. Besides, we had not flown together since last October when we were all at the Thomasville Fly-in. Try as we did to convince her humanoid that it would be all right to spend the day with us, he insisted that he had a trench that really needed to be dug that day and there was no way they could go—even though we offered him sleeping space in one of our tents for one night.

Since our destination for the day was Plains we quickly finished our little chat and the three of us departed with a quick turn to a northerly heading. Yes, 885 did fly a few miles with us before rocking her wings farewell and turning to the east toward her home at Cub Haven. *Work hard, 885, we'll think of you and wish you were here with us. Maybe next time.*

Now that we had been officially dispatched on our trip the routine settled down into the order of the day—getting to Plains as quickly as possible. Yes, there was a forecast of weather to move into northern and central Florida later in the day and we did need to move as far north as quickly as possible.

Williston, our next fuel stop, was not exactly a beehive of activity even though we were invited to spend the morning at this very friendly operation so that we could join in the festivities of a little fly-in that was going to be held that afternoon. It seems they really wanted to have a couple of Cubs such as ourselves on the ramp for all to see. *Thanks a lot, good folks, but we really have a long way to go.* Reluctantly, the locals wished us well on our great adventure and we were once again headed north.

Unknown to us at this time, this repetitive, routine, and somewhat stale portion of our trip was about to change. As in at least 50 percent of our past trips north, we are now rapidly approaching Live Oak, our next rest stop. The weather was beautiful and we actually had a slight tailwind to boost us along our way. In the pattern at Suwannee County airport, we could see that the only aviation activity was some radio control models being flown along the north side of the runway. We wondered at the lack of full-scale activity, and very shortly the reason became apparent.

Rolling to a stop at the gas pump, we were greeted by—*absolutely nothing.* This really came as a shock because Live Oak had always been one of our favorite stops, with its friendly service and smiling faces. (Well, the last one a couple of years ago was a little on the shabby side. But we all have a bad day now and then.) In reality with no radio to talk to anyone, we Cubs are so quiet we do sometimes arrive without anyone knowing we are in the area. Maybe that was what happened this time. Nope—not so—because there stood a young lady to greet our humanoids as they disembarked our cozy cockpits.

The first words uttered were, "Hi there, I hope you don't need gas, because we don't have any." This was not exactly the way two thirsty aeronauts who have just barely started on a very long trip like to be greeted.

Our humanoids looked at each other in disbelief. This could not be. This being Saturday, maybe a load of fuel was on the way to be delivered soon, so the question was asked regarding an ETA of a load of fuel. The female humanoid apologetically replied that she did not know when it would be there as they had not had any fuel in over a week. Maybe someday next week it would come. (Not one of us ever saw a NOTAM stating there was no fuel at this airport.) With that, someone of the bunch suggested that it sounded like the FBO didn't have the money to pay for the fuel from the tanker. To that remark, the young employee just smiled and looked embarrassed.

OK, folks, something has to be done or we will be here forever. We'll never get to Minnesota. The suggestion was made to call someone at Kittyhawk Airport where a number of EAA members reside. Nope, we couldn't do that as nobody had any telephone numbers! All right, let's go back to Lake City, Florida. Nope, we can't do that either because it was a controlled airport and we don't have any radios. Well, we could call them on the phone, but that was the wrong direction anyway. Let's see what we can find further north.

There—there was Quitman, Georgia. It was only forty-two miles further. We've been in the air for about one hour and fifteen minutes. It was about another forty-two minutes to Quitman—provided the wind direction did not change. Hmmmmm—total of both legs was just under two hours. Yes, we could do it. It sure was nice to know that our humanoids planned this trip with some sort of an out if the chips really started falling down.

OK, 726, it was time to put that newfangled GPS of yours to the test. The direct course to Quitman does not have any good checkpoints along the way. Yes, we could follow the road and add a few minutes to the trip, but we might need the gas burned on the longer distance. It was decided that we would start out with the best DR heading we could muster, but 726 would lead the way with her GPS because it had been said that a GPS will deliver you directly to your destination. With that in mind and our plan worked out, we were soon back into the air headed for Quitman. The book said they have fuel and the field was attended. It had to be correct, because if it is not—man, we *are* in deep trouble! Our twelve-gallon tanks would be almost empty by that time.

To no one's surprise, the DR heading worked and the GPS did exactly what everyone said it would do. We arrived over Quitman Brooks County Airport with at least forty minutes of fuel to spare; however, things really looked deserted. Yes, the book told us no problem, but look down there—not a soul in sight and nothing, I mean *nothing*, that gave any indication of anything happening anywhere on the airport! Well, we had to land anyway because we just ain't got enough juice to go any further.

So far, the only nice thing we could say about Quitman was the fact it had a pretty nice turf runway for us to use. Yes, we Cubs do love our grass landing areas. As we taxied slowly toward what we assumed might be a ramp area, we could not see anything that even looked like a fuel storage area or fuel pump. All that was visible were three of our cousins, Thrush agriculture aircraft, which obviously had been ridden very hard and put away wet. I really felt sorry for them because they sat there looking as if they did not have a friend in the world. Seeing their sad condition and enduring the acrid odor emitting from their cargo tanks/hoppers brought back some very unpleasant memories of my own from the time, many years ago, when I, too, was a hard-working ag plane tending fields in New Mexico—a time in my life I would prefer to forget. My heart went out to these poor beasts of burden. I really felt sorry for them. But enough of that, we had our own problems to solve.

The stillness was deafening—especially when we desperately needed go-juice to continue on our way. Our humanoids started searching for someone who could help us take care of our problem. Lyle started across the airport to a private home that appeared to be occupied. He had not gone far when Leighton and Ray discovered a lone attendant coming out of a hangar en route to get in his truck and drive away. He was as surprised to see us—two yellow airplanes parked on the grass—as we were to see him. He had not heard our arrival and was indeed on his way to work on a tractor that had broken down somewhere away from the airport. When he was told of our needs, he invited us to move over to the other side of the hangar where there was a fueling facility and he would be glad to see that our problem was solved very quickly.

That essence of 100-octane low-lead really tasted good. I do not remember when I had been so thirsty as we never deplete our energy supply to such a low level during normal operation. Quitman had come to our rescue and it was nice to meet such hard-working people, but we are anxious to get moving on. So, with a friendly "so long—see you later," our little Continentals were propped back to life and we were on our way.

Now less than 100 miles from our destination for the day, we started to relax a little. We knew we were well beyond the adverse weather, which did move into Florida behind us as we moved northward. Now our thoughts turned to how nice it would be to put our fat little sneakers on the lush grass of Peterson Field at Plains. Not only that, but we knew we will have tents under our wings, which is really what we looked forward to on these trips. Our humanoids were already thinking of Mom's Restaurant in Preston, where they knew Mom would have waiting for them some of the most delicious food they had ever eaten.

Sure enough, Tom Peterson's lovely wife, Martine, was out to greet us as we taxied up to the fuel pump. Tom was off on a charter trip but would be back in time to join us for dinner at Mom's. After very warm greetings between good friends, our humanoids made sure our energy supply tanks were full so that we could get an early start the next morning. We were secured to the nice soft grass on the ramp, and their tents were erected under our wings. By this time Tom had returned from his trip to Alabama and arrangements were made for everyone to depart within an hour to drive to Mom's in Preston for—you guessed it—a feast of fried quail, sweet potato pie, and lemonade. Mmmmm good!

Moontown and Beyond

The shadows were very long and several scattered rain showers had moved into the area by the time our three friends and their hosts returned from their scrumptious meal. Obviously, there would not be any sunset flights this evening nor did the conversation indicate a dawn patrol the next morning. Something about having "plenty of flying ahead of us" precluded these activities. By the time those pesky little showers had dissipated—and missed us completely—the stars were twinkling in the late evening sky and our humanoids were resting snugly in their tents. Sis and I once again basked in the stillness which we almost always find at night on Peterson Airport, situated among the peanut and wheat fields of West-central Georgia. It was extremely relaxing and conducive to drifting off into dreamland.

The sun was just beginning to push the night shadows further to the west when our humanoids started coming to life after a good sleep. As usual, the first one out of the sack was Lyle. A quick look around confirmed his thoughts about an early departure, so he proceeded to roust Leighton and Ray into action. If we were going to make Kentucky Lake, Kentucky, today, we needed to get things started. Before retiring, at the suggestion of Tom and Martine, it had been decided that we would fly to the Callaway Gardens airport, at Pine Mountain, Georgia, for breakfast. We could be in the air within the next half hour if everyone got in gear!

It did not matter that the tents were put away wet (dew from the night air) as they would be used tonight and would dry out then. Besides, only the flies were wet—the tents were dry. Each humanoid took a quick sponge bath in the Peterson's hangar and sure enough, within the allotted thirty minutes, they all seemed ready to depart. One thing remained and that was a weather check.

Locally, things had deteriorated slightly from the very good conditions when everyone got out of the sleeping bags. Still not anything to be concerned about, but it was not one of those see-forever mornings. Looking to the north indicated there could be a slight problem, but looking to the south and west indicated that maybe we should not tarry too long before our departure. The phone call to Flight Service ritual was initiated and things really fell apart in a hurry.

The news was not good. The radar was indicating that what we could not really see to the north was some pretty heavy rain and low clouds. What we could see to the south and west was a very large area of heavy rain with all sorts of low ceilings and visibility. Things were nice to the east and there was a pocket of very good conditions directly over the Plains-Americus area. From all indications, the really bad stuff to the south and west would be in our area within the next one-half hour and that stuff to the north would not clear enough for us to get through for at least one or two hours. Sorry about that gang, but you might as well stay put for a while until something moved on through.

This unappreciated information prompted the two of us to be retied to the ground and our slickers were reinstalled to keep our insides from getting wet. Yes, both Sis and I have a little water-leakage problem when we get rained on, so our humanoids always cover our cockpit areas when it appears we are going to get an unwanted shower. Sure enough, by the time these chores were attended to, it was very evident that the rains and fog were going to arrive shortly. By the time our humanoids had climbed into Tom and Martine's Explorer for their trip into town to get breakfast, we were being soaked by a continuous moderate rain.

A little over an hour had passed when through the rain and light fog we saw the Explorer returning to the parking lot. Each one of our friends uttered some uncomplimentary words about the weather and went into the office. A short time later, Tom joined them and we continued our wait as the rain seemed to come and go at random. Finally at about 10:00 A.M. our ropes were hurriedly untied, our rain gear was removed, and our engines were started. Locally, the weather had improved to good, and from the conversation we were hearing, things would be really good if we could just move another forty or fifty miles north. Tom reaffirmed that we were welcome to return if we could not get through and sent us on our way. He actually stood by to take our pictures as we made a low pass on our departure and once again pointed our spinners north.

Within a matter of minutes, we had once again encountered a little light rain and low clouds. However, flying just above this low scud, we could see the tops of the hills protruding through the thin veil ahead of us. The further north we proceeded, the larger the "holes" became and, sure enough, by the time we were forty miles north of Plains, the low stuff was gone and there was a scattered-to-broken layer a couple thousand feet above. Hey, we were almost back into Cub flying weather again!

Right on flight plan, at sixty minutes and sixty miles out, Calloway Gardens passed under our wings. There was no need to stop now as everyone had already had breakfast. Fifteen minutes later found us putting our fat little donuts on the beautiful grass alongside runway 21 at La Grange, Georgia. Within minutes we were serviced and ready to blast off again. We really needed to keep moving as we were about two hours behind time and Kentucky Dam was a long way away.

The distance to Gadsden, our next destination, was approximately ninety miles. We had picked up a nice tailwind and expected to be able to make the trip in about one hour and twenty minutes. No doubt Sis would be making at least three of her nice big 360 turns on this one. She was getting pretty good at making those things really work out, and I know she enjoyed doing it. It really did keep us together in the air. Once again, we were traveling over an area that we had already explored when the Cub Six-Pack visited Gadsden about five years earlier on our first annual spring trip. However, on that particular adventure, we came up the Coosa River from the south.

A new FBO had been added to the Gadsden Airport since our last visit. The airport now has two operations and, this being Sunday, we were not sure which one we should visit. As we taxied to the ramp area, this problem was quickly solved for us. We Cubs have never been turned away, but, on occasion, we have felt that we were just being tolerated because our service requirements were so small compared to the average transit member of our family. However, we knew that we were welcome at this stop because standing on the ramp at Fisher Aviation (the new FBO) was a young man, wearing a very large smile and waving to direct us to a parking spot.

Our personal needs were tended to quickly and our humanoids were invited into first class offices to check out the weather and tend to other flight planning duties. What a pleasure to be greeted and treated in such a manner in this day and age. It is not often found, especially when you are just a lowly Cub.

Fisher Aviation's new facility had a beautiful glass front that overlooks the ramp area. From where 726 and I were parked, we could watch the activities of our humanoids as they paid for our new supply of fuel and checked the weather on the large TV screen that we could also see. Much to our surprise, we could see some pretty heavy rain areas that had completely covered the route of flight we had just covered while inbound to Gadsden. Also, we could see the scattered rain showers to the north—the direction we needed to go. There was also a fairly solid area of moderate rain located thirty miles or so to the west of our track. If we were going to get any further along our way, we had best be going—now!

This next leg would be only about sixty miles long for two reasons. First, at the speed we were traveling, we needed to stop in about an hour and check another weather radar display to further our education on all of those thunder-bumpers that were starting to form. The second reason was because Lyle just wanted to stop at Moontown Airport a few miles east of Huntsville, Alabama. Many times in the past, he had flown over this pretty little grass field, but never took the time to pay it a personal visit. What better time to do it than right now when we two Cubs could enjoy the experience, too?

Thanks to a nice little breeze blowing on our aft extremities, we found ourselves turning final to Moontown's runway 27 in about fifty minutes. The wind was directly across it from the south, but that really presented no problem even though it was burbling over the high ridge just to the south of the field boundary. Seven-two-six landed first and by the time I had touched down a bit shorter than she, we both rolled up to the energy source island at almost the same time. We had observed a rather ugly dark cloud approaching from our left as we completed the last twenty miles of this leg. Also directly ahead of us was another rather unhappy accumulation of water vapor, dumping some rather impressive amounts of teardrops in our path. Once our mighty Continentals were silenced, we could hear the thunder rumbling in response to the flashes of light we had observed for the last few minutes. Obviously, it was time to become anchored to the ground again, with our rain capes securely tied to our cockpits.

Thanks to the efficient actions of the humanoid who operated the fuel distribution system at Moontown Aviation, our tanks were filled before we were secured in anticipation of the coming storm. Just as the first drops started to fall, Ray, Leighton, and Lyle rushed inside to once again check the weather radar pictures to determine how soon we could proceed further toward our goal for the day— Kentucky Dam State Park. Due to our late start, it was rapidly becoming a question if we would have enough daylight to make it all the way, considering the fact that neither Sis nor I had any navigation lights.

When put into motion, weather radar pictures covering the previous eight or ten hours are quite fascinating to observe. As our humanoids watched, they could see that as soon as that angry little thing that was dumping water on us now passed, we should have relatively good conditions further north. However, that big low pressure area that had been stalled directly over the area where we had been flying for the past two days was now starting to move. The only real problem was that the stupid thing was moving to the northwest instead of east/southeast as it should. Much to our chagrin, it appeared that all of the not-so-good stuff could be attacking us from the northeast in the not too distant future. The great people and laid-back atmosphere here at Moontown were fantastic, but we really needed to say good-bye as soon as possible.

It only lasted a few minutes, but we were extremely glad to have that little shower move away from us so that we could be on our way. (Time and daylight were really becoming a concern now as Kentucky Dam was indeed a long way away.) The wind was still blowing from the south as we raced down runway 27 for take-off. This condition created a little situation that was really not to our liking since we were operating at full gross weight. That south wind coming over the high ridge just to the south of the runway created some very serious descending air over the airport area. We had been able to climb about seventy-five to 100 feet after lift-off when that descending air caused our rate of climb to come to a complete stop. Seven-two-six was a little better off than I was as her weight was somewhat under maximum. This was not the most enjoyable place for us to be as those trees below us were actually quite close to our undercarriage. Even though we were quite low, our humanoids once again helped us move on out by making a gentle turn away from the ridge and we soon ran out of the descending air and were able to resume our normal climb rate.

After flying through a couple of rain showers shortly after take-off, the weather improved to really nice Cub weather. That's right, scattered puffy clouds in a nice blue sky with almost unlimited visibility. What a great way to travel. With the help of the wind on our tails, exactly one hour later we found ourselves parked next to the fuel pump on the ramp at Raider Aviation, located on Maury County Airport, at Mt. Pleasant, Tennessee. The only problem with this picture was the fact that the sun was much too low in the western sky for us to continue, so our humanoids called it quits for the day and started asking questions about erecting tents.

Bob Ballard, vice president of Raider Aviation, thought tents were a great idea; however, he suggested that we take a look at the weather radar before putting them up. He even suggested that some very severe weather was forecast to come through the area and he personally would feel more comfortable if Sis and I were inside one of his nice hangars where we would be safe. We like to think he did not care if our humanoids wanted to spend the night in the tents in the weather, but he sure wanted us to be in a nice hangar. Nice thinking, Bob.

Once our intrepid humanoids took a look at the long-range radar, and Bob informed them that he could arrange a crew rate for them at one of the motels, and he had a big Lincoln Town Car for them to use, they quickly decided to take him up on his offer. The tents still had to go to the motel because they needed to be unpacked and dried. Thus, in very quick order, 726 and I were tucked into a nice large hangar with several locals who made their home there and our three best friends were making all sorts of wisecracks about roughing it as they loaded the car for the trip to the motel.

Considering the forecast of very bad weather during the night, this really was the best way to end another day of great flying. Yes, we had been challenged by the weather on occasion, but that was part of the adventure on a trip such as this. True, we were short of our goal for the day by at least two or more hours of flying time, but what the heck, this is a fun trip and time means nothing at this point. We discovered all of these fine cousins of ours who were sharing their hangar with us for the night were very friendly. We all told each other a little bit about ourselves and our humanoids, but very soon the excitement of the day caught up with Sis and me and we both drifted off into slumberland while the others continued their friendly banter.

Moonshine in a Flask

It was quite difficult to make out much of what was going on in our dark hangar, but we could distinguish very faint lines of gray light filtering through the cracks between the big doors. Cousin Cessna 172 and young brother Cherokee Warrior, who were parked closer to those doors, were whispering to each other about the prospects of early morning departures. Neither seemed very optimistic about such things happening. After listening to their muffled voices for a few minutes, Sis and I informed them that we were awake and very much interested in what they could see on the outside.

The forecasted severe weather had not passed through during the night and now as the first indications of daylight were showing, Cousin 172 was able to peek through a crack and found the ceiling quite low and visibility less than a mile. Obviously things were not conducive for the early departure we had planned to make. Even Quicksilver, the little ultra-light parked in the back corner, was unhappy because he was all set to get a nice bath and go play this morning. It lowered our spirits even more, when we could hear an occasional patter of raindrops on the roof above us. Even worse than that was the occasional rumble, which always announced the presence of one of those mean ol' grumpy clouds somewhere in the vicinity. Obviously, we were going to have to wait until someone opened those doors before we could get a good look at the conditions outside.

We were to find out much later that while we waited, and waited, and waited, our humanoids had been taking care of other necessary chores. After checking the weather situation and finding that we could not go anywhere for a long while, they consumed a very long and leisurely breakfast. Things had not improved much by then, so they spent the next hour or so trying to find some place where they could do their laundry. It was Memorial Day and most every establishment in town was closed. Finally, they did find a laundromat, which was open, so they spent the next hour or so taking care of that little chore. It sure was a good thing that they did not have any horse blankets because huge signs in the establishment advised all DO NOT PUT HORSE BLANKETS INTO ANY OF THE MACHINES. Yes, no doubt their clothes did smell a little like horse blankets, but really, they weren't.

In late morning, the big doors were partly opened and lo and behold, there stood all three of our long-lost humanoids. Beyond them we could just barely make out the ridge about two miles south of the airport. Fact is, it appeared that the tops of the higher ridges were actually still in the clouds. And yes, there was still an occasional raindrop falling. However, there seemed to be a bit of optimism within the group as they proceeded to load all of their luggage and stuff into our eager frames before going back to the office. Maybe things were looking up and we would be going before too long. If that weren't the case, why did they load us as if we were going to depart?

Another hour passed when two strangers opened wide the doors. Little Quicksilver really snapped to attention because these two humanoids were his. Quickly they cleared a path which allowed them to move him up to the door. They did not take him outside. Instead, they stopped right at the front of the hangar where they started their labor of love, cleaning his little airframe as he had anticipated. From what we could see beyond this little group of close friends, we could tell that things were indeed improving in the weather department.

About 2:30 in the afternoon, our humanoids once again returned. This time, they retrieved their sectional charts. Before returning to the office, they stopped to chat with the Quicksilver group for a few minutes. By eavesdropping on that conversation, we soon learned that radar was indicating that in a couple more hours the atmosphere to the north, where we were headed, should be clearing rapidly and we should be on our way. Fact is, if we did not go then, there was a good chance we would not go at all because another very large mass of stinky stuff was moving in from the west. This mass would really block our movement north, so we *must* make our move during that short open window.

One more light rain shower moved through and we were pushed out of the hangar. Tom Caulk, president; Bob Ballard, vice president, and a couple of the great employees of Raider Aviation were on hand to help us get under way. They all had made us feel so welcome and at home here, we really had mixed emotions about leaving so late in the day. Maybe we should stay one more night. Nope—if we do that we might be stuck for a couple more days and we had much too far to go for something like that to happen.

It was exactly 4:30 P.M. when our little fat tires kissed the Mt. Pleasant, Tennessee, runway good-bye. It was indeed late in the day, but it did not get dark until after 9:00 in the evening at these more northern latitudes so Sis and I knew it would be quite late before we called it a day this evening. Our destination for today was Carmi, Illinois, approximately 190 miles to the north. Thank goodness for the continuing light tailwind. With it helping us along it should take a little less than three hours. Even with the two energy stops required, there should be enough daylight to do it. The excitement of today's race with the sun sure was making the adrenaline flow. *Hey, Sis, isn't this great fun to do once in a while?*

About twenty miles south of Waverly, Tennessee, our next stop, we didn't have a care in the world. Cub flying weather prevailed and the landscape was quite intoxicating. Life really was very good to us and we were looking forward to seeing a beautiful sunset as we approach Carmi in about two hours.

On the ramp at Humphreys County Airport in Waverly, we were again greeted by an eager young man who knew exactly what we meant when we told him we wanted a quick turn. (That's jet talk made by the big boys when they are in a hurry to get fuel and be on their way as quickly as possible. Man, we're really hot stuff.) While Leighton and Ray finished taking care of 726 and my needs, Lyle made a call to Kentucky Dam to make sure someone would be there who could fill our energy tanks when we arrived. Actually, it was already closing time for them, but the voice on the phone promised that he would come back after eating his supper just to make sure our needs were tended. Now that is *service*, especially for a couple of Cubs! I do not remember how long we were on the ground, but I do know that a quick turn was completed with haste and now we were once again in the air with our spinners pointed north.

It was just slightly more than seventy miles to Kentucky Dam from Waverly. We would be flying directly up Kentucky Lake so navigation would be a snap. Yep, this will be a leg to really sit back, relax, and enjoy the countryside as it slipped beneath our wings. Right? Wrong!

Within minutes after departure, it became evident that the large mass of weather we knew about was rapidly approaching from the west. Actually, Kentucky Dam was forecast to have severe thunderstorms, after we had flown further to the north. As we continued up the lake, visibility started to come down, finally stabilizing at about five miles. On occasion we could see the white hot flash of lightning off our left wings and this did not help us relax. Finally, the straw that almost broke the camel's back came when 726 discovered that a couple of boats on the lake were going faster than we were. Yes, we had finally lost that nice little tailwind that had been helping us for so long. The need for a very quick transit at our next stop was now becoming more and more apparent. We now had two things working against us—the incoming weather and sunset, which could almost catch us before Carmi with this reduced ground speed.

Entering the pattern at Kentucky Dam, we could see that this weather problem would be solved if we could get a few more miles to the north. As we rolled to a stop at the fuel pumps, our little Continentals became silent and both Leighton and Lyle literally jumped out to start pumping fuel into our tanks. Thunder was rumbling overhead and to the south from whence we had come.

The nice humanoid Lyle had talked with on the phone had lived up to his promise and he *was* there to help with our needs. He also confirmed that it did stay daylight until almost nine o'clock—on a clear day, but with this very heavy overcast, darkness would be coming earlier than that.

All right gang, take it easy now! Things are starting to build for some problems if we don't just slow down and think a little bit. Both 726 and I could detect a bit of get-there-itis starting to develop and it had to be stopped right now! Slow down, there is always tomorrow. As our bills were being paid, the airport attendant wanted to know if we were the two Cubs from Florida. (This little comment brought our humanoids back to reality—thank goodness.) "Yes, indeed, we are from Florida, why do you ask?" It seems that a few hours ago, someone had stopped in at the office and wanted to know if anyone had seen us because we were supposed to have spent the night here last night. We knew right away that it was our friend who lives in Union City, Tennessee. Our friend had said he might be here to see us even though we will be spending the night with him later in the trip. Sorry we missed him.

This little exchange slowed things down enough for our humanoids to start thinking clearly again, which made Sis and me feel much better about continuing our journey that evening. Thus, very shortly, our engines were propped back into life for our departure. Total time on the ground—less than twenty minutes. Not bad considering we had to get our humanoids under control again.

Turning north out of the pattern, 726 took the lead again, only this time she would be using her GPS for real. We really needed to stay on course on this leg. It was seventy-seven miles to Carmi and, without a tailwind, it was going to be a tight squeeze to make it, before we could not fly legally. Within minutes, Cub weather was once again the order of the day even though we did have a light headwind now. Hey, no problem. With this almost clear sky there would be plenty of daylight for our arrival. (We didn't know that, within minutes, all of this would change.)

Twenty-five miles out and approaching the Ohio River, we started encountering low clouds and fog. There was no way we can fly on top of this stuff—it was too thick. Within a very short time, the visibility had dropped to about three miles—in some places even less. Finally, we could see the river and Sis made a turn to the right to follow it for a short distance. By now, I was in the mood to make a beeline for Sturgis, Kentucky, and call it a day. I just hoped the visibility would stay good enough to find their airport as there were no more checkpoints after we left the river.

Sure enough, 726 had come to the same conclusion as I had about Sturgis and she turned directly toward the airport. Her wings never strayed from level as the GPS guided us to the runway. I was amazed at how that little hand-held box knew exactly where we were and where we needed to go. As we proceeded into the gloom, I watched the chart very closely to make sure there were no towers occupying airspace we wanted to use. I had estimated the time to reach the runway from the east river bank to be seven minutes. Sure enough, at five minutes, we could see the beacon and runway. Fantastic! Even ol' doubting Lyle commented, "That gadget is pretty nice," and just maybe he would have to change his mind about getting one—someday.

Our humanoids had been concentrating pretty hard for the past half-hour and this intensive concentration had completely blocked out any hint of the temperature change that had occurred outside our snug little cabins. When they opened the doors to disembark from our cradles of warmth, the very cold damp wind that was now blowing really made them take notice. Remember, these guys are all Florida boys and were dressed accordingly. Lyle always wears long pants so he was not as surprised as Ray and Leighton were because they were dressed in their normal short pants attire. For 726 and I, it was very humorous to watch all three of them dig for jackets! Since leaving Kentucky Dam, the ambient air temperature had dropped at least fifteen degrees and the chill factor from the fifteen- to twenty-knot wind on top of the moisture in the air made it feel really cold. Our first thought was *Do we really want to camp out in this kind of weather?*

Daylight was rapidly disappearing. The thick cloud layer and low visibility was not helping the situation very much either. We needed to get something done soon or we would be pitching tents in the dark! Even though the original program was to camp under our wings each night, the thought of spending the night outside in this cold, wet, and windy environment did not appeal to any of us—especially our humanoids. Obviously, there was no activity of any kind in or around our location, so maybe camping would be the only option available.

Sure enough the office was locked tight. No lights were on anywhere and even the phone book had been taken from the only public pay phone on the property. It looked to me like everything would have to wait until morning when things came to life again. Let's see now—over there was a nice big hangar with the door open. I know where Sis and I would be sleeping. Too bad about you guys!

While our humanoids were trying to figure out just what to do, a car drove into the parking lot. This vehicle carried the White Knight who would come to the rescue of all of us. His name was Mickey Buzzard, and his professed claim to fame here at Sturgis Airport was airport bum. He was just on his way to his all-night job at a local warehouse when he watched us come out of the murk and land. He knew there were not many Cubs in the local area, so he delayed reporting to work just to find out what was going on at his favorite hangout. We soon discovered that if indeed this nice humanoid was the airport bum, he sure had a lot of influence with the right people.

Very quickly, this giant of hospitality made the decision that Sis and I should be put in the hangar out of the weather for the night. We could be refueled in the morning. As we were being pushed inside and the big doors rolled shut, the plan for overnight arrangements for our personal humanoids unfolded in their conversation.

Mickey produced a key that opened the back door to the office and he invited our friends to bring their sleeping bags inside and spend the night on the floor or in the nice leather overstuffed lounges. He knew where the key to the airport courtesy car was located and he would wait while our humanoids put their stuff in the building and then he would lead them to the best restaurant in town where they could get something to eat. (No, he could not join them as he really did have to go to work.) And just to make all of this on the up and up, he would call Tom Hayden, the airport manager, to let him know he had two guests in one of his hangars and three more in the lobby of the airport office building who were also using the courtesy car. He knew that Tom was not at home, but a message on his answering machine would serve the purpose. Oh yes, there was one other thing our White Knight wanted us to do if we could, and that was to talk with—let's just call him Stormin' Norman for anonymity reasons—the local authority on fun things to do with an airplane. Mickey was certain that good ol' Stormin' Norman would be at the restaurant.

Both 726 and I were sound asleep and did not hear nor see the return of our humanoids from their night on the town at Sturgis, Kentucky. However next morning as we were being pushed to the fuel island, we learned the full story as these three nuts, as we call our friends, relived the events of the evening.

It seems that our beloved humanoids were completely accepted by the local patrons of the fine country restaurant to which Mickey had escorted them. As was predicted, Stormin' Norman did appear. Someone had informed him that there were three intrepid aviators, who were flying Piper Cubs out of Florida, eating a late supper at the restaurant. Since our three friends were the only strangers in the building—no doubt in the whole town—Stormin' Norman came directly to their booth, introduced himself, and sat down. Within a very few minutes, he had given them a thumbnail sketch of his aviation skills, among which was doing aerobatics at night in his Cherokee. He also invited them to take a little nip of corn squeezings (mountain dew) from the jug he had in the back of his truck. When that offer was politely refused, he moved to another booth where he joined some of his friends, promising to return to the airport with our three humanoids so they could see his airplane. Thus about midnight, our younger sister, an early model Cherokee, had been awakened from a sound sleep just to be shown to some strangers. I'm sure she was not impressed with the disturbance, but on the other hand I'm sure she liked it better than going out and doing aerobatics late at night. Yep, the jug was still in the back of the truck.

My Humanoid's Roots

Looking out the window, Sis and I could see that it was very difficult for dawn's early light to crack through that persistent low overcast. As the gray light became brighter, we estimated the ceiling to be somewhere around 800 to 1,000 feet; however, the visibility appeared to be at least seven to ten miles. As far as the two of us were concerned, it was at least flyable weather. We would just have to wait until our humanoids showed up to find out what would happen.

Finally at about 6:15 A.M., the big doors were rolled away and there stood our three beloved humanoids. They were all dressed somewhat differently than they had been the past few days. All were now wearing jackets and Lyle was still in long pants as always. Ray had also decided long pants were the dress of the day, but 726's humanoid, Leighton, insisted on continuing to wear short pants. He said something about it almost being the first of June and that meant it was summertime and short pants would be his uniform. Seven-two-six just shook her tail in disbelief as she knew her cabin heater would be of little value as the airflow in her cockpit was diverted by the bulky load she was carrying. I had to agree with her as that brisk northeast wind brought the chill factor well below the low fifties temperature reading on the thermometer. We both hoped Leighton knew what he was doing!

As we were being pushed to the gas pumps, we gathered additional pertinent information about what was in store for us that day. Thanks to another FBO who knew the wisdom of having the capabilities of live weather radar viewing, our partners in this adventure had been able to get a good view of what to expect in the way of weather as we continued our journey to Macomb, Illinois, our day's goal. It looked like once we moved another forty or fifty miles north, we would again be in good Cub flying conditions. Even though the weather systems appeared to be running in reverse, we always seemed to find a way to get ahead of them again. The wind was going to be quite strong from the east-northeast. This would not help us any as we proceeded to Mattoon, Illinois, but once we headed west from there, it would be a great help. The ceiling and visibility certainly were flyable, so it was time to fill our tanks with go-juice and get back into the air.

As advertised, Thomas E. Hayden, the Sturgis Airport manager, came into the office about 6:45 A.M. He was genuinely glad to see us and proceeded to make sure we were properly serviced. He also wanted to make sure our overnight stay had been all right and wondered if there was anything more he could do for us. We assured him everything was great and we really did appreciate his hospitality. Leighton and Lyle were just ready to prop our power plants back into life when our White Knight, Mickey Buzzard, came hurrying out to see us again. He, too, was concerned about our comfort during our visit so he stopped by as he was going home from work. This humanoid had been working all night long, but still felt he should check on us before he went home for some much-needed rest. Talk about hospitality—wow!

All friendly farewells completed and our lifeblood oil warmed to the operating range, we found ourselves charging down runway 04 into the teeth of a rather brisk and cold northeast wind. The air was dense enough that our props could get a good solid bite and our wings felt as if they could lift the earth. Neither Sis nor I had had such an invigorating takeoff in many years—we had almost forgotten how much a few degrees in temperature could affect our performance. This was fun.

A left turn put us on course for Olney, Illinois, and sure enough, just as predicted, within thirty-five miles the sky was clear, the visibility was unlimited, and the wind was quite strong from the northeast. Everything had settled down into another fun-filled journey and all we had to do now was rock along in this gentle turbulence until Olney-Noble Airport came into view.

As Lyle was making some minor adjustment to my trim tab, he made an observation to Ray about a very first for him. He said that this was the first time in our relationship that any of my parts had really felt cold to his touch. He wondered if this meant that I no longer loved him.

Hey, Lyle. This is me—881 talking! The reason I feel cold to your touch now is because this cold air we have been in for the past few hours has cold soaked me enough that it is natural for me to feel cold to your touch. You know that! Don't be silly—I'll always love you.

One hour and twenty-six minutes after departure, our little Continentals were silenced on the ramp at Olney. Since the distance traversed had been about eighty-five miles, we were pretty sure the wind at altitude (800 to 1,000 feet) had shifted more to the east. That was fine with us because it was not slowing us now and would be a big help later in the day. This leg had also given us a brief preview of events to come as our course took us over the intersection where the Wabash and Ohio rivers came together and we then followed the Wabash River for over thirty miles before it meandered east away from our track. Again, it was just one of those little fun things that we Cubs can do to add enjoyment to our life in the slow lane. We wouldn't have it any other way.

Our needs were taken care of quickly and within minutes we were ready for departure. Our humanoids spent more time gabbing with others than was necessary, but what the heck, we are all having fun. Most everyone at the field today, here at Olney, seems to be involved in working with the likes of us, so we were well understood by all. It really feels good to be with humanoids who do understand the simple joys of flight that only we Cubs and our cousins of the same era can produce.

Once again off and flying, the fifty-four mile dash to Coles County Memorial Airport, serving Mattoon/Charleston, Illinois, was easy. Actually, this particular stop was a little out of our way, but there was a good reason for making it. First of all, if the weather had not delayed us way down in Tennessee, and then again in Kentucky, we would have been here to spend the night last night, as had been planned prior to our departure from home. However, the real reason we were here was because this was where one of our cousins lives and he was going to go part way with us on this sojourn down the Mississippi River. He is an Aeronca Chief who was born in 1938, the same year as 726. We have never met him, but have been told he was really quite a nice gentleman. His humanoid was unable to make the trip, but "The Chief" has consented to allow Steve Clayberg to fly him along with us. Three of us for awhile. What fun.

Steve was a personal friend of our three humanoids and they had talked on the phone last night from Sturgis. It came as quite a surprise to all of us to find Steve not ready to go as our last conversation indicated The Chief could hardly wait for our arrival. We were all very disappointed when informed there had been a family emergency in Steve's clan and he would not be able to make the trip. Thus, we never had the chance to meet cousin Aeronca Chief because the wind was so strong he really did not want to come out and join us on the ramp. Actually, it was a good thing because when Sis and I were untied, the wind actually started to move us across the ramp. We had to be held in place while our humanoids boarded and held our brakes. Well, Chief, maybe next time.

It is almost lunchtime and since Ray is always hungry, our humanoids and Steve decide to have something to eat at the restaurant in the terminal building. We could watch them from our location on the ramp. Central Illinois is noted for the breaded pork tenderloin that is served in some of the eating establishments. This eatery was no exception. It had a sandwich known as an "elephant ear," which is a pork tenderloin pounded thin, causing the diameter of the serving to expand to at least twelve or fourteen inches. This was served on a little five-inch bun, which our humanoids chose to call "the handle." Steve suggested that they each should have one and he was sure no one could eat it all. For once, Ray got his food blister stuffed although he ate less than half of his elephant ear. Leighton finished his with a little effort. But Lyle, well, he literally devoured his sandwich and then grabbed the half that Ray could not eat. Steve could not believe what he was seeing.

It was a very sad departure without The Chief, but everyone understood that sometimes things just do not work out. After bidding good-bye, our quick turn to avoid the hospital for a downwind departure must have impressed anyone who was watching. With that rather strong wind blowing on our aft body member, we were really making good speed. The crisp layout of the fields and beautifully manicured homesites of the Amish community to the east of Decatur, Illinois, quickly slipped under our wings. A commuter airliner quietly passed overhead as we skirted the controlled airspace surrounding Decatur's airport. Logan County Airport at Lincoln, Illinois, would soon be our next pause that refreshes and here we would learn more about our trip.

Ever since our departure, four days ago, 726 and I had felt an air of urgency among our humanoids. You know, some underlying current that seemed to be pushing them onward as if there was a time limit controlling our movements. We could not understand this, as from the start, this journey was advertised as a fun trip with no schedule to be maintained. Up to this point, we had not felt that was the case and the weather delays had even made it more evident. Before departing Lincoln, the truth would surface.

With one of their charts in hand, Leighton, Ray, and Lyle stood in front of both Sis and me discussing this final segment of today's flying, which would take us to Macomb, Illinois. Much to our surprise, we heard names such as Havana, Vermont, and Industry. Don't tell us these clowns were thinking of going to the country of Cuba or the state of Vermont now. And this place called Industry—does that mean a lot of factories and their polluted air? We certainly hope not. No, none of the above. It turned out that Havana and Vermont were small towns en route to another small town, Industry, which was just eight miles south of our destination of Smith Field at Macomb. Further listening brought additional interesting information.

The farm where my humanoid, Lyle, was born and raised was about four miles northeast of the village of Industry. We were going to overfly this area before landing at Smith Field. How about that? I am taking my humanoid back to his roots just like he allowed me to return to my roots last year when we journeyed to Lock Haven. Also, it was mentioned that a reporter from the *Macomb Journal* would be on hand to record our arrival at 2:45 P.M. Yes, indeed, a time deadline had been driving us all along. Thank goodness there had been enough slack to take care of the delays we had encountered.

Leaving Lincoln, I would definitely be in the lead. Seven-two-six now had enough running time on her engine that she could easily reduce her cruise rpm to stay in position with me without having to make those delaying turns. Our course would not take us directly to Macomb, but instead we would head for the farm. Havana passed to our right and shortly Vermont passed directly below us. Then as if some powerful force grabbed me, my spinner was aimed directly toward one of the clusters of farm buildings about seven miles ahead of us. Without wavering, we both homed in on the location as if it were a magnetic force pulling us ever toward it. As we got closer, I could hear Lyle talking to Ray, describing how he had been born and raised in that particular farmhouse. How, as a young child, he had played in those fields, which he later would work to earn money to learn to fly. The many long hours spent working the fields within a two-mile square, and the money he earned (five dollars per day from sunup to sundown during the growing season) was all spent learning to fly. He told how he had used these very fields and roads to practice flight maneuvers during his training. Many of the fields had been actual landing sites when his instructor had given him a simulated forced landing. As we circled the area, I could sense the feeling in my stick that Lyle really wanted to land me on one of those fields of the home place, just like he had landed my cousins, Taylorcrafts, in years past when he was learning to fly. The urge to put my little round donuts on that hallowed earth below was almost overwhelming. However, we knew this could not be done because the recent heavy rain on newly worked fields makes for a very soft muddy surface. I certainly did not want mud all over me or worse yet, find myself stuck in the mud, or even much worse than that, find myself laying on my back. No, the pleasure of landing at the farm could not happen.

By the time I had made several sharp turns over the farmhouse, I had lost track of 726. She had noticed that I was completely ignoring her while engrossed with the landscape below, so she proceeded to make large sweeping orbits well away from my spontaneous wild gyrations. Once again having her in sight, she formed up with me and we proceeded four miles further west-southwest to visit the village of Industry.

The number of citizens in Industry was small enough that everyone knew everyone else by first name. Yes, even those who had moved away were still remembered when they returned. Thus, there was no doubt in Lyle's mind that our presence in the sky over the town would announce his arrival back in the area. That strong wind blowing from the east allowed us to park directly over town and enjoy the sights. Once again, Lyle was reliving his youth as he told Ray about attending high school, in a building that no longer exists, and the many other happenings, which fill to overflowing one small section of his memory bank. Our hovering flight lasted for about five minutes and then we headed for the velvety grass that was Smith Field, at Macomb.

Landing into the strong east wind on runway 09 allowed our rollout to take us directly to the ramp in front of the office and main hangar. The whole area was covered by the lush green grass carpet that was ever-present on this airport during the growing season. Standing alongside the runway was Richard Berg, one of the photographer/reporters in the employ of the *Macomb Journal*. He was recording our arrival on film. After about thirty minutes of interviewing and taking additional pictures, Richard felt he had enough information and departed. Our picture and story appeared on page two of the Thursday, May 29, 1997, edition. Now it was time to talk to the rest of the fine welcoming committee that had turned out to greet us.

Henry and Betty Smith, owners of this nice flying field, which is in fact their private home, welcomed us with open arms. Many years ago, when my humanoid, Lyle, was learning to fly from this very same airport, it was owned and operated by Harry Clugston. Harry taught Lyle to fly. As the line boy working for Harry, Lyle had fueled and cleaned the windshield on Henry Smith's airplane many times. When Harry decided to retire, Henry and Betty purchased the property and made it their home. By this time, the city of Macomb had established a new municipal airport. We were going to be honored guests in the home of a very nice hospitable couple who really liked old airplanes like us.

The last, but certainly not least, members of this fine group that had gathered to greet us were Bob and Donna Blansett, Lyle's wife's sister and her husband. Since there were no rental cars available, they graciously loaned their almost-new Ford van to our three humanoids during our stay. Later they would be having dinner with the Blansetts at the Red Ox, a very good local restaurant.

During the past couple of hours, the sky had become overcast by a rather low, dark, ominous-looking covering. The cool temperature seemed to have dropped even further, especially for Leighton who was still in short pants, and the wind was obviously stronger. Besides all of that, a few raindrops had fallen within recent minutes. Henry indicated that the humanoids could pitch their tents almost anywhere they wanted, but he felt Sis and I should be inside the hangar. Our spars quivered with joy when we heard him say, "Nice pretty little airplanes like you should not be outside in this kind of weather." *Thank you, Henry—we have only just met and already I know that you are a very nice gentleman!* Conditions being as they were, our humanoids gladly complied with Henry's suggestion of bedding us Cubs in the hangar and their "tents" would be a motel room in town. Let's face it, it was too cold for camping as far as these Florida boys were concerned.

So this was where my humanoid got started. This hangar in which 726 and I would be spending the next two nights was the very same structure in which he swept, cleaned, repaired, and moved other family members (Cubs, Taylorcrafts, Stinsons, etc.) in and out of in the days of his youth. That runway out there was the same one that he flew from as a passenger on his very first airplane ride at the age of seven years. It is also the one that launched him on his first flying lesson. That strip of grass also caught him as he returned to earth after his very first solo flight at the ripe old age of fifteen years. (Yes, that was an illegal act then as it is now.) This is the place where, as an eager young lad, he went to work mowing runways, washing airplanes, tending chickens, and the many other duties involved in the job description of line boy at a small Midwestern airport back in the late 1940s—who just wanted to be around airplanes. His work was indeed a labor of love because all of these activities were done after school classes were dismissed, when he was not needed on the farm, or when the fields were too wet to be worked. As Sis and I listened to the wind outside and the occasional pounding of rain on the roof over our heads, we could imagine my young humanoid engulfed in his work within these walls as he dreamed of the future.

Wednesday, May 28, 1997, the fifth day of our great adventure, turned out to be the most disappointing day of the trip as far as 726 and I were concerned. We knew that this day was going to be spent here in the area of the land where my humanoid had lived through his childhood and youth. We had anticipated spending a considerable amount of time flying around over this portion of the breadbasket of the world—exploring the sights and sounds of modern-day agriculture. However, this would not come to pass as the weather gods had other ideas.

About midmorning, after consuming a scrumptious country breakfast at the R.F.D. Restaurant in Industry (where they were greeted by many of Lyle's longtime friends), our humanoids appeared in the large doorway of our resting place. Apparently, they had been keeping track of our running time because they were armed with all the necessary items needed to change the lifeblood in our mighty Continentals. Yes, another twenty-five hours had been racked up in our log books. The atmospheric conditions we could see behind them certainly were not going to allow any extracurricular flight activity at this time. It was very gray, with low thick clouds and visibility about one mile, at the most. The wind was still blowing, and an occasional unhappy cloud would go past, crying the whole way, adding to the accumulation of water on the ground. Even the temperature was low enough to encourage use of extra clothes. Ol' holdout Leighton had finally decided it was time to put on long pants!

Henry had given our three friends permission to perform in his hangar the necessary tasks that would confirm 726 and my health to be in good condition. He understood how we really desired our own humanoids to perform these inspections rather than some stranger whom we really did not know. Everyone went to work. Henry pitched in to produced a couple of tools, which had been forgotten when we left home, and furnished the supply of new oil for our full transfusion. Within about an hour Sis and I had all of our vital parts cleaned and inspected and four quarts of new lifeblood installed in our life-support system. By this time, the weather had deteriorated even further and it was decided that our test run, to check for oil leaks, would be delayed until just before our departure the following morning.

As the final fingerprints and grease smudges were being cleaned from our faces, we learned from the banter between our humanoids that there would be no flying for us today. The weather

Preparing for an oil change at Macomb. From left, Ray Olcott, Henry Smith, Lyle Wheeler and 881. Credit, Leighton Hunter.

was just too unpredictable. It was actually more like early fall weather in this part of the country rather than spring as it should have been. Nuts! Our three friends decided to use that nice Ford van and spend the rest of the day touring the countryside, as Lyle put it, "turning over some old stones to find out what is under them." Sis and I would have to spend our time lounging here in this nice cozy old hangar. And from the sounds of the wind and rain outside, I was sure we will be glad we were staying on the ground. Later we would learn that after finding a coin laundry where they generated clean clothes again, Lyle did spend the rest of the day showing Leighton and Ray around all over this farming area where his roots went very deep. As the day ended, Elaine and Herb Bozard, and Georgia and Maurice Litchfield, four very dear friends from Lyle's Industry High School days, joined our three intrepid birdmen for an enjoyable evening of dining, again at the Red Ox. All I can say is that must be one mighty fine restaurant.

Beware, Cowbirds!

It was well past eight o'clock on the morning of Thursday, May 29, 1997, before the big hangar doors were pushed open exposing those of us within to another morning of a gray gloomy sky. At least it was not raining and the ceiling appeared to be somewhere between 800 and 1,000 feet. Thanks to the very brisk wind from the west, the visibility was at least seven to ten miles. Not exactly the most desirable Cub weather, but still very flyable. It was pretty obvious to Sis and me that the temperature was not exactly spring-like and apparently Leighton had finally admitted defeat as far as short pants were concerned because when he came into view, we noticed he was not only wearing his long pants, he also had on his long johns, which in reality was a pair of warm-up pants, *under* his regular clothes. Let's face it, the calendar may say it is almost summer, but the outside air temperature was really telling it like it was! Sis admitted her cabin heater was not working exactly as desired, especially with the load she was hauling in her front seat area.

The Blansetts—Bob and Donna—had brought our humanoids out to the airport this morning so that they could retrieve their van. I know they were very happy and amazed to get it back all in one piece—not even a scratch. The temperature being cool as it was, they elected to return to their home rather than wait around for our departure. However, we would give them a final farewell salute as we passed over their house on our departure. Seven-two-six and I were quickly rolled out onto the lush green grass of the ramp where we were given a quick run to check for any leaks that might have developed during the oil change. Of course we were both completely void of such imperfections, which led to having our energy source reservoirs quickly filled and we were now ready to head further north. Betty insisted on taking portraits of us with Henry and our "clowns" before saying good-bye. Within minutes, our Continentals had been warmed to the proper temperature, and our spinners pointed down runway 27. We extended a final wave to Henry and Betty as they watched our charge down the grass strip giving our wings life as they lifted us back into the air.

A pass over our friends still watching from the ramp with a quick turn to the southwest put us directly over the Blansett's rooftop for a farewell wingwag and then it was a sharp turn to a heading of about 330 degrees. Lake Itasca, here we come! It might take a couple of days for us to get there, but we'll be there.

We had not been on our heading for more than six or seven minutes when I could tell that I was slowly descending. I was in the lead and Sis was dutifully following that lead and descending right along with me. Why this was happening was a complete mystery to us. Neither she nor I knew anything about the area we

Departure time at Macomb. From left, Henry Smith, Lyle Wheeler, Ray Olcott and 881. Credit, Leighton Hunter.

were flying over other than the fact it was all good farmland and any of the fields would make a nice landing area. My throttle remained at cruise setting and this slow descent was causing my speed to increase as we progressed. We were now much lower than we had ever before flown over strange surfaces. What was going on? Suddenly I realized that we were headed directly toward a farm home and would be passing over it at a very low altitude at a much increased speed than is normal for us. Sure enough, as we passed over the top of the buildings, the throttle came full forward and I started a nice slow and gentle climb back to altitude. Our heading did not change one degree. Sis and I had just completed a real no-no. We had buzzed the home of Delwyn and Barbara Combs, some more friends of my humanoid. I hope the FAA didn't see us do that because if they did—we would be in deep you-know-what! *Come on, Sis, let's get these nuts away from here before they get us all into a heap of trouble.*

Even though the ceiling was a bit low, the visibility was very good. We settled down at an altitude of about 600 feet and prepared ourselves for a very enjoyable day of touring the heartland of the United States. The wind was neither helping or hindering our progress over the land and there was very little if any turbulence. The only thing that really concerned us was the forecast of occasional rain and fog, which could reduce the visibility to "marginal and below VFR" at times. Presently nothing like that was in sight.

From this point forward, for the remainder of the trip, there would be no "destination for the day." The only goal we now had is to be back in Venice by June 8th—if possible. Each day will be a new adventure—we will go as far as we feel like going and then stop. The only way to fly—in Cubs.

About five miles southeast of Oquawka, Illinois, (Don't you just love those Indian names?) we start to see the Mississippi River. The next thirty miles would offer a good preview of the big coming attraction as we follow the river to our next port of call, Muscatine, Iowa.

The low temperature (as far as we Florida Cubs were concerned), coupled with the brisk breeze that was blowing, made for a rather hurried refreshment stop at Muscatine. We must admit, our snug comfy cockpits were much more desirable than standing around on the ground in these "fall-like, spring elements" and this prompted our humanoids to be extremely eager to be on our way again. Within minutes, we were once again airborne with our trusty little Continentals pulling us ever northward.

Less than an hour later, after a very enjoyable interlude over the fertile farmland of east-central Iowa, we found ourselves entering the pattern at Monticello, Iowa. True, we had encountered a few minor rain showers with slightly reduced visibility, but it had been another sixty-five plus miles of pure enjoyment. As we lined up for that beautiful grass strip that is runway 23, we observed some rather ominous-looking weather phenomenon to the north— the direction in which we wanted to fly. Even though our weather experience for the morning had been very good despite the low ceiling, Sis and I agreed that maybe some checks should be made before proceeding further.

As we rolled to a stop beside the go-juice dispensing pump, a young woman was observed standing at the pedestrian gateway to the ramp. Upon seeing the white cane, Sis and I realized that this lady could not see us, but she certainly knew we were there and exactly where we were parked. Much to our surprise, my humanoid jumped out and rushed over to give this newcomer a big hug. Hmmm—very strange actions. (I wonder if his wife, Pat, knew about this meeting? We are a long way from home, you know.)

Very shortly, the secret of the mystery lady would be solved as Lyle gleefully brought his niece, Mary Keener, through the gate out onto the ramp to meet us. It develops that Mary resides here in the city of Monticello and she came to greet us as we passed through town. Mary has been totally blind since birth and as far as she was concerned, she did not consider herself sight-impaired—she had come to the airport to see her uncle's pretty little Cub. Hey—that's me!

My introduction to Mary occurred when she very gently placed her hands on the leading edge of my left wing tip. From there, she moved clockwise around my extremities, all the time with her hands gently touching me. When she felt the very slight ridge where my bold lightning bolt zigzag is affixed to my side, she commented, "That must be a lightning bolt—what color is it?" At that point my beautiful plumage was described in detail—even the registration numbers on my tail feathers. When her gentle hands found the

Continental molded into my rocker box covers, she started confirming facts she had read about that mighty power plant. Entering my cockpit, she discovered each and every control, including the gauges in my instrument panel. As her fingers traced each glass, Lyle would explain what the different units displayed. The compass required no explanation as she already knew more about that instrument than my humanoid. As she traced the trailing edges of my wings, she joked about how long my ailerons were and the lack of flaps. She also accused me of having my tail tied on with bailing wire when she saw the flying wires. By now I had really warmed up to this lady and we could now playfully joke with each other. This young woman had spent many hours studying aircraft, among other things, and knew much more about my anatomy and operation than most fully sighted humanoids. What a pleasure to make her acquaintance.

Much too soon, Mary's transportation returned to take her back to town, so we said good-bye and she was gone. The next thing Sis and I knew, we were being pushed across the ramp where we were securely tied to the ground and our three humanoids were departing in an ex-police car—now courtesy car—to obtain lunch down the road someplace. We would learn that the weather to the north was indeed bad—as we thought—and this was nothing more than a delaying tactic waiting for an improvement. Within an hour or so, our well-fed friends would return and confirm a break in the weather to the north had occurred. Our departure was imminent and we were ready.

Seven-two-six would take the lead after we lifted off of Monticello's beautiful grass runway. It was obvious that we had finally found that marginal weather, which had been forecast earlier, and since her new GPS had proven very helpful way back in Kentucky, she would gladly lead the way on this leg with its few checkpoints and likely reduced visibility. Sure enough, the next eighty miles would produce quite a variable mixture of weather from very good, with the sun shining, to very marginal, with rain and fog. One hour and ten minutes after lift-off, 726's GPS delivered us to the Decorah, Iowa, airport. Looking to the north brought some pretty big doubts about going any further today. *Hey, you guys—check the weather real good before deciding if we will fly again today. Remember, we don't have any schedule to keep!*

As soon as our needs were tended, our three humanoids disappeared into the office building. Seven-two-six and I could see the wall of rain and fog rapidly moving toward the airport from the north and, from all indicators, there was little doubt in our minds that this nice landing site here at Decorah was going to be the end of our flying fun for today. Much to our surprise, within minutes after entering the office, our three very best friends came rushing toward us, and we were quickly airborne just as the departure end of runway 29 became engulfed by that wall of inclement weather. Without hesitation 726 moved to the front and we soon found ourselves pointed toward the southwest, ninety degrees west of the direction we needed to be going. *Hey, gang, what's going on here?*

Listening to the conversation between Ray and Lyle, I soon discovered what was taking place. It seemed that once the radar images, weather maps, and weather forecasts had been reviewed, our humanoids decided the best place for us to be was as far west as we could get, as quickly as possible. If this move was not made, there was a very good chance we would be stuck on the ground for at least one day and maybe two. *(Hey—we came on this trip to fly, not sit around on the ground, so we are all for anything that will help alleviate the problem.)* The plan of our attack was to move far enough west so that most of this lousy weather would be to our east as we proceeded further northwest tomorrow. Thus, we were now headed for Charles City, Iowa, about fifty miles southwest.

Once again, Lyle had to admit 726's GPS was worth its weight in gold. The weather report from Charles City was very good. However, there were places along the route to that fair city where the weather was extremely marginal and absolutely no recognizable checkpoints were visible. Along with trying to navigate by dead reckoning, all three pairs of eyes were watching very intently for any uncharted towers or power lines. That GPS had only one duty—knowing where we were—and it did the job very well. By the time we were about fifteen miles from Charles City Airport, conditions improved very rapidly and sure enough, the decent weather they were reporting materialized. Fact is, it was tempting to continue further, but common sense dictated we should stay there for the night.

William R. Kyle and his son, who operate Charles City Aeronautics, Inc., were genuinely glad to see us at their facility. Although it was well past their normal closing time, they really made us feel welcome. The wet atmosphere and continuing cold temperature was really putting a damper on our humanoids' desire to sleep in their tents and Sis and I weren't very excited about spending the night outside with the threat of cold rain falling on us either. I am sure William detected this bit of reluctance on our part, so he volunteered the use of his family van to our humanoids, called the motel for special rate reservations, and even gave them detailed instructions on how to get to some of the best eating establishments in town. His son also mentioned there was room in one of the hangars where Sis and I could spend the night.

With such friendly hospitality coupled with quick service and arrangements, how could such an offer be refused? We were set for the night. However, just before they drove away, our humanoids were shown the wash rack with buckets, brushes, and hoses that were used to clean airplanes. This act was rather unusual, and even more puzzling when they were told we would be needing these items before departing the next morning because of the cowbirds—whatever that might be.

There was still at least an hour of daylight remaining by the time all the humanoids at the airport, including our own three, had left the premises for the evening. This gave 726 and me an opportunity to take stock of who was sharing our quarters with us before it was too dark to introduce ourselves properly. First of all, we were a little concerned about some very messy areas on the hangar floor. From the odor and the consistency of the substance, Sis and I were pretty sure we knew what it was, but did not wish to say anything because after all, we were guests, just spending the night.

As we looked around, we discovered some rather interesting relatives nestled under this roof along with us. Way over there in one of the back corners was cousin Cessna 182. He happened to be one of the first models of his "hatchlings" from way back in 1957. He was all original and looked very handsome. Over in the other back corner was another cousin, little Miss BC-12D Taylorcraft—born in 1946, the same year as me. There was also an assortment of modern-day relatives—you know the ones with the training wheel on the front—resting quietly, watching what was going on. We noted that all of the occupants were keeping an eye on the exposed rafters above us. We would eventually learn why, and the reason would prevent us from getting a relaxing night of rest.

As Sis and I continued in our efforts to get to know our hangar mates, our eyes fell upon a very unusual younger brother of ours resting less than ten feet from Sis's right wing tip. We never did learn what year he was born, but the very unusual suit of clothes he wore was quite faded and worn from many years of use. His basic suit was the normal Comanche attire for his era, but imposed over the top were the names of many cities from around the world. Also emblazed along his side and still very visible was "Around the World 1984," This gentleman's name is N-8998P, a Piper 260 Comanche and he had indeed flown around the world in 1984.

We soon learned that 98P had arrived from Lake City, Colorado, where he resides, just a short time prior to our arrival here at Charles City. He had brought his humanoid, who is a very close friend of the Kyle family, to this location to help one of William Kyle's daughters celebrate her graduation from high school the next day. We would also learn that particular humanoid is Donald L. Rodewald, secretary/director of the Flying Tigers Association, American Volunteer Group—Chinese Air Force. That's right—one of the *real* Flying Tigers. Eight-eight-Papa did not consider himself a celebrity even though he had been flown around the world and was still owned and flown by that same humanoid, who just happened to be one of the few pilots who flew Curtis P-40's in General C. L. Chennault's AVG (First American Volunteer Group in Burma). Well, brother dear, both 726 and I feel you are one of a kind and our hats are off to you. It is an honor to spend the night with you at this quiet little airport here in north-central Iowa. Neither of us ever dreamed of this pleasure.

We would learn the following day that Leighton, Ray, and Lyle did have the privilege of meeting Donald Rodewald in the FBO's (William Kyle's) office and then again at the restaurant where they had dined in town this past evening.

As the evening turned into night, we learned why all of our hangar mates were constantly watching the ceiling above us. The big doors to our room did not close and we were soon to be invaded by many and various species of B-1RDs. (That is *birds* for those folks who do not understand the jargon.) How such small feathered creatures who share their sky with us can make so much noise is beyond us. My they are loud and have no concern about what is below them as they come inside to roost. There really was not anything we could do about the situation—except watch and hope for the best each time one of those very rude creatures decided to take up a roosting position. Yes, Sis and I were exactly right when we thought we knew what all of the mess on the hangar floor might be—it was bird droppings and now that yucky stuff was being deposited upon our upper extremities. How awful—to think we were going to be exposed to this problem *all night long.* Oh my. Yuk. Yuk. Yuk! We are not for sale. Why must they keep putting "deposits" on us. This was terrible!

By the time our humanoids made a showing the next morning, the birds had departed, but their "handy work" was very visible. Some of us fared better than others—depending where we were parked below the open rafters in the ceiling. Sis didn't look too bad, but I had a very prominent area about ten inches wide that stretched diagonally from the trailing edge of my right wing tip to the leading edge of my left wing tip, across the top of my whole wingspan. From the size of some of those deposits, we all knew, in no uncertain terms, what everyone was talking about when they warned us about the cowbirds.

Leighton was able to clean 726 by using a bucket of water and a soft brush. Thank goodness Lyle had been educated about the wash rack and supplies last evening because I really needed it now. As he scrubbed and cleaned I could tell he was not really happy about what had happened to me, but he certainly was not as unhappy as I was, and if I could make him understand what I would do to him if he ever, ever, subjected me to such a thing as this again—well, I'd just—I'd—man 'o man, I hate this stuff. Cowbirds. Yuk!

Lake Itasca—Where the Big River Starts

Not much conversation took place while 726 and I were being cleaned, so we did not glean much information about the day's activities. We did sense that once this job was finished we would be on our way even though the ceiling was not very high, because of an occasional comment about the improved visibility making navigation much easier today. Sure enough, about 9:15 A.M. we found ourselves blasting off from runway 30, bidding good-bye to our newfound friends at Charles City. Just before propping our mighty Continentals into life, we were finally clued in when Leighton, Ray, and Lyle started discussing the observations they had seen on the television weather channel prior to leaving the motel.

Apparently our move to the west last evening was a very smart thing to do. There was a significant amount of unflyable weather that would have kept us on the ground if we had stayed in Decorah. Now, if what the TV was telling them was correct, we should be in nice weather within thirty or forty miles along our track from Charles City. Not only that, it looked like we were in for two or three days of very good Cub flying weather. It was about time.

No matter what the problems or concerns might have been while on the ground, they were quickly vanquished once we got a little air beneath our wings. This was the exact case this morning. Once Sis and I were winging our way northwest over the beautiful farmland, the trials and tribulations of the past night were soon forgotten. The farther we flew, the better the weather and by the time we crossed the Minnesota-Iowa state line, it was absolutely fantastic Cub weather. It was clear and we could see forever. Even the temperature was starting to warm a little—thanks to the bright sun shining on us again.

At our desirable Cub altitude—500 to 1,000 feet—we had a perfect panoramic view of the world. As far as we were concerned, this was the only way to fly and we felt sorry for our relatives who constantly think they need to go high and go fast to enjoy flight. Poor things, they do not know what they are missing! It seemed that all too soon Mankato, Minnesota, Municipal Airport would find us patiently waiting for more go-juice so that we could continue our leisurely journey to the north.

A nice thing about all of these pause-that-refreshes stops we had to make was the fact that we will soon be back in the air again. This last pause was no different—we had met some additional very nice humanoids who had tended to our needs and now we were once again in the air with our spinners pointed almost directly north. Earlier in our last leg, prior to crossing the Minnesota-Iowa border, I heard Ray and Lyle discussing the fact that there did not seem to be any red barns around the countryside as there had been years ago. No, they are now apparently all painted white. However, as we traversed above the southern Minnesota landscape, where large dairy farms seem to proliferate, we note that red barns were once again in vogue. We all agree that red is the more desirable color for barns. Yes, I know this has nothing to do with our trip, but it is just one of the many little details that Sis and I can observe in our low and slow mode of travel.

Eighty miles and one hour fifteen minutes after departing our last fuel stop, we were entering the pattern for landing on runway 31 at St. Cloud Regional Airport, St. Cloud, Minnesota. We were beginning to see and sense the reason Minnesota was referred to as the "Land of 10,000 Lakes." Our first clue came as, in addition to once again crossing over the Mississippi River, numerous lakes had passed beneath our wings. To even further enhance the fact, we now found ourselves sharing the traffic pattern with a couple of cousins (Miss Cessna 180 and Mr. DeHavilland Beaver—both on amphibious floats) practicing their land landings. Seven-two-six was quite taken by "the Beaver" and I think she would have gladly followed him into the wilderness—forgetting that she was on wheels. I, too, must admit to being somewhat excited by the fact that we really were rapidly approaching a more sparsely in-habited part of our great country.

Even though there were absolutely no pressures to continue as quickly as possible, our stay at St. Cloud was very short. The pleas-ant efficiency with which our needs were attended by St. Cloud Aviation personnel was to be commended. They were geared to the big boys operation, but we "lowly Cubs" felt we were wel-come, too. Once again refreshed, the beautiful weather and the siren call of adventure further north prompted us to be back in the air, where we belonged, in less than thirty minutes.

Our track of 332 degrees soon put us in the vicinity of our future guiding line, the Mississippi River, which we continued to follow to the vicinity of Little Falls, Minnesota. At that point, the river meandered in more of a northerly direction while we contin-ued on a beeline for Park Rapids, Minnesota, our next intended port of call. As we continued, skirting just to the west of restricted area R-4301, the populace below our wings became sparse. Within a few miles, the landscape started to resemble part of central Alaska, which my humanoid had spent many hours flying over as a bush pilot years ago. Even though Sis and I were equipped with fat little donut tires and the terrain over which we now traveled was certainly not suited for that type of landing gear, we knew our humanoids trusted us completely. They were totally engrossed in the beauty of this expanse of solitude void of visible civilization. Lyle was actually starting to daydream about flights of the past over the wilderness that we call Alaska. It is flights of this nature that bring the likes of us Cubs into a very close bond with our humanoids. We know they will take care of us and we in turn will take care of them.

The old saying goes "time flies when you are having fun." This flight into solitude was all too quickly interrupted as we found ourselves coasting to a landing on the turf runway 36 at Park Rapids, Minnesota. This would be our last stop before reaching the first goal of this journey—Lake Itasca.

Before continuing, I would like to make a few comments about a very nice feature found at many airports here in Minnesota. Being Piper Cubs, we are always looking for grass runways and airports on which to place our fat little sneakers. Well, the airport gurus of this great state have taken it upon themselves to establish at least one very nice turf runway at a very high percentage of all of their landing facilities where the primary landing runway was an all-weather surface. Not only were these grass runways well maintained, they were extremely well marked. The edges and even the taxiways to these lush green strips of terra firma were plainly marked with reflective markers that make them look like they are outlined by bright lights, even in high noon sun. I do not know how they do it, but their efforts sure make the likes of Sis and me very happy to visit their facilities. I do wish other landing site operators would come to Minnesota and take a look at what can and should be done to further grassroots (no pun intended) aviation. Yes, I knew, we were now flying in a part of the country where the likes of us were quite normal and aviators were not afraid to land on the grass. Anyway, on behalf of 726 and myself, I want to say thank you to those responsible for these great landing areas on your airports. They were fantastic.

Lake Itasca is twenty-five or thirty miles north of Park Rapids and we knew the terrain over which we would be flying was heavily wooded and dotted by innumerable lakes of various sizes. In the interest of safety and efficiency, our humanoids asked some of the locals about getting to this very important landmark. Without exception all indicated that Lake Itasca was indeed hard to find—especially for strangers from as far away as Florida. I personally found these comments very challenging and was eager to prove them wrong—I could find it. However, not to be judged as completely stupid, it was decided that Sis would program the position of the lake into her GPS and I would lead. In the event I got lost, she could take us directly to the lake. In my own mind I knew I had better find that lake as she would never allow me to live down the fact that I had gotten lost. Thus with a full supply of go-juice in our tanks, we once again blasted off and turned north.

Visibility was so good that if we had known exactly where to look, there was really no reason we could not have seen Lake Itasca when leaving the pattern. True, there are many, many bodies of water to choose from, but if the sectional was studied in detail, you could not miss. It was really a "piece of cake" because all that was required was to keep U.S. Highway 71 under my left wing until the proper shaped body of water came into view. Thank you anyway, Sis, but we will not be needing your fancy GPS on this leg after all!

The sectional displayed a very accurate outline of Lake Itasca and at exactly 4:43 P.M. on Friday, May 30, 1997, NC-22726, my sister, and I, NC-87881, found ourselves circling the northwest shore of Lake Itasca, where a very small stream (the Mississippi River) starts its long journey to the Gulf of Mexico. We both felt waves of excitement, joy, and pride surging through our longerons as we realized we had just reached our first goal of this journey.

After several orbits for the purpose of taking pictures, we once again turned toward the northwest keeping that small stream below, the Mississippi River, in sight at all times. After meandering toward the northwest, then north, then northeast, and finally east, for thirty miles or so we found ourselves approaching Bemidji, Minnesota. Along the way we had overflown a variety of lakes, streams, wilderness areas, and at least one log cabin. That tiny structure was in much need of repair and there was no way of knowing how long it had been there—if only it could talk. Could it have been an early pioneer's homestead or was it a trappers' outpost? From where it was situated I am sure no one had visited it for, possibly, many years. If Sis and I had not been exploring the river, I am sure we would never have seen it. This was turning into one grand trip.

Continuing our tracing of this small stream below us, we soon found ourselves passing over the southern extremities of the city of Bemidji and then out over Lake Bemidji to where the river once again departed the lake on the eastern shoreline. After a few more miles of tracking to another unnamed lake, we broke off our path and went directly to Nary National Shefland Airport where we would once again spend the night our favorite way—tied down, with tents under our wings, and our humanoids in those tents.

As our trusty little Continentals were silenced next to the fuel pump, we were greeted by the smiling face of Eric Walter, one of the caretakers of this fine privately owned facility. Once informed of our needs, he quickly gave us approval to establish our campsite on a beautiful knoll overlooking the approach end of runway 35. Leighton made a beeline to the phone to advise the folks at Enterprise Car Rental over at Bemidji Airport that we had arrived and requested that they deliver the four-wheeled conveyance that had been reserved for our humanoids. They were very happy to oblige as the person who delivered it also lived in the close vicinity of our campsite and he would take it back to Bemidji tomorrow morning after our humanoids were finished with it.

The time was rapidly approaching 7:00 P.M., but at these higher latitudes, on a nice clear evening as this was, darkness would not descend upon us until at least 9:30 or later. This being the case, Sis and I were quickly secured to the nice grass overlooking the runway and within minutes the sleeping quarters of our beloved humanoids were erected beneath our wings. The plan was to get our cozy little camp established now because it would be dark when our humanoids returned.

Returned? What are you talking about? Wasn't the program to camp together? What gives?

Unknown to 726 and me, since there was no place closer to Lake Itasca for us to plant our little fat tires, the plan from the beginning had always been that our humanoids would rent a car and drive back to the headwaters, for the express purpose of walking across the Mississippi River. Out of necessity, Sis and I would be excluded from this part of our adventure. It was very disappointing, but we understand and would have to be content with having flown over the site earlier in the afternoon.[4]

It was well after dark by the time our humanoids had refilled their food blisters at a roadhouse, and returned to the trusty steeds guarding our campsite. Needless to say, we were very happy that they did not have to erect tents in the dark, and within minutes, they were all nestled into their sleeping bags, basking in the joy of having completed this major milestone in our adventure.

Our campsite at Nary National Shefland Airport.

I really wished we could go flying again—right then—because it looked as though we could actually touch the stars if we were in the air. *Good night—see you clowns at first light in the morning. We would never tell you guys this, but Sis and I think you are the best humanoids in the whole wide world—especially when we find ourselves in this spot; one of the best campsites we have ever established.* The stillness, beauty, and tranquillity is absolutely breathtaking. Within a matter of minutes, the intoxication of the beauty of our surroundings has lulled all of us off into slumberland. Another great day of flying has just been completed.

Minneapolis Class B Airspace

Hey, Sis, listen. What's that sound? The first dim fingers of dawn were just starting to appear on the northeastern horizon when something other than the sounds of the tranquil night drifted over our serene campsite. The harsh cackle was not exactly soothing, and after hearing it a few times, we knew that it had to be the call of a lone turkey located off in the distance. We were fully convinced that it was indeed a bird in the wild, but, to our disappointment, would eventually learn it belonged to a domestic flock located about one-half mile away. Anyway, this unexpected alarm clock had us wideawake, anticipating the continuing adventure that lay ahead of us. From our vantage point, the weather appeared to be excellent—clear sky, unlimited visibility, calm wind, and a very

Lyle Wheeler standing on the rocks marking the beginning of the Mississippi River. Credit, Leighton Hunter.

pleasant nice cool temperature. My, how we wished our human-oids would come alive so that we could get an early start.

I guess they heard the call of the turkey, too, because, within a few minutes, Lyle crawled out of his tent and departed on his morning exercise of walking four miles. By the time he returned, both Leighton and Ray were out and about. Obviously, all of us were rather eager to be in the air because after a quick breakfast of eat-what-you-brought, the campsite equipment was quickly dismantled and stowed aboard 726. Within minutes, there would be nothing left at the site except our tracks. Just as we were being positioned for engine start, Eric, the friendly welcomer of last evening drove up to make sure we did not need anything. Last minute good-byes were said and quickly we climbed out above the trees as the sun once again continued its climb above the horizon.

Our north-northeast track would have to be held for at least seven or eight miles in order to put us back over the river where we had departed it last evening. As we continued our climb in that direction to our favorite altitude of 800 feet, it was quite apparent to us that the day was indeed going to be fantastic. Not a cloud in the sky, nor a ripple in the air, and we could see forever—Cub weather!

Once again picking up the nice little picturesque stream, which would be our guide for the next 2,000 miles, we turned east. Crossing Cass Lake, we soon found ourselves approaching Winnibigoshish Lake. This is quite a large body of water, so Sis and I decided to stay rather close to the shore as we navigated around to where the river once again exited the lake on the north-east shore. (No, neither of us can walk on water!)

What a beautiful sight to behold as the early morning rays from the sun awakened the world below us. Casting long shadows on the water, it was interesting to watch the many sportfishing boats make their way across the placid water to their favorite fishing holes. The bow wave from each of these small boats moved slowly across the surface making a patchwork of lines on an otherwise absolutely smooth piece of glass. What a peaceful existence they have down there and we thanked them for allowing us to enjoy their morning from the air. However, we did have one question. That is, why did most of the small boats on one side of the lake go to a fishing spot on the opposite side of the lake while those from *that* side of the lake seemed to be going to the other side? I guess it was for the same reason we occasionally fly from our home airport to another one just to get the same soft drink we could have gotten at home. Forget the question—we understood perfectly well why they did it.

Leaving Winnibigoshish Lake, we continued on our way down the river. As we meandered along toward the southeast, we passed a rather large sawmill, which was burning the tailings in a large incinerator. It was fascinating to watch the smoke from that stack ascend absolutely vertically for at least 200 feet. At that point, it simply flattened out as if it had hit an invisible ceiling. Neither of us had seen anything like that in a long time and that was up north in the winter when it was really cold. Yes, I would say, there was no wind this morning.

After forty miles of zigging and zagging we found ourselves lined up for landing on turf runway 28 on Itasca County Newstrom Field, at Grand Rapids, Minnesota. Once again those fantastic markings made it all but impossible to miss the runway and taxiways. And as usual, the grass is well maintained and like a velvet blanket to our little fat tires, as they kissed the surface so gently. Ahhh—what bliss!

Grand Rapids is the birthplace of Judy Garland, a very prominent movie actress of long ago. It was nice to say that we passed through here, but we had no desire to spend any time playing the tourist and visiting the place of her birth. We knew she was a very good actress, quite a beautiful lady, and did a little flying of her own when she was whisked aloft by a tornado in Kansas—you know—when she visited the Wizard of Oz. But we had a great river calling us and we wanted to keep moving on. Thus, we refilled our energy-source reservoirs and quickly bounded back into the peaceful sky where we belonged.

Making a slight left turn after departing runway 16 at Grand Rapids put us directly alongside our guiding stream. Our wings gave us a great platform from which to watch the leisure activities on our river and it was interesting to see it expand and contract as it ambled along, touching other small streams and lakes. It was still hard to believe this tranquil little overgrown brook would develop into one of the most important rivers in our great country. As we continued to follow its meanderings, we found ourselves being directed more toward the south-southwest. It had been decided that we would be making a stop at Crow Wing County Airport at Brainerd, Minnesota. Besides needing refreshments for ourselves, all three of our humanoids felt certain they would be ready for something to eat about that time. So, about noon we found ourselves tied to the ramp, after getting a nice refreshing drink, watching our three good friends as they strolled toward the eatery located in the terminal building.[5]

We passed just to the west of Minneapolis Class B airspace on our way north and this time, if we were indeed going to follow the river, we would be passing directly under and through it. Since neither Sis nor I had any radios for communication or navigation, no transponders, and no electrical systems, arrangements had to be finalized and confirmed.

From bits and pieces of conversation overheard during our preflight inspections, 726 and I learned we had a date with cousin Cessna 172 on Pilots Cove Airport sometime between 2:30 and 2:45 that afternoon. The distance to fly was about ninety miles and it was already after one o'clock. *Hey, gang, I suggest we get going even though we do have a bit of assistance from that north breeze—it will still be rather tight, especially if you clowns decide to take some sort of little side trip along the way!*

Within minutes, we had bid good-bye and were now in a gentle turn to the left off the departure end of runway 30. This departure had put us directly over *our* river, which at this location had grown into a respectable gentle river about eighty to 100 feet wide. The larger, more powerful, pleasure boat traffic had increased considerably at this point in the river's width, too.

Following the river further southwest and then south, we found that we must keep to the east of its course about a mile as we once again pass restricted area R-4301. Yes, the river did drift into the restricted airspace, but since it was now a rather respectable mid-sized stream of water, we kept it in sight at all times. About ten miles further along the winding course, we found ourselves over Little Falls, Minnesota.

Even though Charles A. Lindbergh was born in Detroit, Michigan, at a very early age his family moved to this fair city below our wings, where he was brought up. Of course we all knew of the great contributions that he made to aviation during his entire lifespan. After a little searching on the American Automobile Association road map that Ray was using for navigation, Lindbergh's boyhood home was located and I soon found myself passing directly above it. Both Sis and I were guilty of having shivers of awe pass along our spars as we made a slow orbit of the site. It was not unlike our first sighting of the Wright Monument at Kitty Hawk three years ago. Too bad we don't have the time to visit this historical home, but we do have an appointment to keep.

Continuing further along this journey of pure unadulterated pleasure, we would spend the next hour enjoying the ever-changing landscape as it passed beneath our wings. This beautiful Cub weather we are being blessed with was certainly intoxicating. It seemed that within minutes the north/south grass runway at Pilots Cove came into view. As we got closer, we observed the flash of sunlight reflect from the shiney surface of Cousin Skyhawk, as he turned final for landing on runway 18. By the time his propeller had stopped turning, Sis and I had landed and were parking beside the energy dispensing equipment. Mr. Skyhawk's name was N-3662L and from the smiles on his three humanoids' faces we knew in an instant these good folks were the ones who would be escorting us through the Minneapolis/St. Paul Class B airspace. These three humanoids were Eric Christianson, his wife, Patti, and their son, Brian. Talk about timing—we had never met before and we succeeded in landing together at this neat little grass airport—just as if we had planned it. Wow! I'm impressed!

As always, first things first! Six-two-Lima did not require any service, but 726 and I required our usual five or six gallons of go-juice. This important matter was quickly taken care of and all six humanoids gathered in front of us to discuss the plan of operation for the next sixty or seventy miles. We all agreed that weather certainly would not be a problem, because from the air, we had already seen the Minneapolis "skyline" and it was over thirty miles away. The wind had been helping us during our southbound flight, but it had now tapered off to practically calm—no problems there either.

Since Eric would be the leader of this little formation, he proceeded to conduct the briefing. First of all, he presented us both with "hand-held communication radios." We knew from experience that most of these items would not work in our cockpits because our "unshielded" ignition systems made so much static that nothing could be heard. Since Eric indicated that use of these units was so that we could hear his transmissions to the controllers, we did not tell him they were useless to us—we were just going to follow his lead anyway. He detailed how he had personally talked to Mark Schreier, the FAA controller, and found that he, Mark, would not be on duty by the time we arrived at the core of the airspace. This presented a slight problem because if Mark was not there, our passage through the core might be denied. We would know the outcome at the time we got to the core. If we were not cleared, Eric explained how we would then proceed around it and beyond. We soon would learn that Patti and Brian would also be of assistance during this adventure. Patti would sit in the back seat of 62L and keep her eyes on us while Brian occupied the right front seat, helping his dad watch for other air traffic as we proceeded along the river. Seven-two-six would be flying the right wing and I would be filling in the left-wing slot of this rather unusual formation.

All set? OK. Let's get going!

Now, as this briefing was breaking up, another humanoid—a stranger to me—approached us with a camera in his hand. Our keepers knew exactly who it was—it was none other than Gerry Quilling—the one who had helped us make these arrangements. He and his wife had been told about our passage through Pilots Cove this afternoon and they had driven to the airport, hoping they would be able to see us. Quick introductions and pleasantries were exchanged, a few photographs snapped, and we once again bid good-bye to a good friend before blasting off into the blue.

Taking off and climbing out presented no problem for us two Cubs to stay in formation. However, once we settled down on our easterly course over the river, it became impossible for us to keep up with Cuz Skyhawk. Even with one notch of flaps extended, he did not seem able to fly slow enough. By the time he had gotten ahead of "his chicks" by about one-half mile, he started doing large S-turns, which enabled us to stay fairly close to our proper positions in the formation. (Of course we were not making the S-turns. It was still about all we could do to keep up with him.)

As expected, the hand-helds were absolutely useless, so we turned them off. Even though our little Continentals were operating at a much higher power setting than normal—just trying to keep up—the trip was fantastic. Our altitude was about 1,200 feet above the surface—something about flying over a congested area—the highest we had been during the whole trip. Anoka County/ Blane Airport passed to our left and shortly thereafter Crystal Airport passed to our right. Both of these landing sites are tower controlled so we assume things are going as planned because no one tried to shoot us down.

Our progress carried us further and further toward the core of the wedding cake. We were now passing some very high skyscrapers and, from all indications, it appeared we were going to make it all the way to the center. It was not to be! Just as we entered the core, Cuz Skyhawk made an abrupt turn to the left and we all knew our clearance had been canceled. Too bad. However, we had gotten close enough to be able to see where the river makes a very sharp turn and was coming back to meet us west of St. Paul Downtown/Holman Airport. Now as our wings carried us over the tall buildings of St. Paul, past the Minnesota State Capitol Building, and then past Holman Field, we settled down to thoroughly enjoy the panoramic view below. Even though they had denied our planned route, what we were doing really was not that bad. No sir, not at all. Neither Sis nor I had ever dreamed of seeing the sights which our humanoids were now showing us. You know, we two Cubs really do have a great life!

Once we were beyond the core and again flying under the wedding cake layers, 62L pulled away from us and left 726 and me to our own devices. The plan was to meet at Red Wing, Minnesota, after completing the transition, where the radios would be returned to their owner. Just to the northwest of Hastings, Minnesota, we flew over the first dam/locks we had observed on our river. We also observed that the vessels on the water were becoming much larger now; however, the first barge tow had not been spotted yet. Once again, much quicker than desired, Red Wing came into view. When we landed, we were no longer in Minnesota. Yes, the city is in Minnesota, but the airport is across the river in the state of Wisconsin. Sis and I now had another state recorded in our logbooks.

Rolling up to the ramp, we noticed that 62L was parked quite a distance from the active ramp area—as if he had been abandoned for some reason. We did not like seeing him in such a lonely setting so we insisted that he join, us for refreshments at the fuel pumps. Reluctantly, he did join us and we spent the next hour or so, just enjoying friendly conversation about the events of the day.

As is always the case, time kept marching on and it was decided that we should press onward for at least a little more river exploring before calling it a day. Lifting off of runway 09 we gave a final wingwag salute to Cuz Skyhawk sitting on the ramp, and to the Christianson family as they photographed our departure from beside the runway. We had met less than four hours ago, but we all felt these were additional names we could add to our long list of friends. They had made it possible for us to complete one of the

A Cub's-eye view of the city of St. Paul, Minnesota. Credit, Ray Olcott.

details of this little adventure and their help had been freely given. Maybe someday we can return the favor. I sure hope so.

Our quick right turn after takeoff put us over the north end of Lake Pepin, which was a twenty-mile-long integral part of the Mississippi River just south of Red Wing. Because it was Saturday, many recreational boaters were enjoying the waning hours of what had been a glorious spring day in this part of the world. Fact is the air temperature had reached a level that now caused both Leighton and Ray to vow that on the morrow they would both be back into their short pants uniforms. After all, tomorrow would be the first of June—and *everyone* knew that means it was summertime. No more long pants.

The low-riding sun in the west, generating ever-elongating shadows across the fascinating riverscape below our wings, created an atmosphere of complete relaxation for all of us. It was as if we were indeed on a magic carpet whisking us along to our next destination. Now that we were away from that congested area we could once again get back down to our desirable altitude of 800 to 1,000 feet above the river. It was a mere fifty miles or so to Winona, Minnesota, our planned overnight stop. The smooth air coupled with a light tailwind evaporated those miles in what seemed to be very short order and we soon found ourselves in the pattern at Winona Municipal/Max Conrad Field.

Whoops. Watch it brother. We're here, too. Yes, I know that looking into the sinking sun and trying to see a couple of little yellow Cubs can become a problem, but that is why we are all looking out the window. I was in the lead as we flew our pattern for landing on runway 29 and 726 was about one-quarter mile behind me. I had just turned final when Brother Piper Cherokee zoomed past us directly below me as he also turned to final. We would learn later that he had not seen us until the moment he passed below and to my right. At that point, Bro made a go-around and landed on the next time around. He could have landed out of the first approach even though we were on final because of his much faster speed, but it did no harm for him to go-around either. Later he found us on the ramp and apologized for almost cutting us off. We all laughed about the incident—joking about how there was room for all of us up there.

Two strong factors influenced our humanoids' decision to spend the night here on Max Conrad Field. Location was one as the field was situated next to our river and we had arrived here with plenty of daylight remaining to get our campsite erected before dark. The other deciding point was that Winona was Max Conrad's hometown. Max set many long distance records with some of our brothers and sisters and we thought it would be fun to spend the night on his airport. We later found a large wall, in the offices of the FBO who took care of us for the night, literally covered with interesting photographs and storyboards about some of the interesting feats that Max accomplished. Boy, he sure flew L-O-N-G legs on some of his trips.

We were greeted by a very pleasant, smiling gentleman as we approached the CFI Aviation ramp. He made sure our needs were attended to and made us feel absolutely at home within a very few minutes. We would soon learn that this genuinely caring person was George Bolon, Ph.D., Department of Physics/Aviation, at Winona State University. It was interesting to learn that this FBO had been purchased by the Winona State University and it was in the process of making it a showcase operation at which students could be trained in the fine art of FBOs as well as all areas of flight training. The goal was to have students actually run the operation—with faculty supervision of course. Sounded like a good idea to us—if the type of service Sis and I were receiving is any indication of the quality of the finished product they hope to produce.

When Dr. Bolon, or George as he preferred we call him, learned of our desire to be tied in the grass with tents under our wings for the night, he quickly indicated where this could happen. However, he was sure that our humanoids would find it much more comfortable bedded down in the administration building where they could spread their bed rolls on the floor of separate rooms if they wanted to do so.

Ahhhh, come on, George. We want those tents out here with us! Give us a break. We knew what our so-called barnstormer pilots were going to do with that offer. *Well, Sis, we can at least look across the ramp and see them through the second story windows. Nuts.* Only two nights together under the stars so far and we had been on this adventure eight full days. Nuts. (Unknown to us at the time, those two nights would be the only nights we would have tents under our wings during the entire trip.)

Sure enough, shortly we found ourselves secured by tie-downs in the grass where we could watch the activities of the evening. Seven-two-six was soon relieved of her burden of sleeping bags, air mattresses, and those wet tents from last night. They would be erected inside the building for the purpose of drying out. Even the ground cover was draped across the security fence to dry. *I don't know Sis—maybe having our humanoids sleep inside is a good idea after all—at least you won't be hauling all that wet, dew-*

soaked, equipment in your front seat. When we were able to see Leighton and Lyle looking out two second-floor windows and Ray at one of the ground-floor windows, we decided maybe this arrangement would be better after all.

George came up with instructions on how to reach a very good eating establishment in town, and the last we saw of our three crazy friends, for the evening, was as they took his personal station wagon and headed for some chow. Well, actually, when they did return, Leighton and Lyle came back out to where we were tied and made sure we were comfy and cozy for the evening. They have a habit of doing things like that whenever Sis and I aren't in some nice cozy hangar. We appreciated the gesture.

Once all good nights had been said, 726 and I settled down to enjoy being here together under the stars. It was fun watching students working on their night takeoffs and landings. Even Dr. Bolon—ooops—George, gave an FAR Part 135 check ride to one of his pilots during the very late evening hours. He took his station wagon when he went home after completing that task. Sis and I laughed about that because now our friends could not go anywhere unless they walked or had us fly them out. Life was very peaceful now and as the events of the day were reviewed—especially the Minneapolis/St. Paul Class B Airspace transition—we were overtaken by the sandcub.

Back into the Weather Again

Sunday June 1, 1997—we awoke to another absolutely beautiful sunrise. From our vantage point in the grass, Sis and I could watch the first light of dawn rolling back the shadows of night as the sun crept from below the eastern horizon. Looking across our river and above the bluff on the far side, we could tell that this day again was going to be great Cub flying weather—at least in this part of the world. As we knew they would, our humanoids had enjoyed another breakfast of eat-what-you-brought and were now walking toward us from the west while the sun cleared the low hills to our east. We knew the temperature was going to be nice because Leighton and Ray had returned to their favorite costume— short pants. Yep—it was summertime again.

This morning we would learn a lesson about how things have changed since we were young, eager Cubs. (Keep in mind that was in the late '30s and '40s.) Back in those good ol' days, we never knew of any landing facility that did not give service to all travelers from daylight until dark every day. It also seemed that every humanoid associated with aviation was performing a labor of love and the clock meant nothing. My, how things have changed.

Occasionally, the only way that we Cubs can learn of things that happen in our lives is to listen intently to our humanoids as they banter back and forth while tending to our needs. As Sis and I were being loaded and prepared for flight we gleaned bits and pieces of information that painted a picture of the planning that had gone into this first leg of our journey for this morning.

Checking the distances on the sectional chart, it was decided we should make our first rest stop at Prairie du Chien, Wisconsin. This would be a nice little ride down the river and our ETA should be about 8:00 A.M.—a normal opening time. The airport information book was then checked and lo and behold, the place was only open from ten o'clock in the morning until four in the afternoon. That wouldn't work because it would be an absolute shame to waste all of this good early morning air. No big deal—our guys just looked a little further down the river and found the next available port of call would have to be Tri-Township Airport located just south of Savanna, Illinois. True, the distance was a bit longer than normal, but with this nice wind blowing on our aft extremities, we could make the big jump with no problem. However, there was a statement in the airport information book that did not sound too encouraging and it was "hours attended: not reported." In order to clear that problem, Lyle had made a phone call to Tri-Township Airport and discovered that they didn't even have any fuel they could sell to us. *All right, gang, what do we do now?*

Further study of all available material revealed our only out would be to continue down our river to just above where the Wisconsin River joined it and then proceed east to Boscobel, Wisconsin. After getting some go-juice there, we could return to the Mississippi River and continue to Clinton, Iowa, for our next pause that refreshes. Yes, this plan would take us away from our river for a short distance, but at least we could see what we were not actually going to be flying over. All concurred with the plan of attack and Sis and I were actually looking forward to visiting the Wisconsin River anyway.

Finally back into our element, we found the air to be perfectly smooth. It was always a joy to be airborne on beautiful clear mornings such as this, especially when you have a sister beside you and your cargo is humanoids you really like. All of us were out to see the sights and we were not disappointed. The landscape below was a continuing thing of beauty with the rolling hills cradling the river as it wended further southward. Shortly after passing slightly to the west of La Crosse, Wisconsin, (we had to stay out of the controlled airspace at La Crosse Municipal Airport), we found one of many barge tows we would encounter during our journey. This particular raft of barges was only three wide and five long with one tug boat pushing them—really quite small compared to some that would display themselves further down the river, but it was the first we had seen and felt it worth remembering. About ten miles north of Prairie du Chien, we took a long hard look at the river ahead and turned east toward Boscobel where that only available energy supply was waiting for us.

Boscobel Airport sat beside the river, between bluffs on the north and south. It really was quite a picturesque setting and we were really happy this little detour was forced upon us. Flying the downwind leg for runway 01, we are sure the FBO is closed because there was absolutely no activity anywhere to be seen. True, it was rather early on Sunday morning, but the book did say "attended—daylight." Our fears were soon relieved because as our mighty Continentals ceased to roar at the energy pumps, we were greeted by the very friendly older couple who operated the facility. Much to our surprise, the second statement from the lady, after a very cheery "good morning," was "would you like 80-octane?"

Eighty-octane? Yes! As it turned out, this was the only drink of that great tasting red stuff that would be offered during the trip. My how good it did taste. Even though it came as no surprise, it was still disappointing to hear the lady explain how this was the last "load of 80-octane" she would be able to get. The supplier was no longer going to handle it and she could not find it anyplace else.

After paying the bill and seeing pictures of some really neat fly-ins held on this nice little airport in the past, we bid this very friendly couple good-bye and once again found ourselves back in the sky above this great land of ours. It was still such a beautiful clear morning that we decided to climb high enough to be able to see the Mississippi River and then turned south to intercept our river a little further downstream. We could still see it from our position and the panoramic view of those clean-cut farmlands below our wings really made it all that much more enjoyable. Within a matter of minutes, Old Man River had again taken his position below and was leading us ever southward.

Dubuque, Iowa, quickly passed on our right and from here the Ol' Mississippi continued southeast for about thirty-five miles before making a long sweeping curve to the south. By now, the river had grown enough to accommodate much more commercial traffic and it seemed we spotted another raft of barges either going up or downstream about every twenty minutes. As we passed above the northern outskirts of Clinton, Iowa, we made a slight right turn to take us the four or five miles west to our next refreshment stop at Clinton Municipal Airport.

The wind sock was standing almost straight out and it was somewhat difficult for us to stand still as we were silenced on the ramp, facing into the wind. What a nice little airport this seemed to be; however, there really didn't seem to be anyone who cared that we are gracing their ramp with our presence. Oh sure, there was that gentleman over there, less than fifty feet away, giving his truck a bath, but obviously he was not interested in two pretty yellow airplanes parked on the ramp—needing chocks. Good grief. Finally, he decided maybe he should leave the truck and see if he could give us a little service. In due time, we were chocked and our energy reservoirs were replenished with essences of 100-octane low-lead.

This landing facility seemed to be quite nice as far as the physical properties are concerned. The office/terminal building appeared to be quite new, but the attitude of the two individuals taking care of the operation this particular day really left much to be desired. We certainly were sorry we interrupted the truck-washing operation. Anyway, none of us could find a reason to tarry any longer at this thriving center of indifference so it was back to our river for some more exploring.

Seven-two-six and I had no doubts about there being a strong wind from the northeast helping us along our way. As we followed the river southwest from Clinton, it seemed we covered the thirty miles to Quad City area in nothing flat. This area is made up of Davenport, Iowa, plus Rock Island, Moline, and East Moline, Illinois. Due to the Class C airspace around the Quad City Airport, we had to detour a couple of miles north of the river, as we followed it to the west for the next thirty miles.

Approaching the ninety-degree bend in the river at Muscatine, Iowa, we ran a quick ground-speed check and found it to be 110 miles per hour. *Hey, Sis, it would seem that the SST had better watch out because we will soon be catching up.* Obviously that would be impossible for us Cubs, but it sure was fun going this fast once in a while. An amazing thing about this high wind is the fact that even at our altitude of less than 1,000 feet above the ground, turbulence was really quite light. The sky was clear, and the visibility was unlimited. Thank goodness we were not trying to go up the river because if we were, I am sure the tugboats and their barges would be passing us—even those going upstream.

As our spinners are pointed south again, way off on the southern horizon we could detect the faint signs of cloudy skies stretching all the way across our route of flight. Even though this phenomenon was still a long way off, it confirmed what our humanoids had observed on the Weather Channel earlier in the day—we would once again be flying in marginal weather. The forecasters had predicted that we would find light rain, lowering ceilings, and much-reduced visibility as we moved further south. Yes, it did appear that the fantastic weather of the past few days would vanish as we caught up with the same weather system we had traversed on the northbound trip. *Well, what the heck, let's not worry about it now. We'll cross that bridge when we get to it.*

Muscatine Municipal Airport slipped beneath our right wings as we found ourselves over a portion of the Mississippi River we had seen on our way north. How we had missed the dam and lock complex about fifteen miles south of the city, I do not know, but this time there was considerable activity to watch as we passed overhead. Obviously the locks were not large enough to accommodate all of the barges that made up a tow at one time. It was very interesting to see how some of the barges were moved into the locks and then unhooked from the main group, which then backed out of the lock to wait for the next opening. It must take a considerable amount of time to make the passage, but Sis and I did not care to hang around for the whole operation to be completed. As we continued our journey down the river, we would have the opportunity to observe several more lock passages of this nature.

Assisted by that nice tailwind, we soon found ourselves turning more to the southwest as we once again passed Oquawka, Illinois. Soon Burlington and Fort Madison, Iowa, were history and as the river led us back south again, we could see Keokuk, Iowa, Municipal Airport—our next go-juice stop. However, before making our approach to landing, we decided to take a look at that neat little town over there on the Illinois side of the river, just south of Fort Madison.

In my earlier years—fact is in a whole other life—I had spent a considerable amount of time in the western United States. Three days after my birth at Lock Haven, I had been flown west and did not return for many, many years. While in the west, I had heard of a place called Salt Lake City. That little town nestled over there on the east bank of the river has great significance when talking about Salt Lake City, Utah. Yes, we did need to take a closer look.

The name of the object of our attention was Nauvoo, Illinois. Joseph Smith, the leader of the Mormons, established the town in 1838. By the early 1840s it had become the largest city in the state of Illinois with a population of 20,000 inhabitants. (The present population is around 1,000.) Smith was killed by a mob on June 27, 1844, at which time Brigham Young became his successor. In 1846, mobs once again attacked the Mormons and forced them to move out of Illinois. Brigham Young departed Nauvoo in midwinter of that year, leading his people west to establish their homes in the Great Salt Lake valley in what is now known as Salt Lake City.

Yes, I know that little history lesson has nothing to do with our trip, but Sis and I found these little tidbits of information, which we gleaned as we crossed the miles, to be very interesting and educational. It is amazing what we Cubs can teach our humanoids—all because we insist on flying low and very slowly. Well, thanks to this tailwind—today was just slow, not *very* slow.

Now back to the task at hand—landing at Keokuk. As we circled the field, we could easily see that the wind was very strong and splitting the runways —almost exactly. No matter which runway we used, it would be one large crosswind. I was about ready to help my humanoid, Lyle, remember a lesson he must have learned sometime in the past. Either he had forgotten it, which I seriously doubt, or he chose to ignore it. I was going to demonstrate to him what happens when the maximum crosswind for landing limit is exceeded. He knew very well that when all of the rudder movement had been applied—and there wasn't any more available in that direction—my longitudinal axis had better be parallel to the direction of landing or things are going to happen.

Lined up on final for runway 08, it was necessary to carry at least a twenty-five to thirty-degree crab angle in order to hold the extended centerline. Our ground speed was quite slow and my little Continental was still producing at least one-half power as my sneakers inched ever closer to the runway. As expected, my left tire let out a small voice of complaint about not landing on grass, as the rubber came in contact with that hard concrete surface. As we balanced on one wheel, we rolled true—straight ahead down the runway with full right rudder and full left aileron being applied with vengeance. However, as my speed started slowing down, my control surfaces became less effective. Even as my tailwheel was forced to the ground and we continued our rollout on two wheels, there would be no stopping that strong crosswind from weathervaning my nose into the wind. The short bursts of power from those mighty horses under my cowl, applied in an attempt to regain rudder control, did nothing more than increase the rate at which we were continuing our turn into the wind. *Sorry about that, Lyle. You have just exceeded my maximum limit for a crosswind landing. Hang on because I'm taking you for a ride.*

Not that I had very much to say about it, but there were no runway lights in the way and the grass beside the runway was very good, so no harm was done as I continued my turn to about thirty degrees off the runway heading. Leaving the runway, I continued my slow roll out directly into the wind. This little excursion continued until I found myself sitting peacefully in the grass ready to roll onto the taxiway to the ramp. The runway and taxiway lights were just as happy as I because I had not made contact with any of them during this little side trip. The only real complaint anyone had were the ones my little fat donuts made as they were doing their best to keep us on the paved runway. Even they were happy when they finally rolled into the nice soft grass.

As I continued to taxi back to the ramp, I watched with envy as 726 touched down *diagonally* across the big intersection of the two runways in the center of the field. She had absolutely no problems because, landing as she did, her crosswind component was almost zero. I waited for her to catch up so we could arrive at the ramp together. (Thank goodness for the big hangars that gave us protection from the wind as our energy reservoirs were replenished.) I hated to admit to her that my little excursion was *not* planned. She was surprised to hear that, because we often land on the grass beside runways and she assumed, at the last minute, I had decided to use the grass in order to land into the wind. *I'm sorry Sis—I wish I could say that was the case, but I must admit my humanoid really screwed up on that one and I saved his bacon. I'll bet he remembers maximum crosswind landing limits now.* Thank goodness no one else saw my performance. How embarrassing.

While comparing notes about the last leg, we discovered that our average ground speed had been slightly over 100 miles per hour and Sis told of an occasional reading of over 110 miles per hour reading on her GPS. (Yes, she was using her new toy as a back up for our pilotage navigation.) Not bad for a couple of old Cubs.

Departing Keokuk proved to be much less exciting than our arrival. The wind was still as strong and from the same direction as on our arrival, but the extra blast from my propeller at takeoff thrust created enough air movement over my rudder that I was able to keep things lined up. Once off the ground, we quickly established a nice big crab angle and were again on our way down the river.

As we turned south, it was very obvious that in the not-too-distant future we would be flying beneath an overcast. This cloud cover was at 10,000 feet up, so it would not create any problems; however, it did clue us in that we were rapidly catching up with the marginal weather our humanoids had been cautioned about early in the morning. From the latest radar observations that they had seen, it had been determined we really needed to be south of St. Louis by the end of today, if we planned on being able to fly anywhere tomorrow. It seems there was a weather system moving in from the west that would definitely create problems north of St.

Louis. All indications for the rest of this day pointed to some light rain or drizzle, reduced visibility, and low ceilings awaiting us in the vicinity of Alton, Illinois, exactly as had been predicted.

A very interesting side note to this weather situation is the fact that not once since leaving Kentucky have we heard any Flight Service specialist tell us that VFR is not advised—not even as we approach obvious marginal conditions to our south. Each one has treated us as if we know what we are doing and it is up to us to decide if VFR is or is not advised. Hmmmmm. I wonder if their lawyers know about this? How nice it is to receive briefings that are applicable to Cub-type operations. It would be interesting to know what training program these specialists attended and if there are openings to retrain those we work with in the deep south. Very interesting.

There was absolutely nothing we could do about the weather, so Sis and I decided that we might as well get back to exploring this great river. As we continued our southward trek, we discovered some rather long expanses of new and rebuilt levees separating the fertile land from the mighty river. This new construction puzzled us until we realized this was the area that was so devastated in the big flood of 1993. Historians say that was the worst flood in the history of the United States. After seeing all of the new levees and remembering what we had seen on television at the time, we had to agree with them.

Zipping past Quincy, Illinois, our ground speed was still more than 100 miles per hour, and, our imaginations started painting some very pleasant pictures as the river took on another new meaning. *Hey, Sis, see that old cabin over there? Yeh, that one. Doesn't that look like Tom with his bucket of whitewash for the fence and isn't that good ol' Huck talking to him? What about that cute young lady skipping rope toward them? Isn't that Becky? Oh look! There's a raft pulled up on the west bank of the river.*

Yes, indeed we were rapidly approaching the home of Samuel L. Clemens (Mark Twain) in Hannibal, Missouri, our next port of call. Even though Clemens was born in Florida, Missouri, his family moved to Hannibal when he was very young and this was indeed his home. The stories he wrote about the adventures of Tom Sawyer, Huckleberry Finn, and Becky Thatcher generated all sorts of fantasies about this part of the mighty Mississippi River for people all over the world. Seven-two-six and I really enjoyed observing the riverscape below and experiencing our own fantasies.

Both Sis and I had plenty of go-juice remaining as we idled up to the fuel pump at the Hannibal Municipal Airport. No, this stop was being made only because, even with that nice tailwind, we could not make it all the way from Keokuk to the next available fuel stop, beyond Hannibal. There were several landing sites, but none of them had fuel and our little tanks did not hold enough to continue. Well, what the heck. We got to meet some more nice humanoids and our three nuts have a chance to check the weather once more before venturing into the low stuff we know was waiting for us down the line.

A gentle right turn after an intersection takeoff from runway 35 positioned us back over our river with a panoramic view of the city of Hannibal to our right. Now that the river was leading us in a southeasterly direction, the wind was not as effective in its efforts to push us along over the ground. Oh, Sis and I were getting lots of help, but not as much as the last couple of legs.

Our progress down the river was becoming more and more evident by the ever-increasing barge traffic below our wings. It seemed that we had at least one and sometimes two or more tows in sight every ten or fifteen minutes. They also seemed to be growing in size—not width, due to the locks—but in length. It was interesting to watch these massive floating warehouses as they met in the channel of the river, passing ever so close, but still at a safe distance.

We had departed Hannibal under an estimated ceiling of 3,000 feet with unlimited visibility. Now, fifty miles further down the river, it had become a very gloomy day as the ceiling had thickened and descended to 1,200 to 1,500 feet, visibility had lowered to six or seven miles, and occasionally we felt the sting of raindrops on our leading edges. Still very flyable, but certainly not preferred Cub weather. The last information obtained from the man with the Ouija board was for these conditions to remain fairly stable until passing St. Louis. If he was right—no problem! If not, well, who knows what!

We were rapidly approaching the second of the five Class B airspaces mentioned earlier. By the time the thirty-mile veil of the St. Louis, Missouri, Class B airspace had engulfed us, another rather large river had come into view about four miles to our left. Sis and I recognized it as the Illinois River, which joins the Mississippi less than two miles from our next point of physical contact with earth. Fifteen minutes later, the two runways at St. Charles County, Missouri, Smartt Airport were beckoning us to taste their wares.

Entering downwind for runway 36, a sense of discouragement surges through our longerons. From our vantage point, it appeared that the whole airport was deserted. Well, we needed fuel so we might as well land anyway. We entered the ramp at the most convenient FBO to our landing and sure enough there was a note on the window that indicated it was closed (something about "gone flying") but would return sometime after five o'clock. It was now 4:15 and we did not really want to wait that long so preparations were made to move to the north end of the field where another FBO apparently existed; however, it, too, appeared to be closed. As Sis and I were being pushed around for engine start, the humanoid who belonged to one of our cousins—Cessna 172—tied down on the ramp, came around the side of the office building and suggested that the best place on the field to obtain the service we required was at the Confederate Air Force, Missouri Wing, hangar located about 1,000 feet to the south of our location. It had self-service fuel available and, furthermore, there was a nice restaurant located in the building next to the hangar.

Hey, that sounds good to us. Sis and I can have a nice drink of go-juice and our humanoids could replenish their food blisters at the same time!

Even though it was a very windy, dreary day, quite undesirable for most fun flying, Sis and I were pushed away from the self-service facility before our three friends disappeared into the eatery. You never knew who might need fuel and we certainly did not want to be an obstruction to the gas pump. No tiedowns were available, but Sis felt very comfortable sitting in some tall grass facing directly into the wind. With my tail tucked very nicely into the corner between two hangars, and chocks under my sneakers, I, too, had a feeling of comfort and safety. We thought we would be here a very short time, but Mother Nature had other ideas and it was well over an hour before we could depart.

As is always the case, Sis and I learned many details about the planning that went into our next leg as we listened to our humanoids discuss very recent events as we are prepared for flight. We already knew the main goal for today was to get south of St. Louis because of incoming weather. After partaking of a very late lunch, while viewing pictures of and listening to stories about flood problems that plague this nice little airport, thoughts once again turned to flying further down the river.

Festus Memorial Airport at Festus, Missouri, was chosen as the day's final destination. This facility was located just outside the mode C veil, directly south of Lambert/St. Louis International airport, and according to the book met all requirements for a nice overnight stay—including tents under our wings. However, due to the weather, there was considerable doubt about placing our tents there for the night.

The chart makers had come up with a fantastic chart for the St. Louis VFR Terminal Area Chart. Not only did it have all the normal things you find on such a chart; it also has "suggested VFR flyways" printed on the back. In this rather marginal weather it was of great help to us. I can just imagine how convenient it must be to use on a clear day. *All* chart makers please take note!

Anyway, our next destination was not more than fifty miles away, but the visibility had deteriorated to less than five miles and those raindrops seemed to be increasing in frequency. When consulted, the Flight Service specialist was pleased to announce that even though it was marginal, there really was no reason we should not go. I guess we would have departed at that time except the actual report from Scott Air Force Base was well below VFR minimums with indefinite ceiling, visibility two miles, in fog. That particular installation was less than fifteen miles east of our proposed track and common sense dictated we wait at least until the next sequence report was printed.

Within the next forty minutes the new weather was checked and it indicated a slight improvement in visibility at Scott Field. Festus Airport did not report weather, so Lyle called for the current conditions from someone who worked there. It was not real Cub weather, but still flyable. Thus it was decided to press onward.

OK, Sis, fire up that new GPS of yours and take us to Festus! There were indeed some restrictions on this leg, which we must not violate, and since Sis now had the capability of close-tolerance navigation she would lead us on this leg. In addition to staying out of the core, St. Louis Regional Airport and St. Louis Down-town-Parks Airport control areas must be avoided. The Gateway Arch, Bush Stadium, and state hospital were important landmarks that needed to be identified as well. It was obvious the visibility was not going to be excellent nor the ceiling way up there on this segment of our little adventure and it was very possible we would need all the help we could get if things became difficult. *When you are all programmed, Sis, let me know and we'll be on our way.*

As is normal, I departed runway 36 at St. Charles County ahead of 726 but she quickly overtook me and then slowed down to my speed. Due to the congested area we would be traversing—we would be flying directly over downtown St. Louis—our altitude must be at least 1,200 feet above the surface. Reaching that alti-tude, we were pleasantly surprised to find the ceiling to be about six hundred feet above us. Within five miles, the clouds above had became very sad and their stinging teardrops were slamming against our leading edges. By the time we reached the junction where the Missouri River joins the Mississippi River, we had passed our first obstacle—St. Louis Regional Airport.

The rain had increased and reduced the visibility to about three or four miles and the flags we observed on the ground were stick-ing straight out toward the south. Yes, we still had that nice tail-wind working for us. Our average ground speed for this leg—including the fifteen or twenty miles that we flew ninety degrees to the wind—worked out to be over ninety-six miles per hour. Thank goodness we were not going north. Following the river was no problem and finally we both relaxed a little more and enjoyed the trip. Eventually the Gateway Arch and tall skyscrapers of down-town St. Louis took form in the murk and it seemed they were all extending above our altitude. Visibility was now steady at three or four miles and it quickly became apparent our altitude was enough to clear all obstructions if we chose to fly directly over them. How-ever, in order to remain clear of the St. Louis Downtown-Parks Airport control area, it was mandatory that we pass the arch and downtown buildings slightly to their west.

About ten miles further south, something must have happened to cause that dark overcast to cheer up because no more teardrops were falling and the visibility had increased to at least eight or ten miles. Both Sis and I wish the crying had stopped before the arch and downtown slipped past our left wings because the view would have been much better. Oh well, maybe next time. Minutes later, our presence was gracing the ramp at the Multi-Aero, Inc. FBO, located at Festus Memorial Airport.

Something again upset those dark gloomy clouds overhead because shortly after our arrival, as our little energy reservoirs were being refilled, they started crying. Thank goodness, a quick decision was made to have Sis and me spend the night in T-hangars while motel accommodations were arranged for our humanoids. None of us wanted to spend the night outside in the rain.

When inclement weather elements are creating a rather high level of discomfort for our humanoids, they tend to get things done in a hurry. Thus, even before needed luggage was off loaded, 726 and I were pushed into our own T-hangars. Neither of these structures had any doors on them, so our shelter would be completely open in front of us. We would be safe, as ropes secured us to anchors in the dirt floor and there was no way we could blow away. No, our only real worry was what if the cowbirds returned? We certainly did not want that to happen again. No way.

When Bill Rodgers, Multi-Aero's chief pilot, came by to pick up our humanoids and their overnight luggage, everyone expedited boarding the van because the rain was really falling now. They quickly drove off and the last we saw of our three friends were the taillights on their transporter as it took them into town. One task we knew they would take care of during this overnight would be doing their laundry. It had been four days since the last time and believe me—it was time to do it again.

Even with our totally open front doors, Sis and I really appreciated being under a roof for the night. The wind had died down considerably and there was enough overhang on the roof to prevent any raindrops from reaching us. These were not the best accommodations we have occupied, but they would be adequate. Due to the dense overcast, which had moved in, darkness came quickly and the continuing drops falling from the sky seemed to have settled in for the night. We wondered if our dash southward today had put us far enough in that direction to be able to continue our adventure tomorrow. Well, I guess we'll know in the morning. The fatigue from the day's adventure coupled with the steady patter of rain on the roof soon had us drifting off into slumberland.

A Fantastic Home-cooked Meal

Hey, Sis, smell that—clean clothes. They really did do their laundry last night. Thanks to the weather gods our humanoids had plenty of time to take care of that little chore. Here it was after 10:00 A.M. and our three friends had just now returned from town! In reality, there had been no need for them to get here any earlier because Mother Nature had deposited fog and low-flying clouds over our area as the trailing edge of last night's storm moved eastward. By this hour, things were improving rapidly and as our preflight inspections were being administered, Sis and I learned of much-improved conditions forty or fifty miles further down the river. Yes indeed, we had succeeded in moving far enough south to avoid the bad stuff approaching St. Louis from the north. We also discovered that today was going to be a very easy day. Our final destination would be Union City, Tennessee, less than 200 miles away. Oh yes, even the cowbirds were not around last night so we didn't need a bath this morning either—thank goodness.

Some of the most interesting and beautiful sights in life are fleeting glimpses that can be missed and lost forever if the observer is not at the proper place at the right time. Such was the case as we departed runway 36 at Festus Memorial Airport. Due to her location, off of and above my right wing, 726 did not have the opportunity to witness this very unusual display which was presented to us in a New York minute.

By the time we took flight, the clouds were dissipating quite rapidly and the sun was making strong inroads into becoming the dominant element of the sky; however, at this time there were only holes in the overcast. Climbing straight out to sufficient altitude for a safe right turn around the end of a bluff back over our river caused us to pass directly over an area that evidently had been used as storage for crushed or ground glass. The stockpiles had been removed and it appeared to be just barren earth below. Just as we passed over this area, a break in the overcast allowed the sun to shine unrestricted on this small area of the earth. When that happened, it appeared that thousands of tiny flash bulbs were flashing on and off, bidding us farewell. The scene lasted no more than two or three seconds, but the beauty of those tiny brilliant lights flashing in that pitch-black patch of terra firma was absolutely fascinating. It was extremely tempting to make a couple of orbits just to see it all again, but ol' Mr. Cloud had other ideas and quickly closed the hole.

Ol' Mississippi River was now leading us toward the southeast and by the time Chester, Illinois, had drifted beneath our left wings, we were experiencing good Cub weather again. It is not excellent Cub weather, but certainly much better than what we had while passing through the St. Louis area. Hey, maybe those crystal ball things work after all. *They* said it would be good weather down here.

We no longer had that strong movement of air assisting us along our way so there was more time to relax and watch the panoramic view of the environment slip beneath our wings. About eighteen or twenty miles north of Cape Girardeau, Missouri, a very large cross is observed, about ten miles to the east. Sis and I were not sure why it was there and we did not venture in that direction because it appeared to be located in the Bald Knob Wilderness Area over which low flying was not encouraged. Even from this distance, it was a very impressive structure and really deserved further investigation.

Ten miles south of Cape Girardeau, we saw the two sharp 180-degree turns our river made as it prepared to receive the water from the Ohio River just south of Cairo, Illinois. Within minutes, we were entering the pattern to land at the furthest-south landing site in the state of Illinois.

Seven-two-six was in the lead as we lined up for landing on runway 32 at Cairo Airport. All information that we had told us that the FBO was open from 8:00 A.M. until 5:30 P.M. every day and the present time was about 12:45 P.M. Should be no problem—right? Wrong!

We suspected all was not as it had been written when we could see nothing moving or indicating anything was happening while we flew the pattern. Once our little Continentals were silenced at the energy dispensing island, the only sound we could hear was the grass growing, and the birds, bees, and the breeze in the trees. No one came out to see what we two pretty little yellow Cubs wanted or anything else.

Leighton walked over to the FBO office and found it locked. A note hung on the door declaring CLOSED ON MONDAYS. *OK, gang, what do we do now because there aren't any other places within our fuel-remaining range. We could use auto gas, however, that would be illegal and besides, where is the nearest gas station?*

Sis and I could do nothing except sit there on the ramp and watch the frustration level within our humanoids climb almost to the breaking point. Actually some of the events which took place within the next hour or so were quite entertaining. Once presented with a problem, these three friends of ours will go to great lengths to solve it.

After a brief period to cool off and start being rational again, things began to fall into place. First of all a pay telephone hanging on the outside wall of the hangar was discovered. Posted beside this phone was a list of telephone numbers to call in case they were needed. At the top of that list was a number to call for *service*. Aha! That is exactly what we needed—service—so Lyle dropped in a quarter and dialed the number. The phone started to ring—*inside the hangar, directly through the wall, which supported the pay phone from which the call was being made.* After four or five rings, an answering machine—apparently also located inside the hangar—answered the phone with a cheery message asking the caller to leave a message. Lyle's frustration level went over the top as he slammed the phone back onto its hook and stormed across the ramp mumbling something about calling the police.

Overhearing that "calling the police" comment, Leighton turned to the list next to the phone and sure enough there was a number listed for the police department. Sooo, he dropped in his quarter and dialed it! He had the police dispatcher's office on the line by the second ring. Now at least we had another humanoid to tell our troubles to and just maybe something could be done. Leighton explained the situation about two aircraft on the ground at the airport, unable to proceed further because they both needed fuel. How does the police department intend to help us? The pleasant female voice on the other end of the line admitted she did not know what could be done, but she would find out and call back. She did! Within two or three minutes, the pay phone rang and this very helpful voice informed Leighton that one of the members of the airport authority was on his way to the field to help us get fuel.

Fantastic! With service like that, we all needed to take back those ugly thoughts we had just minutes ago. Now all we had to do was wait until Mr. Airport Authority arrived. Things weren't as frustrating now, as this was a rather nice peaceful quiet little airport. Besides, Union City was only about sixty miles down the road—oops—river, and that was as far as we were going today. We had plenty of time, so Sis and I just sat here on the ramp and relished the tranquillity of this nice little country airport. *Take your time folks, this is a great little breather.*

It had been at least twenty-five or thirty minutes since they were told that help was on the way and our humanoids were on the verge of calling the nice voice at the police department again when an older pickup truck was turned off the main road onto the airport access road. When the rather rotund older gentleman (probably about my humanoid's age) dislodged himself from this slightly beat-up truck, he informed us that he was indeed a member of the airport authority and he would be very happy to get us what we needed and send us on our way. He seemed a little surprised that the airport office was closed, but that would be no problem. He possessed a key.

Sure enough, his key worked fine and within seconds entry was made into the lounge area of the terminal building. However, it did not take very many minutes for this rather jolly humanoid to have a change of attitude when he discovered his *only* key did not fit the lock to the office door. In the office was the switch that would allow him to turn on the power to the gas pumps. The longer he fiddled with the lock, the more frustrated he became until finally, he literally broke the lock off and forced entry into the office. His anger and frustration level was rather high, but it was not directed toward us or our humanoids—thank goodness for that.

Now all he needed to do was turn on the circuit breaker that powered the gas pump. Well, once again things did not go as expected. The circuit breaker box was also locked and our authority member friend *did not* have a key for that lock either. This man was not about to be stopped. He went to his truck, whipped out his toolbox and proceeded to dismantle the circuit breaker box in order to get to the switches inside. Once inside, he discovered the only breaker in the off position was the one that controlled the fuel pumps. He could only stand beside us and shake his head in disbelief as our go-juice reservoirs were refilled. We thought the situation was rather funny in light of the fact that we really were not in any hurry.

Our experiences at Cairo were not over yet. The fact that this very helpful person did not know how to operate the fuel pumps was no problem as our humanoids *always* take care of filling our energy supply tanks themselves and they are well versed on the operation of many types of refueling devices. Once this task was completed, it was time to pay our bill and continue down the river. This proved to be another interesting event of this *unique* pause that refreshed.

Once back in the office, our humanoids were standing around with credit cards in hand, waiting to be told what the damages were, but nothing was forthcoming. Finally, this fine gentleman who had been so helpful suggested that he had no idea what to charge us for the fuel. With that, one of our humanoids asked him if he knew how much the fuel cost per gallon. He did not. With a little more prodding, he rummaged around in some papers and came up with a figure that sounded reasonable. Then, he was confused as to what good that information was to him, so he handed his calculator to Lyle and said, "Here—you figure out what you owe me." With that, our tabs were quickly computed, rounded to the nearest "correct change dollar," (nobody had any change) and the legal tender exchanged. (It is a good thing for him that our humanoids are honest!) Now all that remained to be done was—depart.

We all expressed our concern about all the trouble we had caused the man—calling him away from his work, the broken door lock, the dismantled circuit breaker box, and the confusing paper work—but our newfound friend just laughed and assured us that *things would be taken care of* and we should come back again sometime soon. He waved a cheerful good-bye as our wings lifted us back into our natural realm to continue our journey. After take-off, a quick turn to the right sent us in a southeast direction with the Mississippi River on our right and the Ohio River on the left. Within five minutes we had flown over the big junction of the two rivers and were once again on our way.

As we continued down the river, it was obvious that we had seen the last of the dams across the river. Commercial traffic on the river had increased tremendously and the barge tows were much, much longer than they had been further up the river. The river traffic we were observing could be destined to proceed up the Ohio, Missouri, Illinois, or Mississippi rivers, as well as several other tributaries along the way. It seemed we had one or two large barge rafts in sight at all times now, as our wings carried us along above this very interesting water lifeline to the heartland of the good ol' United States of America.

Much too soon, Hickman, Kentucky, drifted past our left wings and as we rounded a large bend in the river, to the west we could see New Madrid, Missouri, beyond Sassafras Ridge, Kentucky, where once again our river made a sharp turn to the south. This was an easy landmark for us to pick up the next morning when we resumed following our dream.

Once this navigational reference point had been established, Sis and I made a gentle left turn to the southeast, away from the river, toward our next destination, which we had been anticipating ever since leaving home. We would be spending the night at Union City, Tennessee, at the invitation of humanoid friends of ours by the name of John and Linda McShane. Sis and I needed the life-blood in our mighty Continentals changed and our three human-oids had been promised sleeping facilities at the airport, but much more important than that—John and Linda had given them a special invitation to their home for a home-cooked meal. Knowing our three lovable nuts as well as we did, we knew there was no way on earth they would pass up that invitation.

Rolling toward the ramp of Everett-Stewart Airport, Union City, we could easily see that John had made all the preparations as he promised because, in his very proper military form, he personally was directing us toward the gas pumps. He knew we would want to replenish our energy supply before proceeding to the hangar in which we would be spending the night. His preparations were so complete that all the necessary equipment and supplies were in place for the transfusion both Sis and I needed before continuing our little adventure. We had flown just over twenty-five hours since the last such medical procedure had been done way back in Macomb. Talk about personalized service—John had really done his stuff. Not only was he concerned about our comfort and needs here at his hometown, we learned that this very caring friend of ours had indeed been the humanoid asking about our progress at Kentucky Dam Airport as we were traveling north more than a week earlier.

Sis and I found that we would be sharing a rather large, doorless hangar with several of our cousins this night. Thank goodness there was no possible place for the cowbirds to roost above any of us at this facility. This would also be the structure in which our oil would be changed and as soon as we had been maneuvered into position, our cowls came off and the old "blood" was soon being drained from our bladders.

How would you feel if a complete stranger walked in on you when you were partially disrobed in preparation to attending to some personal hygiene matters? Well, that was how Sis and I felt when young Rosemary Jacobs, a reporter from the *Union City Daily Messenger*, introduced herself. Not only did she interview our three humanoids as they continued to expose our vital parts during the oil change, but she also insisted on taking pictures as well. How embarrassing to be photographed with our cowlings removed and various internal parts and hoses disconnected!

Someone had informed the local newspaper about our adventure and arrival at Union City, and she was here for the story. It was nice to think we were newsworthy, but couldn't she at least hold off on the pictures? After she had finished her interview, we convinced her that she should return early the next morning prior to our departure. She seemed to understand our concern about not having half-naked photographs floating around and promised to return the next morning—if her boss would give her permission.

The way John, our host for this evening, kept looking at his watch as Rosemary departed, it was very apparent evening chow time was at hand. Our humanoids assured us that after they had finished their evening meal, they would return and complete this task of changing our oil. We had also learned that a meeting of the local Civil Air Patrol would be taking place in our hangar this evening and this group of future aviation leaders wanted to learn all they could about the two of us and our little trip. With one last check to make sure our scattered parts would be safe, everyone vanished around the corner of the hangar, en route to John and Linda's home on the west side of town. Sis and I could do nothing except wait for their return and hope no strangers walked in and saw our state of disarray.

It was a little over two hours before John returned our three characters back to us. We wondered if they would ever get around to completing our oil changes because all we could hear was Lyle moaning about eating too much and the rest of the gang yanking his chain about eating all of the chicken casserole and fresh corn. Linda, John's lovely better half, had really given our gang one grand home-cooked meal. All were in agreement that it was the best meal any of them had eaten in a long, long time. Knowing how our three guys like to eat, it is a wonder they didn't try to finagle another such dinner from her before leaving town.

Even though it seemed like a long time, it was only a matter of minutes until major progress was taking place to complete our transfusion. John was one of the officers in charge of the CAP cadets and he soon had them all around us talking to our humanoids as they tended to our needs. What a joy it was to have these young and eager minds absorbing all the information they could about the likes of us. It really brought back fond memories of our younger days when both Sis and I were engulfed in teaching other young people the fine art of flying.

The sun had long gone and the dark shadows of night were in command by the time Sis and I were back together and ready for the air once again. The final check for any stray oil leaks would be made before departure in the morning. John had made arrangements for Leighton, Ray, and Lyle to spend the night in luxury, sleeping in the administration building. They would even have a shower available. Yes, tents under our wings would have been much more fun, but then our accommodations were quite nice too—soooo—there would be no complaints from us either.

Even though today had been quite easy on us, both 726 and I were quite content to drift into slumberland almost as soon as our dear friends had departed with their sleeping bags and other overnight equipment. We knew our adventure down the Mississippi River would continue on the morrow and we wanted to be ready.

Old Man River, Just Keeps On Rollin'

Many small airports around this great land of ours have some very interesting activities going on during the night, and Everett-Stewart Airport, Union City, Tennessee, is one of them. In the very wee hours of the morning our slumber was disturbed by the distant sound of some rather large round aircraft engines. Even though the roof above our wings prevented us from seeing the glowing lights as they passed overhead, we had absolutely no doubts about that sweet sound coming from a couple of Pratt & Whitneys, each one swinging a three-bladed Hamilton-Standard prop, bolted on the front spar of a Douglas DC-3. As young Cubs, fresh out of our jigs, that unique sound had been a mainstay of our everyday life as the DC-3 plied the nation's airways tending to the air travelers' needs. To think that after all of these years, just maybe—maybe—either Sis or I would recognize this long-lost vision from the past if he actually came up and parked outside our door.

Sure enough, in short order, we heard the almost-forgotten sound of those big tires scrubbing on the dry runway as they gently touched down, while in the background we could hear the low, throaty POW as unburned fuel found its way into the hot exhaust-collector ring and exploded as those beautiful Pratts slowed to a slow idle. Seven-two-six and I both were elated to be awakened by such pleasant sounds from our childhood. However, much to our chagrin, from our location in the hangar we only had a glimpse of that ghost from the past as he went by the door. Nuts. If only we could get out to the ramp. Darn.

Neither of us were able to return to the land of slumber for the rest of the night. First of all, the big trucks that seemed to be coming and going around our night visitor were very noisy and second of all we certainly did not want to miss a single sound as those two big, round engines returned to life and propelled the ol' reliable DC-3 back into the night sky. Oh, how I wish we could see what is going on.

Sis and I watched with anticipation as the dark of night slowly turned into the gray of dawn. Our big cousin on the ramp hadn't come to life yet, so the possibility of us seeing him still existed— provided our humanoids pushed us out on the ramp in time. I think mental telepathy must work because it was just barely light enough to see across the ramp when our friends were standing in the big door to the hangar, making ready to push us onto the ramp in preparation for the day's activities. As we rolled across the track in the threshold, we could see him—our long lost cousin—the Douglas DC-3. No, neither of us knew him personally.

There he sat, with a big eighteen-wheeler backed up to his side while workers transferred many boxes into his fuselage. Even though he was not bright and shiny and did not carry a large corporate logo, it was obvious that his everyday needs were being taken care of by the three young pilots flying him. We soon would learn that Mr. Douglas was working under contract with General Motors engine division and almost every night he made a round trip from Flint, Michigan, to Union City. He was transporting engine parts from Flint to Union City, where some sort of seal was installed on them. That accomplished, the parts were then taken back to Flint. Big Doug admitted it was not the best job in the world, but it would do—considering what the alternative might be. We had to agree with him because old airplanes like us do have a very limited opportunity market and therefore must be satisfied with whatever comes our way. Most of us will do anything to keep flying during our advanced years.

As the eighteen-wheeler roared away, cousin Douglas settled down, getting ready to carry his load back to Michigan. All preflight duties completed, his big radials shook the sleep from their systems and made ready for action. Just watching the cloud of blue smoke belch from the exhaust stacks as these two beautiful power plants roared back to life was enough to send shivers up and down our longerons. In a few short minutes we bid good-bye to this vision from the past as his sturdy wings lifted him into the overcast as he passed by the ramp on his initial climb after takeoff. Already, his visit seemed like a dream. Yes, a very pleasant dream indeed, bringing back many great memories of the past. *Hey, Sis— it was almost like being a kid again—wasn't it?*

John had corralled our humanoids and taken them into town for breakfast and now all of us were just waiting for the clouds and fog to dissipate so that we could depart. As we waited, Rosemary Jacobs, the newspaper reporter who took those nude pictures of us last night, came around the corner of the hangar. After we were posed, she snapped several pictures and wished us well as she departed for her office. Eventually, John would forward a copy of the Wednesday, June 4, 1997, issue of the *Union City Daily Messenger*, which carried our story and picture on the front page. Guess which picture they used! That's right, it was one of those half-naked shots she had taken of us in the hangar. How embarrassing, and on the front page, too.

Now that we were all ready and primed to continue our journey down the river, it seemed the weather gods were very intent on working against us. The two hours or more elapsed time since Cuz DC-3 departed had seen a steady decrease in both ceiling and visibility. Each time Leighton or Lyle returned to the ramp where we waited, they would be muttering something about if only we could get a little further south, all of this low stuff would be gone. Finally, at about 10:30 A.M. we could see some local improvement and the last check with Flight Service indicated conditions in all directions were quickly improving. With this encouraging news, we bid farewell to John and all the gang at Union City, as our mighty Continentals were once again brought back to life.

Our altitude remained at twenty feet or less as Sis and I completed our famous Cub formation takeoff from runway 01. Passing the ramp, we gave our friends standing there one last wingwag salute of thanks as we pointed our spinners west to rejoin our river. Climbing to a respectable altitude of about 500 feet, we found the top of our rudders sticking into the overcast. Visibility was even less than expected, but having checked the sectional very closely, we knew that no tall towers were charted between us and the river. Once headed south over the river, from experience, we knew there would be no towers to grab us as we made our way the few miles further south to good weather. Thus, even with some doubts as to the wisdom of doing so, we continued on our way with me in the lead.

Ten, and then fifteen minutes passed without finding a single recognizable checkpoint. Since the light breeze was blowing directly out of the north, I adjusted my heading a few more degrees to the right just to make sure we got back to the river at the proper location. Finally, after about thirty minutes, our big ol' guiding stream of water came creeping out of the murk. My last drift correction had been more than necessary and we found ourselves about five miles further up stream than intended. Be that as it may, at least we now had our good friend, the river, back under our wings showing us the way to better weather further south.

Both 726 and I will admit to the fact that flying conditions at this time certainly left much to be desired. The ceiling was extremely ragged and at times we could hardly see each other so we really did not get in much sight-seeing on this segment of our river journey. Actually, I was sure we would have paid the good folks at Caruthersville, Missouri, a visit if our charts and books had indicated they could replenish our energy source, but they did not indicate such service to be available. That being the case and the weather seeming to have stabilized, we opted to continue about twenty miles further down the river to Blytheville Municipal Airport, at Blytheville, Arkansas. Considering the fact that we were rapidly approaching Memphis, Tennessee, Class B airspace and the weather had *not* improved as much as forecast, common sense dictated we should grace the ramp at Blytheville for another weather check and wait it out if necessary.

By the time we had drunk our fill of essence of 100-LL, it was quite obvious that conditions were rapidly improving—especially to the south. The nice voice at Flight Service confirmed good weather in the direction we were going. (She never once mentioned anything about VFR not recommended.) That was all we needed to make a hasty exit for some more fun flying. Sure enough, by the time the big Mississippi was once again tucked securely under our wings, Cub weather was the order of the day and all we had to do was sit back and enjoy life.

Once again the riverscape had changed character. Now the Muddy Miss seemed to be leisurely meandering back and forth through very rich, fertile, flat, floodplain country. I was sure this same type of scenery existed further upstream, but we were too busy to enjoy the gradual change as we traversed the area of questionable weather. As Osceola, Arkansas, slipped slowly past our right wings, our thoughts turned to preparations for negotiating the Memphis Class B airspace—the third encounter of such areas during our adventure down the Mississippi.

As usual, there really was no problem traversing these controlled airspaces without any radios—not even a transponder—as long as our humanoid pilots paid attention to what they are doing and stayed out of them. Our river route would take us to within six miles of the Memphis International Airport—within one mile of the core—but as long as we remained at our normal cruise altitude of 1,000 feet or less, there would be no way we would enter any of the controlled area. Since the major part of the city of Memphis would remain east of the river, there would be no reason for us to be concerned about the FAR regulation about minimum altitude above congested areas either. Nothing to it and we never had to leave the river.

We were still at least ten miles north of the big bridges, which carry interstate highways and the railroad across the river, when they came into view. Passing General DeWitt Spain Airport, the panoramic view of downtown Memphis dazzled us with metropolitan beauty. Sis and I both wonder if it would be possible for us to find the exact spot where Hernando de Soto first saw this mighty river back in the year of 1541. Yes, that place is here someplace, but who knew exactly where? Seven-two-six and I feel tingles of honor surging through our frames as we flew above that beautiful white building just southwest of the bridges. This sudden surge of pride stemmed from the fact that inside that building was one of our great and famous relatives of the past. We had been told that domed structure protects the *Memphis Belle*, our Boeing B-17 cousin who helped write history with her brave and gallant service in the sky over Europe during World War II. I wished we could stop in to visit her for a while, but that would have to be on the next trip.

Flying out from under the Memphis wedding cake, our companion, the river, led us in a southwesterly direction. We made no attempt to follow every curve and bend because the serpentine

Cub weather at last! Credit, Leighton Hunter.

meandering would have us continuously making 180-degree turns if we literally followed the river. It was really quite interesting to observe the hundreds if not thousands of crescent and horseshoe lakes that had been formed over the many years as this mighty river changed its channel. This, in turn, creates some rather unusual state boundaries, as the river may have originally formed that boundary, but since eroding through some hairpin turn it no longer was that border line. I was sure glad I was not responsible for keeping track of land ownership in this part of the world.

Our reception at Thompson-Robins Field, at West Helena, Arkansas, was really very nice. Coasting to a stop at the refreshment pumps, it was quite apparent that much agricultural activity went on around here. The tie-down area was crowded with many different makes and models of our hard-working cousins who tend the crops around the country. Obviously, today was not a pressure day for them as their humanoids all seemed to be gathered around hangar-flying to pass the time. Our presence on the ramp prompted several of those humanoids to come over and admire our plumage and originality. This group of critics understood the likes of us who travel great distance without avionics. What a joy to hear conversations that were more about how much fun we must be having and wishing they could join us, rather than how weird we are to be doing what we are doing without all that fancy electronic stuff. However, all felt it was a good idea when Sis did admit she was carrying a GPS and I declared it had been a very valuable tool on a couple of occasions. The whole group, even our own three close friends, really enjoyed discussing the joys of aviation, which the likes of us—two little yellow airplanes—were able to impart to anyone who would listen. We were a little disappointed when our tanks were filled and it was time to depart. This gabfest was fun.

Leaving West Helena, things settled into a routine that was both pleasant and still a little boring. Well, I should never say the "b" word, because there is absolutely nothing about flying that is boring. No, let's say the river continued its constant meandering through beautiful flat, fertile, land along which had been built miles and miles of levees. (We learned there are over 1,600 miles of levees along the river.) Now, there was a constant flow of barge traffic up and down the river. Some of these moving islands were so large they required two very large tugs to push them along their

Southbound over Memphis, Tennessee, and the "Memphis Belle." Credit, Leighton Hunter.

way. The river was wide enough that two-way traffic was no problem; however, it was very interesting to see two large tows meeting within one of the many sharp bends in the waterway. It became a game with us to count the number of barges rafted together and 726 came out the winner when she found one that contained fifty-three—yes, fifty-three—barges being pushed by two tugs.

Having decided that Lake Village, Arkansas, would be an ideal spot for our next rest stop, we carefully worked our way into the traffic pattern between a couple of ag planes that were part of a fleet working from the field. Parking in front of the office building, we find that the FBO also owned and operated this very impressive fleet of beautiful new or almost-new Thrush equipment. In my past history, I, too, have served a few years as a crop sprayer/duster, but never had I seen such nice, clean, well-maintained equipment. I must say the ramp area was very noisy as those beautiful workhorses with their big turbine engines rolled in and out of the loading area. Even with all the activity, our needs were attended to in a very friendly and efficient manner. We felt our welcome was sincere, but we also knew our presence on the ramp did create a cramped maneuvering area for our working cousins, so we quickly said good-bye and departed. Even these hard-working cousins seemed happy to have seen us as they politely made way for our departure during their beehive operation.

The ol' Mississippi had adjusted her course to a more southerly direction now, even though she still made lots of switchbacks. The almost constant flow of traffic on her surface as well as the ever-changing panoramic view of the countryside still intrigued us as we moseyed toward the end of our journey. Soon we said so long to Arkansas as Louisiana presented itself on our right, with the state of Mississippi still on our left.

Come on you guys—you know you shouldn't even be thinking about doing it. Maybe several years ago you could have done it, but not in this day and age. Both of us could sense the ever increasing pull of temptation as we passed over those beautiful long, wide, sandbars that had become more prominent in the river. We could feel the tingling in our control sticks as Leighton, Lyle, and Ray, all three, contemplated how much fun it would be to put our little fat 800x4 sneakers on that temptress down there singing to us. What fun it would be to drag the area and make a sweeping turn back around to end the approach by making wheel tracks in that virgin sand in the middle of the river. Just the solitude of being there would be fantastic. But alas, we all know—in our youth, nothing would have been said about the event, but now—it would create a stir all the way to Washington. *An unauthorized off-airport landing. Heavens. Those pilots must be crazy. Ground 'em. They aren't safe anywhere around or in an airplane.* Nope—as much as we all would like to spend a few minutes on one of those beautiful sandbars—it just was not worth the hassle. Darn.

Turning back to something we could legally enjoy, we found some of the actors on this river stage below us had been developing an interesting comedy/drama. We noticed while passing some of the larger settlements upstream and as we approach Vicksburg, Mississippi, a new character has been added to the cast. This little guy appears to be nothing more than an overgrown rectangular box that scurried around any place that the large barge tows were being assembled or disassembled. These little boxes reminded us of worker ants as they maneuvered to position those big barges into a raft. From our vantage point, we found it humorous to watch as they raced across open water to a waiting barge and then churned the water like crazy as they slowly nudged those big, heavy floating containers into position beside another vessel or loading dock. At times, two or three of them would be attacking one barge—not unlike the mighty ant summoning help when he finds something too big to handle.

Twenty miles or so southwest of Vicksburg, it was time to bring out the Houston Sectional and start looking for Tensas Parish Airport, in Louisiana, our next port of call. Actually, both Sis and I had enough energy to make Natchez, Mississippi, but we thought it would be nice to drop into this little place for the fun of it. This was almost a mistake.

On downwind leg for runway 34, we could not see any of our relatives nor even a fuel island although all information we had told us the services we needed were available. However, much activity could be seen around the small office and hangar at the north end of the runway. Rolling to a stop adjacent to the vehicles from which fertilizer and chemicals were being unloaded generated absolutely no interest from the humanoids working so diligently in the area. Finally, Lyle found one of them who seemed to be the boss and inquired about the possibility of obtaining a little fuel for us two Cubs now gracing the ramp.

This young man was very courteous, but admitted that he knew nothing about the airport as he and the rest of the workers were employed by the firm that was delivering fertilizer for the ag planes that operate from the field. However, he was more than happy to call the man in charge who was located at the Newellton Airport about six miles north. Since it was now past 6:00 P.M., we were advised that someone would be right down to attend to our needs. Within minutes, we could hear the ever-increasing volume of the voice of a powerful 150 Lycoming engine approaching from the north. Quickly a very well-known front silhouette came into view just above the treetops and, within seconds, one of our exuberant young brothers—a Piper PA-18 Super Cub—flashed overhead and made a crop duster turnaround for a short landing and rolled onto the ramp. This energetic young whippersnapper coasted to a stop behind the big truck and we were not introduced properly; however, we certainly knew he was there.

Bounding around the obstructions, this newcomer humanoid greeted us with enthusiasm and indicated we should be pushed toward the side of the hangar as he ordered the fertilizer unloading equipment to be moved out of our way. Shortly, both 726 and I were positioned very close to the one and only fuel storage tank located against the side of the hangar. The pump was turned on and Lyle was given the go-ahead to refill my energy reservoir.

Being the nitpicker that he is, Lyle took a quick look inside the hose nozzle before inserting it into my filler neck. Well, he usually does that anyway, but this time it was indeed a good move as he observed a considerable amount of dirt and crud inside the fixture. Needless to say, I did not want all of that stuff in my energy system, so a container of some sort was requested to catch the fluid used to clean the nozzle. Much to our dismay, Lyle was told, "Oh, just squirt it on the ground." (Oh well, from the looks of the ground many gallons of other things had been dumped there so a pint of so of aviation gas will not matter, I guess.)

It was only a matter of a few minutes before Sis and I had again drunk our fill of essence of 100-LL and our bills had been paid, in cash—rounded to the nearest even dollar—as no change was available. Stuffing those newfound cash dollar bills into his pockets, the "gas man" yelled, "Thanks for tonight's beer money and a chance to fly the Cub," as he once again bounded around the big fertilizer truck on his way back to our waiting brother, the Super Cub. As soon as "bro's" big Lycoming came to life, the power was up, and away they raced for the runway. A quick dash down the strip brought his bright yellow wings to life as they hovered ever so low with his black "sneakers" just barely above the asphalt. All the while, those mighty 150 horses pulled them faster and faster. The sharp pull-up and another crop duster turnaround soon had our young brother passing directly above us once again and then out of sight beyond the trees to the north. Actually, he reminded us of the Lone Ranger of yesteryear. He always came to the rescue from nowhere and just as quickly disappeared into nowhere when the job was done. With a hearty "hi-yo Piper Cub," he flew off into the sunset. *Have fun dear brother I wish we could have gotten to know you better.*

By the time this latest fueling experience had been filed in our memory banks, the long shadows of late afternoon were taking shape. Further in-depth study of the Houston Sectional indicated to all concerned that Natchez should indeed be our final destination for the day. All available information indicated the facilities at their airport were exactly what we needed for this evening's activities—provided we could have tents under our wings. Thus, thirty minutes later and twenty-seven miles further down the river, the smiling face of the only visible humanoid welcomed us to the ramp on Hardy-Anders Field, Natchez-Adams County, Mississippi. Robert was the name of this fine young man and he was extremely helpful to all of us as we settled in for the night.

By the time 726 and I were serviced and ready for the departure tomorrow morning, Robert had pointed out where we could be secured for the night and where tents could be erected. Neither location was to our liking for several reasons. First of all the tie-downs were arranged for much larger members of our family—namely business jets, as Robert called them. Besides that, the lines were so rotten that one of them broke when Lyle picked it up off of the ground. No other area was available, so both Sis and I used the lines from our own tie-downs to keep us safe for the night. Next, the location for tents certainly left much to be desired. It was overgrown with tall grass or weeds and seemed very bumpy, as our three friends explored the area.

Ray to the rescue. Of the three lovable humanoids traveling with us, this one is the least shy of all. He marched over to the office and asked if it would be possible for the three of them to put their sleeping bags in the building for the night. Robert felt it would be a great idea and pointed out the conference room on the second floor as the most desirable location for sleeping. This room proved to be almost as good as tents under our wings because the wall exposed to the ramp area was entirely glass—floor to ceiling— and they had a panoramic view of the whole airfield, while Sis and I could watch over them during the night while they slept. Really a neat arrangement—a great view for all of us—except when our three clowns disrobed for bed and then we turned our gaze to another direction. No modesty at all.

Now that the sleeping arrangements were settled, all thoughts turned to *food*. Robert offered the use of the "Airport Cadillac" and made several suggestions as to good places for Ray, Leighton, and Lyle to refill their food blisters. It was decided all wanted ribs, so Robert drew a map showing how to get to the best place in town for such cuisine. The restaurant was located directly on the river bank adjacent to the Lady Luck Casino River Boat. The trip would be at least seventeen miles, one way, and cab service was not available, thus the offered transportation would be used. Sis and I had a good laugh when we saw our three humanoids drive out of the parking lot in a vintage Chevy station wagon that was the color of rust, had lots of noise coming from a worn-out exhaust system, and from what we could tell—very bald tires. Yes, the Airport Cadillac was really something to behold. However, it did have the city/county crest still visible on both front doors, which indicated to us the vehicle had been some governmental department's limousine earlier in its life. We sure hoped it gets our buddies back before morning.

Sometime around 11:00 P.M. we could hear the rumble of the old station wagon rounding the curve and a couple of unaimed headlights came into view. Yes, it was our intrepid birdmen returning safely after all. Since Robert had been so helpful and knowing that he would be on duty most all night, our humanoids thought it would be nice to bring him a big order of ribs for his lunch. As soon as that delivery was made, all three of them came out to retrieve their sleeping bags and give Sis and me one last loving caress to confirm our security. Within minutes the lights in the conference room blinked out as we bid farewell to another great day of exploring our river.

So Long, Ol' Man River—Thanks for the Trip

The serenity of early morning at a country airport was absolutely intoxicating. The stillness, the sweet-smelling air, the awakening of all that was around us as the golden dawn traced the eastern sky, was enough to make any flight-loving Cub quiver in anticipation of each new day. These were some of the feelings surging through our airframes as Leighton and Lyle gave 726 and me our daily thorough preflight inspection. The first one of the day is always very complete—all the rest at each fuel stop are a quick once-over before departure—unless something unusual is found— then look out! Things really get inspected then.

About halfway through this early morning ritual the low throb of a big round engine could be heard in the distance to the west. This sweet song kept getting louder and louder until suddenly the beautiful yellow, bi-winged, vocalist burst over the tree tops just to the southwest of our location on the ramp. The big constant speed propeller and the throaty exhaust of that round engine produced one of the sweetest-sounding duets ever to echo through the hills.

Passing less than one-fourth mile south of us, this proud bird made an abrupt left turn and in less than a minute one of our hardworking cousins, Ag Cat, N-8253K, was parked beside us. His humanoid jumped out and approached our intrepid flyers while Cuz 53K patiently waited with his big power plant slowly ticking over in a very melodious idle. We soon learned that 53K's humanoid recently had owned a Cub, but had sold it in order to purchase the big Ag Cat. Seeing the two of us together here on the ramp was just too much and the situation demanded a short stop to view our attributes. Both Sis and I enjoyed the admiring eyes and gentle touches as this knowing airman drank in our beauty. Almost as quickly as he had come, he said thank you, waved good-bye, and blasted off down the runway. Moments later, the big Cat was very low, directly overhead with its big prop beating the air unmercifully, followed by a graceful sweeping turn eastward over the treetops as the melodic crescendo faded into extinction. It was a fantastic gesture of farewell. *Hey, Sis, when I grow up, I want to be an Ag Cat.*

Mr. Sun popped above the eastern horizon at about the same time our fat little tires gave runway 18 a final good-bye kiss. What a great time for the likes of us to be in the air—especially on a morning such as this, when the sky is clear, visibility unlimited, and not a bump in the air. A gentle turn to the west soon had us passing the river boat casino for a couple of pictures and then it was down the river we went! The early hour with the attending smooth air made our enjoyment of the passing kaleidoscope below even more enjoyable. In this particular area of its journey, the river seemed to meander back and forth in ever-increasing sweeps, seeming to make the water flow and the river traffic travel at least twice as far as would be necessary if straight line movement was available.

Everything seemed to be going well until Lyle tried to use his camera after loading new film. It was working fine up to that point, but now it would not operate—no matter what he did to it. Finally it was decided that the battery must have died during auto rewind. No spare batteries and still a long way to go. Nuts! Well, wait a minute. We were not far from False River Air Park, our next port of call, and it was just two miles from New Roads, Louisiana. Shucks, it was such a nice day. Sis and I would lounge on the ramp while our humanoids went into town for a new battery. Even if they had to walk—it is only four miles round trip! Sounded good to us.

The sign on the door read CLOSED and a quick check of the latch confirmed it was locked but that really did not seem to be a problem as we were parked next to the self-service fuel-dispensing equipment. However, after several tries during which the instructions were followed to the letter, the system would not work. Now what? It quickly became apparent that getting go-juice was much more important than trying to get a battery for a camera.

The large hangar located less than seventy-five feet back of the fuel island seemed to be a beehive of activity. Several county (Ooops that is "parish" here in Louisiana) mounties were having their vehicles serviced inside the structure. Yes, indeed, it was the parish service facility and many things were going on within the area—including servicing police helicopters, cars, and trucks, and the construction of a large barbecue grill, which was needed for an upcoming social gathering. A couple of these uniformed gentlemen noticed our predicament and came to the rescue, which consisted of a couple of hard flips of the switch followed by a swift kick to the switch box and the pump started operating. Yep, that thing needs some work. Sis and I continued to chuckle about the quick fix the entire time our reservoirs were being filled.

With our needs satisfied, thoughts once again turned to the battery. The two deputies had been so friendly and helpful with the fueling problem that Lyle decided to follow Ray's example of not being so shy. He boldly asked if anyone knew how far it was to the nearest place where a camera battery could be purchased and the best way to get there. The chief, who was welding on the new grill, looked up and replied with the answer we all know Lyle wanted to hear.

"It would be the Wal-Mart located in town and that deputy over there will be very happy to drive you to the store and wait to bring you back out to the field."

As the deputy's truck disappeared down the road, Sis and I relaxed in the gentle breeze while Leighton and Ray made small talk with the police officers and mechanics in the area. In about twenty minutes Lyle was back with the new battery and as he started to install it, he made a very embarrassing discovery. The reason the camera would not work was because the new roll of film he had put in was not properly positioned. He felt so stupid that he could not bring himself to tell the kind, helpful, police officers of his error. With that little revelation, Sis and I were propped back to life for a quick exit!

Once again at our breathtaking altitude of 700 feet, we could see Baton Rouge, Louisiana, about twenty miles to the southeast along the east bank of the river. The Class C airspace around Baton Rouge Ryan Airport did not present a problem; however, we would be required to fly a couple of miles west of the river for a short distance to avoid the core. Another interesting aspect of this area is the fact that the bottom of the outer layer of the wedding cake is at 1,300 feet msl, while within the southwest quadrant, located inside the circumference of that layer, were two very tall towers that stood as high as 1,749 feet msl—extending from the surface up into the controlled airspace. Obviously, that made a portion of the airspace completely unusable for the likes of 726 and me. Oh well, I guess it further proved that politicians make the rules rather than actual users of the airspace.

Plaquemine, Louisiana, slowly slipped beneath our right wings, signaling the passage of the last of the big tall towers in this vicinity. Now we could concentrate on the ever-changing drama performed on the river stage below.

By now that tranquil little stream we found in northern Minnesota has turned into a bustling thoroughfare with thousands of movements taking place at one time. Petrochemical plants and oil refineries lined both sides. Intermingled were grain elevators storing some of the bounty from the heartland farms, stockpiles of various products, as well as warehouses filled with who knows what. The agricultural and industrial products would be loaded on ocean-going freighters bound for foreign destinations or on barges

The False River fuel island. One kick fixed it.

headed up stream. It appeared that both sides of the river were lined with barge rafts waiting to be moved, while ocean-going freighters plied the main channel as they moved to and from loading docks. It seemed impossible for a small clear stream at the northwest end of Lake Itasca to grow into something as big as all of this. It has to be true because Sis and I have watched it happen. We were both awestruck as we rapidly approached the last pause that refreshes along our river— St. John the Baptist Parish Airport, at Reserve, Louisiana.

Seven-two-six and I both felt something was bothering all three of our humanoids as they disembarked from our cozy cockpits at the fuel pumps. I think the fact that we were very near the end of our journey down the river had finally started to show its ugly head. Just prior to landing here, we had flown through the western-most arc of the thirty-mile veil of the New Orleans Class B airspace, the fourth and last one along the river. (Those words "last one" really are not what any of us like to hear.) Actually, the airspace was not the problem, it was the fact that unless a suitable landing site south of New Orleans could be found, we would not be able to escort our traveling companion—the big river—all the way to the Gulf of Mexico.

Listening to Leighton, Lyle, and Ray discuss the situation, we learned that where we were parked was the only place where go-juice was available. It was more than 120 miles from our location to the settlement of Pilottown at the very mouth of the river. Oh, sure, we could get out there, but how in the world were we going to get back when there were no facilities along the way? Even if we were equipped with avionics and could talk to the control tower at Lakefront Airport, we still did not have enough endurance and range to make the trip out and back. Well, there was Tiger Pass Sea Plane Base at Venice, Louisiana, but Sis and I knew our fat little sneakers would never keep us above water—we needed floats to land at that facility. Our only hope was to find someone who knew of a private, unmarked, facility that we could get permission to use this one time.

Returning from paying the fuel bill, our three friends seemed to be in a more jovial mood than when we last saw them. They had indeed asked many questions and talked to several of the local humanoids about finding nourishment for 726 and me further out toward the mouth of the river. Nobody knew anything about any facilities where the needed fuel could be obtained. Our three intrepid birdmen had resigned themselves to the fact that we would not be able to explore the last seventy or seventy-five miles of the river. Too bad, but with only twelve gallons of go-juice on board, we Cubs did not have long enough legs to make the trip. Sis and I were really concerned because we will do anything we can to please our humanoids. It was just that there were limits as to what we could do sometimes. Thank goodness our three lovable characters understood and did not hold these limiting factors against us.

Before proceeding any further under the New Orleans wedding cake, a conference was held under our wings. This was a mandatory meeting because we would be passing in close proximity of three controlled airports. At one point the river would lead us to less than five miles from New Orleans International/Moisant Airport. We knew we must avoid the controlled airspace at both Lakefront Airport and Naval Air Station-New Orleans. There would be no problems in making this passage provided we paid close attention to our location at all times. The point along the river where we would terminate our southbound journey was also determined. Now that everyone was in agreement, our faithful little Continentals came back to life and we were once again on our way.

Within two miles, our 180-degree heading found us over our river directly south of St. John the Baptist Airport. A ninety-degree left turn had us following this amazing body of water further downstream as it continued to display much versatility in the activities taking place on its surface and along both banks. For the next forty or so miles, as we proceeded literally through New Orleans, this mighty river demonstrated what a great international seaport she had become. The multitudes of barges—both loaded and empty, tug boats, ocean-going freighters, those ever-present little box tugs scurrying here and there, and an occasional pleasure craft, reminded us of some of the busiest thoroughfare we had observed flying over landlocked metropolitan areas. As downtown New Orleans slipped beneath our left wings, we watched in awe as the masses of humanity, vehicular traffic, and tall buildings blended harmoniously with the hustle and bustle below.

Taking into consideration the headwind component we would have after turning toward the northeast, it had been decided that Chalmette, Louisiana, would be the point where we would say good-bye to the river. Even at that point, we did not know exactly how far we could go without making a refreshment stop. It had to be either Slidell or maybe Picayune, Mississippi. Much too soon, we found ourselves over Chalmette.

It was with much satisfaction and some disappointment that we took one last look down our river as she continued southward on her journey to the Gulf of Mexico. The visibility was very good and we could see at least twenty miles further south to the next big bend as its course meandered further toward the southeast. This was the spot where my humanoid would terminate his dream of more than twenty years. Thank goodness, he waited for me to come into his life before making that dream come true, because I have enjoyed this adventure more than any previous outing in my life.

So long Ol' Man River—it has been a fantastic journey! You have given us memories that will never be forgotten and stories to tell that will last a lifetime. We do not know if you can experience feelings or not, but we sure hope you have enjoyed having us two little yellow Cubs scooting along above you for the past five days. Mighty Mississippi River, we thank you—it has been a great trip. With one last wingwag salute, we pointed our spinners north-northeast which marked the start of the last stage of this adventure—heading home.

Ole Ugly and Billy Roy

Following Interstate 10 and the railroad across the east end of Lake Pontchartrain enabled us to determine that the wind was indeed holding us back by as much as ten or twelve miles per hour. Calculating our time in the air and the distance remaining, the humanoids decided to proceed to Picayune, Mississippi, for our next stop. Besides that, our three humanoids had a mutual friend who might be in that area and they thought it would be fun to just drop in on him.

Picayune Pearl River County Airport was really our kind of airport. The inhabitants were all laid-back, relaxed, and living life the way it should be done. Everyone seemed to be our long-lost friend even though they do not even know us. The likes of Sis and me gracing their ramp was considered a visit of royalty to their facility. Much to our chagrin, the friend we all hoped to visit was not in the area at this time. It seems that he was in Florida.

By the time 726 and I had again drunk our fill of essence of 100-LL , it was long past lunchtime and all three of our jokers were complaining about being hungry. Much to our surprise, the man in charge (I'm sorry, Lyle lost the piece of paper that had his name on it.) called to one of his customers and told him to mind the store because he was taking these three guys to "Don's" for lunch. With that, we watched them vanish in a cloud of dust.

At least an hour had passed and Sis and I were beginning to wonder just what might have happened to our friends. Even the man in charge had not returned which made us even more concerned because we assumed he would not leave one of his customers in charge for too long. Nobody else seemed concerned, but then these good folks really did lead a relaxed lifestyle. Actually, we had nothing to fear because in due time, the four wayward lunchers returned and Leighton, Ray, and Lyle were extremely happy with the great, fresh fish sandwiches they had eaten at Don's Seafood Restaurant. It never ceased to amaze us how these so-called barnstorming pilots of ours found such good food to eat.

Now that all food blisters were filled and energy reservoirs replenished, it was time to depart from this haven of newfound

The Mississippi River flows past the New Orleans riverfront.
Credit, Leighton Hunter.

friends. An in-depth study of the New Orleans Sectional had proven that Wiggins, Mississippi, only forty miles up the road, would be our next mandatory fuel stop. There were just not many facilities suitable for no-radio aircraft with very short legs in this part of the country so flight planning required thinking about not just one leg, but at least one or two more. One more important feature of this particular leg was that very few good checkpoints existed, which meant we had to rely on good dead reckoning navigation. Well, Sis did have her GPS and she would use it, but just for the fun of it, I suggested navigating the old-fashioned way through DR navigation.

Departing from runway 05 at Picayune launched us almost directly to our no-wind heading of fifty-five degrees. As is usual, I departed ahead of 726, but due to her extra speed, she had no problem catching or overtaking me within a very short time. Usually, if the runway was wide enough, we made our famous Cub formation takeoff as we did this time. However, in the event the runway was narrow, Sis charged after me and as soon as we were both airborne, she pulled up beside me as a farewell gesture to those who may be watching. During cruise, we moseyed along at a very comfortable distance from each other so that we could both enjoy the scenery.

Following Sis and her GPS over the trackless countryside had us approaching Dean Griffin Memorial Airport, at Wiggins, Mississippi, in less than forty minutes. (That GPS gadget sure makes me lazy as the extent of my DR navigation was just to determine some sort of ETA.) As we came closer to the traffic pattern, we could see things were really happening. It looked like the place had been invaded by a horde of Ag Cat dusters and they were literally all over the place. The wind was favoring runway 35, but these busy workers paid no attention to wind direction—their main

726 and 881 on the ramp at Picayune, Mississippi.

concern was how quickly they could take on a load, depart, spread their fertilizer, and return for another load—repeating the procedure over and over again.

It was obvious that these busy big Cats were communicating with each other as their sequencing on the runway was extremely smooth—even though some operations were head-on procedures. Seven-two-six and I wondered how our entering the pattern was going to work since neither of us could communicate with anyone connected to this beehive. From past experience, we should have known there was nothing to worry about. As always, those ag plane cousins of ours were some of the most courteous creatures in the sky and when one of them saw us two little yellow Cubs entering a normal into-the-wind landing traffic pattern, they all went into orbit until we were safely on the ramp out of their way. It all worked like magic—even as we taxied onto the ramp where they were taking on their heavy loads, they moved aside and allowed us to slip right in there with them next to the gas pump.

We never did figure out just how many Cats were in this ever-moving choir performing around us, but the melodic roar changed pitch frequently and the volume was really quite loud. We loved every note because they were the beautiful sounds of members of our family enjoying what they were doing, and the music could not have been sweeter. Since Sis and I had not seen any cultivated fields anywhere around the area, we had to inquire as to just what or who was the recipient of these many loads of chemicals. We soon learned that several thousands of acres of forest were being fertilized and when the crew was through working from this airfield, they would be moving on to another area.

Since 726 and I were not allowed to follow our humanoids into the offices and were not privy to flight planning ideas until after they were finalized, we must pay close attention to their good-natured banter to learn vital details as they preflight us. Apparently the walls of the cluttered office inside the old hangar were lined with antique "household and home" radios—most of which supposedly worked. The owner of this FBO was a collector of this old equipment and some of it was even older than Sis, if you can imagine that. During our travels, we had found some very interesting things tucked away at various off-the-beaten-path landing sites we visited. It was too bad our modern-day relatives considered the speed and altitude they travel to be more important than the "roses that grow along the way." Once again some would argue that we ol' Cubs had outlived our time. I don't think so.

Finally our intense listening disclosed the last destination for today—Atmore, Alabama, just a couple of miles north of the northwest corner of the Florida panhandle. Once again we would be proceeding about 102 miles further northeast instead of going directly east toward home. This prolonged detour was required to keep us out of controlled airspace further south and avoid flying over fairly large expanses of water if a southern route had been selected. We knew that departing Atmore tomorrow, it would be downhill the rest of the way home.

Falling in behind one of our cousin Ag Cats as he taxied out with his heavy load, we waited on the taxiway as he back-taxied to make his takeoff into the wind. As soon as he cleared the runway, another big Cat landed downwind, stopping short of our position until we could move onto the runway for our back-taxi for takeoff. As we passed, the humanoid occupying his big glass cockpit gave us a thumbs up along with a big grin. As soon as we saw these warm friendly gestures, we knew these hard-working Cats were watching out for us as we prepared to depart their busy beehive. Sure enough, as we made our quick climbing turn to the right from runway 35, we could see one of them in orbit at the north end of the pattern and another on close final at the south end of the runway. What a great bunch of birds. It is too bad this kind of courtesy does not exist at many, much more sophisticated, landing sites—including our own home field.

Proceeding leisurely along our way over the heavily forested landscape below, Sis and I felt as if we did indeed have wings of magic. Just a few hours earlier, we had been over the mighty Mississippi River and now here we were, treating our humanoids to a beautiful panoramic view of some of the most pristine woodlands we had ever seen. We observed the clean-cut angles of areas, which had been harvested alongside still-standing growth. We could see the rows of new seedlings that had been planted to replace recently harvested mature trees. Mixed in among these two extremes were areas of new growth trees in various stages of maturity. This fascinating panoramic display extended from horizon to horizon. Now we knew why so many of our Ag Cat cousins were working so hard back at Wiggins—they had a lot of trees to feed.

The sun still had more than an hour to go before dipping below the western horizon when Atmore Municipal Airport came into view. A sudden flash of sunlight from polished wings brought our attention to "Cuz" Cessna Skyhawk as he banked from the south side of the airport toward town, northwest of the field. The time of day was very conducive for sight-seeing activity and a mental note was made of this possibility as concerned our 172 cousin. I was following Sis at a normal quick-sequence landing distance as we prepared to enter downwind for runway 36. We had been watching the movements of Cuz and it came as no surprise when he also entered the pattern—directly behind 726. Of course, this action caused me to make a long extended pattern while he slowed to safe spacing behind Sis. If he had followed me in the pattern, he would have been on the ground almost as quickly and would not have disrupted the flow of traffic. I refuse to believe his was an intentional act, but was done out of reliance on talking on the radio and not looking out the window. We are sure Mr. Cessna had seen Sis but did not observe me following her. Not that we would have said anything, but it was interesting to see how fast Skyhawk was rolled into the hangar and his humanoid vanished into thin air.

The peace and quiet surrounding us as our little Continentals clicked to a stop was overwhelming. Even though that was a hard-surfaced runway, we knew this was our kind of airport. The grass beside the runway was suitable for the likes of us and if that nice gentleman walking toward us was as friendly as he appeared—well, it might not get any better than this.

Sure enough, Mickey Parker lived up to his appearance and proved it by doing all in his power to make us feel welcome. After another big drink of essence of 100-LL, Sis and I were securely tied down for the night. I was lucky because my spot was in some nice soft grass, while 726 was stuck with sleeping on the hard concrete ramp. Once again, tents could have been erected near us, but our intrepid birdmen chose to sleep on the lobby floor of the administration building. (Wow. These guys sure are not roughing it much on this trip.) Mickey further explained that in addition to helping with the airport operations, he owned and flew a Cessna Ag Wagon during the cotton and corn dusting/spraying season. We were to meet Mr. Ag Wagon very briefly the next morning as he and Mickey prepared for some serious crop tending. What a fine clean specimen he turned out to be—it was obvious that he was in good hands.

In the midst of finalizing overnight arrangements, another very pleasant and jovial humanoid appeared on the scene—Billy Roy Parker, Mickey's brother. Since it was too late to find a good place to eat their evening meal, our three characters were very willing to accept Billy Roy's offer to drive them to his favorite eating establishment. Within minutes, Sis and I found ourselves alone and resting easily on this very tranquil ramp in southern Alabama. We knew our beloved humanoids would be returning because Billy Roy had insisted he needed to take care of some errands in town and would be happy to bring them back after they had eaten. We had not anticipated the interesting display of unusual flying ability that would be shown us by little Miss Motorized Parachute. Her performance was interesting to watch, but I prefer my strong solid wood spars to that folding mass of cloth she calls an airfoil.

The sun had slipped below the western horizon when Billy Roy's truck came through the gate next to the office building and stopped just short of the ramp. In less than two minutes another truck pulled in directly behind his and out stepped Mrs. Billy Roy Parker. (I do wish I could remember her name.) This was indeed the beginning of a good old hangar-flying session, conducted in the cool of the evening while watching the antics of a small aircraft. The touch-and-go landings performed by the buzzing parachute had also enticed several passing observers to pause and enjoy the camaraderie at the local small airport. All could have been seated on the office building porch where several rocking chairs were available, but much to 726 and my pleasure, they were congregated near to us where we could listen to the conversations.

The passersby were extremely interested in watching little Miss Paraplane perform, but the Parkers and our humanoids were engrossed in serious hangar-flying conversation. Billy Roy and his wife were the sole operators of an aerial crop-tending service. He was the pilot, and, she, the official loader. In addition to all of the necessary ground equipment, they owned one big Ag Cat, affectionately referred to as "Old Ugly." It was very interesting to hear how, over the years, the cotton boll weevil has been greatly reduced—so much so that this year may be the last year Old Ugly would be working the cotton fields. Billy Roy and his wife both attested to the fact that over the past few years the need for their service has been reduced until now Old Ugly was flying less than one-half what he flew last year. They were both thankful for the decline in the weevil presence, but it was more difficult to make a living.

On this trip, our first encounter with crop dusting/spraying aircraft had been at Quitman, Georgia, where the pungent odor and the beat-up appearance of the aircraft jolted my memory to the days of long ago when I too served as a beast of burden, tending fields in West Texas and New Mexico. It was a period of my life that I wish to forget. However, as we progressed along our way, we have encountered many ag operations at which our hard-work-

ing cousins—many of them very young—were living a very shel-
tered and enjoyable life. They were doing what they like doing
best and being cared for and flown by humanoids who loved them.
Now I surmised that we had found the ultimate in humanoid/fly-
ing machine relationships—very much like the one I have with
Lyle.

I made this observation because each time Billy Roy mentioned Old Ugly his eyes lit up like a kid on Christmas morning.
You can tell he loves that big Ag Cat and I will bet you anything
that Ag Cat loves Billy Roy just as much. How nice it was to be
referred to as Old Ugly in an endearing manner rather than just the
Cub as was my case those many years ago. As further proof of the
affection Billy Roy has for his flying machine, Leighton, Ray, and
Lyle were each presented with new caps with Old Ugly's full-color
picture embroidered on the front. *Cuz—I wish it had been possible
for us to meet you as I know we would have liked you, but as that
was impossible, we want you to know the caps touting your picture were worn all the way home and now occupy places of dis-
tinction in the homes of our humanoids.*

Bright twinkling stars had taken command of the heavens by
the time this friendly band of humanity decided to end the day.
Once again, newfound friends said "so long" and Sis and I were
given one final check by our three very dear humanoids as they
made their way to the lounge floor. The serenity of the setting and
the low soft night sounds surrounded us as Sis and I remembered
today's adventure and contemplate what might be in store for us
on the morrow. Could we be going all the way home tomorrow? It
might be possible, you know.

Homeward Bound

The gray dawn of Thursday, June 5, 1997, brought proof that
weather conditions at Atmore Municipal Airport had greatly deteriorated during the night. It was hard to understand how things
could be so grim considering how beautiful conditions had been
when we all retired. We had no actual measurements, but the ceiling could not have been more than 500 or 600 feet and the visibility not much more than two miles. Obviously not good Cub
weather around here. I wondered what conditions are like further
to the east?

Our three humanoids consumed another one of those eat-what-you-brought breakfasts and proceeded to make ready for departure just as soon as Mother Nature permitted. Mickey Parker rolled Cousin Cessna Ag Truck out of his hangar and prepared him for a day of tending cotton. Cuz was a picture of perfect health and the mighty roar of that big Continental under his cowl left no doubt in anybody's mind. Improvement in the weather conditions had to be imminent considering all the activity taking place.

Soon Leighton, Lyle, and Ray came out the door of their sleeping quarters carrying their belongings. They were obviously ready to be in the air once again. As Sis and I were being prepared for flight, we gleaned details of what lay ahead of us from overheard bits and pieces of conversation between our three eager airplane drivers. It seems that Flight Service had been called for weather information and, as expected, VFR was not recommended because of very marginal conditions over a large area. However, nothing really serious would be encountered until we got in the vicinity of Tallahassee, Florida. Well, what the heck—with this strong headwind we had to work with, it would be at least five hours before we got that far east and lots of things could happen by that time. Yes, this reduced visibility would make navigation a little difficult, but the magic GPS that Sis now possessed sure would be a big help. Thus, with that fancy box programmed and 726 in the lead, we blasted off for points southeast.

As expected, the headwind made for very slow, rough, going, and the visibility made anything except DR—and the GPS—absolutely useless. As we progressed further to the east and those checkpoints kept materializing, as if by magic, out of the murk, Lyle finally admitted that I should have a GPS before we take another long trip. Finally, the old man has realized modern technology really has something to offer. It was about time. Even though it did nothing to smooth out the bumps, just the thought of finally getting through to him made life much easier.

The destination of this first leg of the day had originally been De Funiak Springs, but the farther east we traveled, it seemed the stronger the wind became and the rougher the ride. A close watch of our fuel consumption indicated that, even with these increased winds, that original destination could be reached with no problems. Eventually, Bob Sikes Field, at Crestview, Florida, came into view and, much to my surprise, 726 entered the pattern for landing on runway 35. This was very unusual for her to arbitrarily change the game plan, but I knew she did it for a reason so I followed her to the ramp. Sure enough she had a very valid reason for making this unscheduled stop. Later, we would learn just how vital it was to make this stop even though that reason had never crossed her mind.

Since the winds had increased somewhat and the ceiling and visibility remained marginal, Sis made the wise choice of landing at Sikes Field while we still had plenty of fuel remaining. She did not want to go all the way to De Funiak Springs and then have trouble finding the airport when our go-juice was at a very low level. *Good thinking, Sis. Good thinking.*

We had no reason to tarry long at Crestview, so after once again checking the weather and learning that some very heavy rain was moving toward the northeast, through the Tallahassee area, the little Continentals under our cowls launched us on our way. The remaining run to De Funiak Springs was only about twenty miles, but it took us thirty minutes to complete the trip. Hey—that's only forty miles per hour. Not much wonder all of the surface traffic going our direction is whizzing past us all of the time. One thing is for sure—there is no way we could go nonstop to Quincy under those wind conditions!

Anticipating a quick turn (Once again, that's the fancy way our big hot-shot cousins say, "Hurry up and take care of my needs 'cause I'm too important and busy to hang around.") as we rolled to a stop next to the gas pump, it was a real shock to hear the FBO manager inform us that we could not get any fuel from him. Oh, he had plenty of fuel all right—it was all in the ground directly below where our little fat sneakers were resting but he had no way to get it out of the ground. It seems the pump had been broken for more than two weeks and the city officials refused to get the pump fixed. He would be happy to drain some gas from some of his own fleet, but that source had been depleted a couple of days ago.

It is too bad that politics play such a integral role in our lives, but obviously that is what is going on here. The city officials were too dumb to understand the value of a full-service airport and were content to let it die or kill it off themselves if it would not die. Thus, the pump was not getting repaired.

Now what should we do? Together, 726 and I would need less than five gallons of gas to fill our tanks. That is not much, but we need all we can hold to make the next leg, considering the wind direction and velocity. Leighton and Lyle spotted a Citgo Gas station directly across the street and as if on cue they both exclaimed, "Let's do it!" The "it" they were referring to was putting automotive gas in our systems even though we did not possess the proper FAA paperwork for doing such a deed.

Returning with five gallons of premium *mogas* presented another problem which back in our day—fifty years ago—never existed. Transferring the liquid from the gas can to our reservoirs was no problem provided proper equipment was used. When queried about the availability of a funnel the friendly FBO attendant replied that he did not have one but there was a plastic soft drink bottle somewhere around the gas pump area that was modified to serve as a funnel. Fifty years ago, a funnel could be found anywhere mechanical devices were serviced.

When the homemade funnel was finally found, it was so dirty that there was no way it would be inserted into our filler necks. Some of the precious fuel was used to clean the dirt from the bottle and then our energy source tanks were topped off with the remainder of the mogas. The fueling completed, we thanked the young man for his concern—even though he gave no service— and made like a bird.

Politics, politicians and political power. Yuck. If only we could get it all to stay out of our lives. Thank goodness we had made that stop in Crestview because if we had not done so, our tanks would be almost full of illegal mogas instead of a couple of gallons mixed with the legal stuff.

The run from De Funiak Springs to Quincy was just under ninety-five miles, which meant that we needed to pay very close attention to our ground speed during the first part of the leg. If it continued to be at forty miles per hour, we would have to divert up to Marianna, Florida, to have our go-juice tanks refilled. Mother Nature decided to smile on us because as Sis and I passed the quarter-way checkpoint, visibility and ceiling had improved considerably and the wind direction had shifted to the north, reducing our headwind component. Another twenty-five miles found us flying through almost good Cub weather even though it was very rough and bumpy because of the strong wind, which by now had shifted even more to the north so that our groundspeed now equaled our airspeed. Quincy, here we come.

Standing beside the gas pump and directing us toward him was the man with the perpetual smile on his face—Dennis Mathews, the operator of the FBO located on Quincy Municipal Airport. We had met this fine gentleman in the spring of 1995, when 726 and I attended Quincy's annual fly-in. At that time, we had camped for a couple of days next to the trees just north of his ramp. Dennis recognized us from that visit and we, too, knew exactly who he was because of his ever-present smile and eager-to-help attitude. It sure felt good to be welcomed back by good friends.

Reminiscing and talking about current happenings is always fun, but it was obvious that our humanoids were eager to keep moving. Nothing had been said, but we had all come to the conclusion that we could make it home tonight—weather permitting. Dennis confirmed that some bad weather had passed through just a few short hours earlier. Flight Service confirmed that Tallahassee had just started to improve after passage, toward the northeast, of some very heavy rain. Marginal VFR conditions were reported from all stations and of course the standard "VFR not recommended" warning was issued. Accepting the invitation to bring us two pretty Cubs back to camp at our old campsite if we could not get through the weather, our humanoids thanked Dennis for his kind hospitality and propped our little Continentals back to life.

Considering the information, our humanoids decided to make the next fuel stop at Perry. We had not visited Perry in a long time because they did not have fuel available, but a phone call had confirmed they now had a new self-service facility available. We could make it all the way to Cross City, but perhaps the stop at this new facility would allow us to overfly ol' big nozzle there. Besides, with this headwind component the shorter leg would be more conducive to a relaxed journey.

Back into the air, we were rapidly approaching what we like to refer to as home turf. Having flown over the upcoming area of this planet many times, finding familiar checkpoints for navigation became a pleasant game. Passing Tallahassee Commercial Airport the visibility was down to not much more than three or four miles. As long as we stayed out of the Class C airspace around Tallahassee Regional we would be legal because we were now flying clear of clouds. Passing a point about thirty miles east-southeast of Tallahassee, Old Man Weather decided to give us a real break. Obviously, we had passed beyond the band of really stinky stuff and by the time Perry-Foley Airport came into view the ceiling was at least 1,500 feet and visibility was six or seven miles.

Sis and I were beginning to really appreciate the self-service fueling stations, such as the one now operating here at Perry-Foley, as they become more popular around the countryside. They are extremely convenient and efficient—when they work. However, on this trip, we have found manned facilities have been much less reliable! We did not know it now, but we had one last bad experience with a so-called friendly manned-service facility waiting to trick us before this day was over. With our thirst for go-juice once again satisfied, our thoughts turned to determining our next port of call. We are getting close to home now, so no matter where we chose to go, it would not be a destination that was new to us.

Much to our dismay, 726 and I soon learned our next landing will be at Cross City. We hated that place. Well, it was not the people or place—it was that stupid huge nozzle they use to dispense energy into our tanks! Why must it be so big?

There are two reasons for making this particular stop. The first and most important is because the headwind component was a bit of a question mark, leaving some doubt as to how far we could safely fly on our little twelve-gallon fuel supply. The second reason seemed to be that ol' big nozzle did have a restaurant located on the field which was a very strong selling point as our humanoids were getting hungry again—especially Ray. The wind was now directly on our beam which caused us to use fifty minutes to complete the forty-two mile run from Perry to Cross City. Sure enough, as we coasted to a halt next to the fuel hose, ol' big nozzle could plainly be seen. Someplace along the line on this trip—I think it was in Iowa—Sis and I found one of these big old things that had been modified with a reducer so that it fit inside our filler necks and did not spill go-juice all over us while filling our reservoirs. The only thing that needed to be remembered was the fact that the nozzle still had about a pint of liquid in it when the valve was closed. If that was not considered, it might overflow—still, that was much better than using this unmodified unit.

While consuming their very late lunch, Leighton, Ray, and Lyle decided there was no reason why we would not go all the way home. The sun did not call it a day until about 8:30 P.M. and the weather forecast indicated Cub conditions the rest of the way home. Our only concern was being able to obtain one more tank of energy at some point because our little supply certainly was not enough to make it all the way to Venice.

Perusing the Jacksonville Sectional for a suitable rest stop all eyes fell on Hernando County Airport at Brooksville, Florida. Since we all had visited this nice little landing spot many times in the past, we knew all services that we required were readily available at this location. A few quick mental calculations brought to our attention to the fact that because of the leisurely pace that Sis and I cover the ground, our ETA at Hernando County would be very close to 6:00 P.M. Recent experience had demonstrated that many FBO operations open and close by the clock rather than by the dawn-to-dark policy that was almost universal when 726 and I were young Cubs. For this reason, Ray made a long distance call to the FBO at Brooksville, giving them our ETA. Ray had been advised that someone would be waiting for us even though our arrival was programmed to be at their lockup time—6:00 P.M. Yes, they would wait for us and make sure Sis and I received the necessary service.

As mentioned a long time ago, there would be five Class B airspaces for us two no-radio Cubs to contend with on this trip. Hernando County Airport is situated exactly on the northern most arc of the thirty-mile veil of Tampa International Airport Class B area. Thus, this one was the fifth of the trip. Actually, we had traversed this one several days ago as we started on this journey, but since we played around under this wedding cake most of the time anyway, no thought or concern was ever given to it other than to remember where the boundaries and altitude limits were located. Really no problem at all for the likes of us.

Now that our realm of operation was over home turf, we more or less just relaxed and enjoyed the scenery as we continued further southeast. Things were going very nicely, thank you, until about ten miles after passing Crystal River. This being Florida, it really was not a surprise when we found two very angry dark clouds crying their little hearts out directly in our path. As was usually the case, with a little care, Sis and I were able to work our way around them by moving a few miles to the east. Of course this little detour would add a few minutes to our travel time, but there was no need to worry because the nice folks at Brooksville were going to wait for us. Right? Wrong!

As we pivoted to a stop in front of the office, Sis and I could see the clock on the wall inside, and it was indicating eighteen minutes past the hour of six P.M. We had our suspicions as we rolled onto the ramp where everything was deserted and as our humanoids entered the office, our worst fears were confirmed. A manned service facility has failed us again.

Watching intently and reading lips we observed and heard a very interesting exchange—especially since all concerned knew our ETA, which was less than twenty minutes earlier than our actual arrival time. That was pretty good for a couple of old lady Cubs. It was quite apparent that our three birdmen were cooling their heels while the young lady behind the counter finished her personal phone call. This took at least two or three minutes at which time she made the statement, "I guess you are the Cubs that want gas! Well, I'm sorry everyone is gone. We close at six and I could not keep them any longer. I just stayed around to tell you everyone is gone because I knew you were coming."

Nice gesture, my dear young lady, but it sure doesn't help the situation any. Hey, we were here just eighteen minutes after you normally close and someone promised to wait for us. We had to go around a couple of thunderstorms which cost us those extra minutes. Doesn't anyone care about keeping a promise around here?

Without saying another word, Leighton, Lyle, and Ray stormed out of the office and made a beeline for our cockpits. Self-service fueling at Zephyrhills Airport, here we come. This unfortunate detour was going to make getting home tonight very interesting because neither Sis nor I could legally operate in the dark and it would appear we were now in an all-out race with the dark shadows of night as they pushed the fading light further west. There still might be enough time. Certainly no time to goof off here on the ground.

Our humanoids normally were very conservative in their ground handling of us, but this particular departure was a "wings-on, gas-on, hang-on operation," which neither Sis nor I appreciated. I am sure less than a minute passed from the time our trusty Continentals came to life and we were in the air off of runway 20. As soon as we cleared the trees, our noses were pointed directly toward Zephyrhills Municipal Airport and just twenty minutes had passed by the time the self-service facility on their ramp was giving us another much-needed drink of essence of 100-LL.

Departing Zephyrhills just as quickly as we had arrived, we were back in the air with our spinners pointed toward home, Venice, in much less time than we had anticipated. The stopwatch on Lyle's wrist suggested the time was 7:05 P.M and the sun would not sink below the horizon until about one hour and twenty-five minutes from now. *Hey, Sis, we're gonna make it! It'll be close, but we're gonna make it.*

Sitting very low in the western sky, the sun produced a fantastic panoramic display of ever-elongating shadows on the ground. This, coupled with unlimited ceiling and visibility plus satin smooth air created a fantastic wind-down leg for this great adventure we experienced for the past thirteen days. Of course, like all good things, we hated to see them end, but on the other hand if they didn't, how could we ever start something new and different that just might be even better than the present?

Always ones to have a good time in the air, Sis and I jockeyed for posing positions as we expended the few remaining picture frames in our cameras. It seems we are always striving to get that perfect air-to-air shot which can only be found during the subdued light of a sunset or dawn. Besides, what we were doing helped relieve the pain of having to admit this great adventure was rapidly coming to a close.

The soft smooth grass beside runway 4 seemed to be saying welcome home as our little fat sneakers softly kissed it hello. The time was exactly 8:18 P.M in the evening. Our race with the sun had been won with plenty of time to spare!

Rolling onto the self-fueling ramp to top off our reservoirs before being put to bed, we were pleasantly surprised to be greeted by Dale Kraus, the general manager of Venice Flying Service, and his entire family. Seeing us two yellow Cubs in the pattern as they were driving past the airport, was enough for them to want to be the first humanoids on the field to welcome us home. *That's very nice of you Dale.*

Well, Sis, as much as we hate to admit it, this fantastic adventure is over. We certainly have had lots of fun and we now know the Mighty Mississippi River is one mighty long river. Gosh I'm glad the two of us could make Lyle's twenty-year-old dream come true. I wonder where we can go next.

It has required thirteen days, during which we have traveled more than 4,200 miles, visited fifty-five different landing sites, and flown sixty-four hours and fifty minutes, to fly the Big River. We have more dirt and grime covering parts of our anatomy than has ever been the case since Sis and I have been owned by our present humanoids, but as far as we are concerned, it was all clean dirt and very shortly both of us would have a nice bath. It always happened that way. I knew that as soon as we were cleaned up and had a good night's sleep, both of us would be ready to go again.

The closing of my hangar doors brought down the final curtain on this grand adventure. As I settled in for some much-needed rest, my mind started wondering—wondering just where would our next long journey take us. Then I remembered Sis's humanoid came from the state of Vermont—I wonder how long it has been since he took her back to his roots? Had the two of them ever explored the Hudson River through metropolitan New York and beyond? How about the Statue of Liberty? When did she see that landmark last? Then there is the next Sentimental Journey event at Lock Haven. We could combine it all with another visit to our roots. Hmm. I must drop a few hints tomorrow, when we get back to our mental telepathy communication system.

[4] Lake Itasca State Park, the headwaters of the Mississippi provided we humanoids with information about the mighty river. We decided that after bedding down the Cubs, we needed to go back to spend more time there.

It was well past 7:00 P.M. when we finally got under way back to Lake Itasca. By this time the mosquitoes had started to search for something to eat so repellent was a definite necessity for one and all. Actually, I think two or three of them would have been able to carry either 881 or 726 away, if they had not been tied down. The skeeters are *big*.

The thirty-five or forty-mile drive back to the Lake Itasca State Park is very enjoyable and by the time we arrived in the parking lot at the actual headwaters, it seemed we have the whole place to ourselves. The park did not close until 10:30 so there was plenty of time to accomplish what we wanted to do. Following a very wide walkway for about 200 yards through the woods brought us to the actual starting point of the Mississippi River. Here, the river is twenty or twenty-five feet wide and about eighteen inches deep. At this time in the evening, with the sun quite low, the setting is absolutely beautiful. All three of us walked across the river on the stones that had been strategically placed for that purpose. We could have waded in the water, but we were too lazy to remove our shoes and socks. The water is crystal clear and, in fact, I did drink from the water at the point where it was flowing out of the lake, starting that long journey south. It was fascinating to think about the fact that the water we were watching exit this beautiful lake here in northern Minnesota would travel 2,348 miles to the Gulf of Mexico, where it would be part of the yearly discharge of 145 cubic miles of water, which also carries 10.6 billion cubic feet of sediment. It was also hard to believe that this small twenty-foot-wide babbling brook would become about a mile wide and over 100 feet deep in many places.

The next hour or so was spent enjoying the surrounding environment and reading much information that was presented at the tourist information facilities located nearby. This was quite an education for all of us.

Lake Itasca is situated 1,680 feet above sea level and has an area of about two square miles. It was established in 1832 as the headwaters of the Mississippi River by Henry Rowe Schoolcraft, an explorer. The river was discovered by Hernando de Soto near the present location of Memphis, Tennessee, in 1541.

Coupled with the Missouri, Red, Arkansas, Illinois, and Ohio rivers, plus about 250 other tributaries, this great river drains most of the territory between the Rocky Mountains and Allegheny Mountains—an area of about 1,257,000 square miles. The Falls of St. Anthony (sixty-five feet high) in Minneapolis, Minnesota, are the head of the river navigation. The U. S. government constructed dams and locks around obstructions to navigation at Rock Island, Illinois; Keokuk, Iowa; and north of St. Louis, Missouri, to accommodate the barge traffic carrying goods up and down the Mississippi River. A system of storage reservoirs near the headwaters and a series of flood-control dams along the river and its tributaries help maintain an even flow of water. After being joined by the Minnesota and St. Croix Rivers, the Mississippi River becomes the boundary of ten states—Minnesota, Iowa, Missouri, Arkansas, and Louisiana on the west, and Wisconsin, Illinois, Kentucky, Tennessee, and Mississippi on the east.

[5] Before getting into the Minneapolis Class B airspace program, I would like to tell you about the really nice eating facility located here in the Brainerd airport terminal building. The food is very

good and the young proprietress, chief cook, waitress, et al., is really very entertaining. If you have ever watched the sitcom, "Wings" on television, you will have seen the character, Helen Chapel, who operates the lunch counter at the airport. Well, Helen Chapel, in person, operates a very similar establishment here at Brainerd.

We had decided that we would like to have breakfast, which included eggs; however, when Leighton asked if we could have them, we were informed in no uncertain terms that "no, we could not have eggs because I have cooked enough eggs for today." This response really took us by surprise and I responded, "Is your name Helen?" Evidently this question was the icebreaker because the young lady could not keep from laughing and then offered to cook us eggs. Just to be obnoxious all three of us refused to have eggs and opted for hamburgers instead. Believe me, they were very good—so—if you are ever in Brainerd, Minnesota, be sure and see "Helen" for some real good "vittles." (Yes, she did know who "Helen" is and where she works.)

Hearing of our plans to go through Class B airspace, many skeptics have told us that is impossible to do in Cubs that do not have communication radios or navigational electronics in them. We have also been told that it is foolhardy and a little bit stupid to even think of such extended trips in these old unequipped air-planes. True, this trip with the involvement of Class B airspace does present some problems, but anything can be solved with a little clear thinking, common sense, and planning.

Lake Itaska, the beginning of the mighty Mississippi River.

The Minneapolis/St. Paul Class B airspace is one of five such areas that we would become involved with on this trip down the Mississippi River. It is the only one in which we would need to penetrate the core in order to follow the river, so it did require some advance planning. (Transiting the remaining four would not require actual entry into the "controlled airspace" as we would stay below the "layers" and outside the core.") This planning phase was facilitated by help from Gerry Quilling, a friend of ours who lives in the Minneapolis area, when he gave me the telephone number of Marlan J. Perhus, safety program manager, FAA flight standards district office, at Minneapolis.

About a month before our departure, I called Marlan and, during the next day or two, several phone calls were made to various people in the Air Traffic Control System associated with the MSP Class B airspace. Within this short span of time, we had received tentative clearance for our two Cubs (NC-87881 and NC-22726) to follow the river all the way through the Class B area—right through the middle of it. All that was required was a phone call before we actually entered the area. Fantastic.

The day before we departed from Venice, ATC at Minneapolis was advised that we were on the way and would be calling them for final clearance in about a week or so. They knew we were flying Cubs so understood our ETA very well. Late in the evening on the second night out, I received a call from Pat, my wife, telling me that I should call a certain telephone number in Minneapolis immediately because it was the FAA and very urgent that I talk to them. That telephone number was the home of Mark Schreier, the air traffic controller who was working with us on this project.

He was waiting for my call and he had bad news for us. It seems the powers above him had turned down the idea and we could not come through the airspace. However, Mark had already set in motion a plan, which would work for us. He had arranged to have an escort with all the necessary radios, transponders, etc. ready and waiting to take us through. He supplied me with the home phone number of the gentleman who would fly the escort with us. Talk about assistance—you surely do not normally find that kind of help anywhere in the FAA!

That same evening, I called the number Mark had given me and the very cheerful voice of Eric Christianson came on the line. Yes, indeed, he was aware of our problem and yes, he would be more than happy to escort us through the Class B airspace! A series of subsequent phone calls to coordinate our movements were made and thus, here at Brainerd, the final call was completed, establishing a meeting time at Monticello, Minnesota. Now all we had to do was finish our lunch and make that rendezvous!

About Lyle Wheeler

Lyle Wheeler was born and raised on a farm in West Central Illinois. He learned to fly at a small grass airport near Macomb, Illinois, soloing a BL-65 Taylorcraft at the age of fifteen (illegal then as it is today). His formal education was completed at the University of Illinois where he was employed as a flight instructor at the age of eighteen. Flight instructing continued to be a vital part of his life. By the time he was twenty, he was employed as a pilot with a major airline and continued in that employ until forced retirement in December 1991. As a commercial pilot he was employed by Northwest Orient Airlines, Reeve Aleutian Airways, and during the last thirty-seven years of his career, with Pan American World Airways. While flying for Reeve Aleutian Airways, Wheeler also flew small aircraft in the bush in Alaska. Through the years he has accumulated more than 42,600 logged hours in many different aircraft, from the Piper J-3 Cub on the small end up to and including the Boeing 747 on the large end. He continues to be an active pilot, flight instructing, flying for pleasure and personal enjoyment.

About NC-87881

Piper J3C-65 Cub, NC-87881 was born at Lock Haven, Pennsylvania on January 14, 1946. Immediately thereafter she was pressed into service as a pilot trainer and airplane ride-giver at El Paso, Texas. Until May 1953, she served several fixed base operators in Texas and New Mexico. At that time, she was sold to an agricultural operator.

During the next four years she served as an aerial applicator working the fields around Portales, Roswell and Carlsbad, New Mexico. In July 1957, retaining the big eighty-five horsepower engine under her cowl, she was sold and converted back to her original configuration so that she could once again teach humanoids to fly. This started her on a thirty-year journey of a multitude of owners living in Texas and North Dakota until finally she was left to "die" behind a hangar in Montana. It appeared her life was at an end until she was rescued by a gentleman from Bloomington, Illinois, who purchased her and resold her as a "basket case" to her present humanoid who resides in Florida. Before making the trip to her new home, she was completely restored, returning the sixty-five horsepower engine to her nose. This restoration produced two coveted awards at the Sun-'n-Fun EAA Fly-in at Lakeland, Florida. Today, she continues her happy life in retirement doing what she does best—giving pure unadulterated joy of flight to those around her.